I0112567

MARKETING ANALYTICS

MARKETING ANALYTICS

Essential Tools for Data-Driven Decisions

RAJKUMAR VENKATESAN,
PAUL W. FARRIS,
AND RONALD T. WILCOX

DARDEN BUSINESS PUBLISHING
University of Virginia Press
Charlottesville and London

UVA Darden Business Publishing, an imprint of the University of Virginia Press

© 2021 by the Rector and Visitors of the University of Virginia

All rights reserved

Printed in the United States of America on acid-free paper

First published 2021

9 8 7 6 5 4 3 2 1

Library of Congress Cataloging-in-Publication Data

Names: Venkatesan, Rajkumar, author. | Farris, Paul W., author. | Wilcox, Ronald T., author.
Title: Marketing analytics : essential tools for data-driven decisions / Rajkumar Venkatesan,
    Paul W. Farris, and Ronald T. Wilcox.
Description: Charlottesville : Darden Business Publishing, University of Virginia Press, 2021. |
    Series: Darden business publishing | Includes bibliographical references and index.
Identifiers: LCCN 2020037900 (print) | LCCN 2020037901 (ebook) | ISBN 9780813945156
    (hardcover ; alk. paper) | ISBN 9780813945163 (ebook)
Subjects: LCSH: Marketing—Management. | Marketing—Statistical methods. | Marketing research.
Classification: LCC HF5415.127 .V453 2021 (print) | LCC HF5415.127 (ebook) | DDC 658.8/3—dc23
LC record available at https://lccn.loc.gov/2020037900
LC ebook record available at https://lccn.loc.gov/2020037901

Cover art: PictureDragon/Shutterstock

Contents

Foreword

There's a lot in this book that I wish I had known when I was building my first company. You can read about that adventure in chapters 5 and 9, although I recommend that you work your way there rather than just jumping ahead. We first called the company "Retail Relay," and back then, when we were growing it, the authors of this book wrote a case study about it for the University of Virginia's Darden School of Business. They had been my professors when I was there—teaching me both marketing and marketing analytics—and as they wrote and I worked, they become my mentors. The advice and guidance that they gave me, a newly minted MBA with a big dream, was invaluable.

However, as I read the case study now and think back about the company, I am embarrassed at all of the mistakes we made, even with that guidance. A book like this, one that lays out the fundamentals of marketing analytics, would have made a real difference as I built the marketing capabilities at Relay.

"Half the money I spend on advertising is wasted; the trouble is, I don't know which half," said John Wanamaker (1838–1922).

Back in the nineteenth century, when Wanamaker is supposed to have made this famous statement, there really was no way to know how a company's marketing was affecting its sales. Marketing analytics has changed all of that. Its techniques let marketers know what brings in customers, what keeps them connected to the company, and what they like (and don't). This knowledge allows a company to make the most effective use of its marketing dollars, and, with that, to grow and increase its chances of becoming a real success.

If you don't already know about marketing analytics, you will discover as you start to read and interact with this book that marketing analytics is a critical field, and a growing one. *Marketing* is about how to place your product so that it will have the most exposure and gain the most customers. *Marketing analytics* involves using the data that you can glean from customer decisions to determine how a company should use its marketing money to achieve the most fruitful results. You will see that the more effectively companies employ marketing analytics, the more effectively they can deploy their marketing resources, the more quickly they grow, and the more successful they will be. The research on this is impressive and convincing. If your company is serious about acquiring customers at scale, it needs to take full advantage of the information that marketing analytics can give it. It is one thing to collect data; it is another to use marketing analytics to understand them and make them actionable. Or, as the authors put it, "The tools that open that treasure trove of data are marketing analytics."

This book will be an invaluable resource for any chief executive, head of marketing, or head of marketing analytics, as well as for anyone who is interested in developing a sense of how a company should allocate its money—its marketing spend—for the ultimate effectiveness. This is a good book if you have experience with marketing but need to be more robust in your understanding of how to use data. You should read it if you are part of the decision process around how to spend money, if you are a marketer, or if you are a graduate student trying to decide whether this is how you want to spend your career.

You can get a lot out of this book even if you don't have a marketing background (although you will find that having some math and statistics fundamentals is helpful). It will give you a good introduction to the concept of media channels; it walks you through real-life problems, step by step; it presents key words and technical concepts; it teaches you how to design an experiment and how to collect the data you need. It helps you learn to work with both quantitative and qualitative analysis. With this book, you will learn how to interact with the largest, most prevalent platforms, because it will show you how to bid, and how to leverage your viewing numbers and ad words. It will give you a strong understanding of the big players in the search world, which is something that every marketing and marketing analytics person today needs to know.

If you are already a practitioner, and even if you have been working in the area for a long time, this book will challenge you to think more broadly about the field. The case studies can help even the most seasoned professional think through fundamental concepts more practically, refreshing your perspective and helping you to maintain your peak creativity and agility when considering how best to use data for your company.

If any of this is what you are looking for, this is your book. It is not a dry but informative textbook, announcing concepts and hoping that you can handle the math.

Much better, it is an engaging discussion about how to make marketing decisions based on the growing body of data that is available. The book is interactive; it teaches through the case method, training you in how to think through marketing problems and make more focused and more accurate decisions.

Companies are spending many millions of dollars in marketing. In the past, a marketing manager would put ads on television and in the paper, circulate flyers, post on billboards, or rely on word-of-mouth support from customers, and then try to estimate, based on surveys and sales data, which approach had been the most effective. There was no realistic way to ascertain a direct correlation between the marketing output and the sales numbers. Today, a company can pour money into a direct response campaign and end up with a volume of data that is almost unbelievable in its richness, quality, and sheer volume. But once you have it, analyzing this data becomes critical; it can make or break a company. It is the magic of marketing analytics that will allow you to develop a clear attribution of how your company's spending is affecting your customers' decisions.

I have come a long way from Relay. After heading eCommerce Technology for the international division at Walmart, I am now the Chief Product and Technology Officer at Stubhub. I was less involved with marketing analytics at Walmart, but since joining Stubhub, I have become more sophisticated in my approach to marketing data; I had to, because the marketing analytics department reports to me. At Stubhub, we spend a significant amount of money on marketing. We have a marketing team that makes the final decisions about our spending, but it is our marketing analytics team that informs the spending recommendations—where to put that money, how much to put where, and when to increase or decrease spending. Without an impartial marketing analytics group at Stubhub, there is no doubt that our financial returns would be on a different scale entirely.

Throughout my career, I have watched the advances in marketing analytics with awe. The quality of the data has improved. Marketing attribution (understanding what impels a customer to respond to which ad, directly or even indirectly) has moved closer to being an exact science. It is now the case, more than ever, that if your company relies on marketing to grow, you need marketing analytics to make yourself sustainable and successful.

If you are going to study the field of marketing analytics, there are no better teachers to guide you along the path than these authors. As professors at Darden, they are standouts—engaging students, challenging their thinking, pushing them to improve their decision-making frameworks. Each is, in his own way, an innovator, stretching boundaries about how and where to teach, and always thinking about which subjects matter. All three make a point of keeping current and staying in touch with the latest developments. They reach out of their theoretical academic towers to make sure that they are teaching the most sophisticated techniques and conveying the most modern information.

As I read this book now, years after Relay, I can see it triggering questions that I want to ask, and new directions that I want to pursue. It reinforces some of my deeply held concepts, but it challenges me to reexamine others. This is definitely a book that I want to keep handy so that I can refer to it to refresh my thinking about marketing analytics and how we use them at Stubhub.

I am excited about the potential that this book has to help current and future executives, and am endlessly appreciative of the efforts to which Raj, Ron, and Paul have gone to make sure that you can make this field your own.

Arnie Katz
Chief Product and Technology Officer
Stubhub
February 2020

MARKETING ANALYTICS

Introduction

I n 2012, SoQuera, a Frankfurt-based online marketing agency, reported that its clients had improved their returns from marketing by 21% after the agency optimized its search engine advertisements. From 2007 to 2008, Jetstar, a low-cost airline, increased its market share by four percentage points and its profits by $28 million by improving service design and price competitiveness. The same year, IBM increased its revenue by $20 million by reallocating sales resources to its more profitable customers. In 2008, Bayer increased profits in a $4 billion unit by $685 million through a dynamic allocation of marketing resources. The performances of Jetstar, IBM, and Bayer are even more impressive when we remember that 2008 was the start of the Great Recession.

The common element in these success stories is the sophisticated and careful application of analytics to marketing. Used wisely, analytics can transform marketing efforts and substantially increase the profits of both major corporations and smaller companies.[1]

WHAT IS MARKETING?

At its core, marketing is a relationship. A business creates a connection with a customer and engages in a dialogue with them in hopes of building value.

Three strategic aspects and four tactical elements characterize the marketing process. The strategic aspects are segmentation, targeting, and positioning. We can think of these broadly as relating to the customer part of the dialogue, or how the business finds its conversation partners and engages with them. The tactical elements relate more to the business's part of the dialogue, or what the business says to its customers. Often referred to as the **four Ps**, these tactical elements are product, price, place, and promotion. Marketing also involves financial considerations, which are often used as metrics to gauge the success of the dialogue. These include return on marketing investment, customer lifetime value, and brand equity.

To begin to get a picture of how the strategic aspects work in practice, consider the case of Airbnb. Segmentation refers to the way that Airbnb categorizes its customers. It can group them by, for example, age, income, and whether they are leisure or business travelers. Targeting refers to the particular segment of customers on whom Airbnb would like to focus its business and marketing activities, say leisure travelers. Finally, positioning refers to the value proposition that Airbnb offers the target segment. One positioning could be "live like a local on your leisure trips."

Turning now to the tactical elements, Airbnb's products are the different properties that the hosts provide for rent and the photographs of those properties. Price means the daily rental rates posted for the properties. Place refers to Airbnb's website and mobile apps that connect guests with the hosts. Promotions include reviews of the properties and guests, as well as Airbnb's television and online advertisements.

Finally, appropriate financial metrics for Airbnb would be the rental frequency of properties and the lifetime value of its guests and hosts. Airbnb can use these metrics to assess the effectiveness of its marketing.

WHAT IS MARKETING ANALYTICS?

If marketing is a dialogue, it is safe to assume that a business is well aware of its own part of that interchange—its marketing spend that leads to the tactical decisions, the details of each advertising campaign, the wording of each slogan—but until recently, the only part of the customer's response that a firm could know was purchasing behavior. And it couldn't even be sure that this behavior was a response to its marketing overtures, because it couldn't connect a given purchase directly to its advertisement.

Before the internet took over the marketing landscape, television and print were the only media available to advertisers. A firm knew how much it invested in advertisements, and it knew the subsequent sales of products every month, or sometimes even every week or every day. But it could not be certain that a customer had bought an item because of a particular ad for that item. Much of the inference between advertisements and sales was merely correlational: if a firm saw higher sales in the same week it advertised its products, it might assume that the new ad had led to those sales. Some marketing managers might have used tools such as regressions or A/B testing to find this correlation, but it was difficult, if not impossible, to establish a causal relationship between advertisements and sales. Marketing managers relied on long experience and honed managerial intuition, since the hard facts at their disposal were relatively few.

The advent of the internet brought an explosion of data and gave firms access to a huge amount of granular information about customer behavior. But "big data" are incomprehensible and unusable without ways to analyze them. *The tools that open that treasure trove of data are marketing analytics.*

Sophisticated econometrics, combined with rich customer and marketing-mix data, now enable firms to bring science into a field that has traditionally relied only on managers' intuition.[2] Indeed, in this age of big data, marketing analytics is absolutely necessary for businesses to be able to use the huge amounts of information available in order to best market their products and services.

To be fair, marketing analytics is not entirely new. Marketers started to use conjoint analysis in the early 1970s. Regression, which marketing adopted from statistics, has been around since mathematicians Adrien-Marie Legendre and Carl Friedrich Gauss invented it in the eighteenth century.[3] Experiments have helped marketers in a variety of contexts for a long time. However, the rise of big data not only changed how they used these and other existing tools in marketing, but also catalyzed the creation and customization of an abundance of new marketing tools. With the growing array of marketing analytics techniques, businesses can optimize the value-creation potential of their relationships with customers, both existing and potential.

Data-driven marketing rests on three interconnected pillars: analytics, experimentation, and intuition.

Managers use analytics to make hypotheses, which they can then test with experiments. They then need to weigh the results of these analyses and experiments against managerial intuition and the feasibility of marketing campaigns. Intuition is also a key ingredient, as it directs the analytics to focus on the questions that are of strategic value for the firm.

Marketing analytics tools like regressions, experiments, text analytics, and segmentation—all of which we introduce in this book—enable companies to move beyond reports about *what* is happening in their field to the point of actually understanding *why* something is happening.[4] All the techniques in this book rely on company data about its actions and its customers' reactions. Without data about firms and customers, it is not possible to use these techniques to inform marketing decisions.

A 2013 report in *Forbes* magazine covered a survey of 211 senior marketers at large companies; the survey indicated that the companies that employed analytics and big data to understand customer behaviors found significant success.[5] More than half (60%) of the organizations that used big data a majority of the time reported that they surpassed their goals. Almost three-quarters of companies that used big data a majority of the time were able to understand the effects of multichannel campaigns, and 70% of that group of companies said they were able to target their marketing efforts optimally. Companies that used big data only occasionally reported significantly less success. However, only 10% of the senior marketers in the survey reported using data analytics in a majority of their marketing initiatives.

Four years later, in 2017, more than 53% of companies surveyed responded that they used big data.[6] By 2019, the surveyed companies reported using marketing analytics powered by big data for about 43% of their marketing decisions, the highest percentage in six years of surveys and a major increase from 2013, when respondents indicated using analytics for decisions only 30% of the time.[7] The surveys point to a growing trend among companies toward using big data for analytics, while at the same time suggesting huge potential for growth. The consumer insights that these companies obtain through big data and analytics reliably help them outperform their competitors that use this approach less. But despite this demonstrated success, marketing analytics is underused. This disconnect is likely due to the twin barriers of lack of knowledge—which this book aims to change—and unwillingness to implement the changes necessary to use marketing analytics in the real world—which the final chapter addresses.

Companies that use marketing analytics are no longer in the dark as to the exact effect of an advertisement on customer purchasing behavior. With the widespread use of email and web-based advertising, firms can now closely connect their inputs (for example, ad placements) and outputs (whether the target of the advertisement made a purchase). In today's marketing dialogue, the firm can not only hear what the customers say, but can connect those responses directly to the firm's outreach to them. This produces a large amount of behavioral data. These data, in turn, allow companies to model existing customer behaviors and predict future behaviors more precisely, informing the firm's next outreach and helping it shape the conversation.

It is important, however, to note that with big data come big problems. A firm that relies on data without the benefit of managerial experience or understanding of some principles of statistics runs the risk of finding false positives, or of seeing patterns among chance events.[8] We should also emphasize issues of customer privacy and the responsible use of data for marketing decisions, although these ethical dilemmas fall outside the scope of the current volume.

While big data and marketing analytics give businesses tools to develop concrete, evidence-based insights into customer behavior, managerial intuition is still essential to successful marketing. Intuition, honed through experience, helps managers avoid making mistakes with big data or misusing marketing analytics tools. Business intuition enables marketers to select the correct inputs and outputs for a model, and to choose the appropriate analytical tools for the business goals. Used thoughtfully and appropriately, analytics empowers a company to take traditional static and historic dashboards of customer reactions, firm investments, and marketing metrics and turn them into predictive and dynamic entities.

Marketing analytics is the engine that drives effective marketing decisions.

WHAT IS IN THIS BOOK

This book provides an overview of the analytics tools that enable marketers to collect, analyze, and interpret data in order to guide decisions and optimize the different components of the marketing process. These tools can be descriptive, predictive, or prescriptive. **Descriptive analytics** summarizes historical information, answering questions like *What happened? When, where, and how often did it happen? Why did it happen? Was it abnormal or typical?* **Predictive analytics** forecasts outcomes, answering questions like *What will happen if I do this?* Finally, **prescriptive analytics** recommends actions, and answers questions like *What can I do to maximize revenue from this?* We focus mainly on descriptive and prescriptive analytics, as they are used most frequently by marketing managers looking to change customer behaviors, not just predict them. Toward the end of the book, we also provide some discussion of predictive analytics in the context of artificial intelligence.

The book begins with an overview of resource allocation, the endgame of analytics. Chapter 2 is a review of K-means clustering, a common method for segmenting customers and identifying appropriate positioning for the segments. In chapter 3, you will learn about conjoint analysis, a tool used for designing products and finding the optimal price for these products. As explored in chapter 4, marketing-mix regressions allow managers to identify optimal price and promotion budgets for brands. In chapter 5, we examine customer lifetime value, a key integrating metric for customer management. Chapter 6 is a discussion of various types of marketing experiments, or ways to determine which promotions will be most effective. Paid search advertising, the focus of chapter 7, is a deeper dive into a type of promotion that relies on and generates a huge amount of data. In chapter 8, you will learn how text analytics provides managers the sophistication to use digital data to optimize price and promotions. In chapter 9, logistic regressions provide predictions of customer churn, an important component of customer lifetime value, as well as offering managers new insights into products and promotions. Chapter 10 explores how collaborative filtering enables managers to develop recommendation systems that personalize their website interface (the tactical element of place) to many customers. Finally, chapters 11 and 12 offer a look ahead, first through an overview of some of the ways in which the rapidly advancing field of artificial intelligence informs marketing, and then by an exploration of practical strategies to implement marketing analytics in your own work.

HOW TO READ THIS BOOK

This book grew out of the authors' extensive experience teaching graduate business students and executives using case studies, and its organization is rooted in case method. **Case studies** are business situations that are unresolved in some way, and therefore require readers' active engagement. **Case method** puts you in the shoes of the case protagonist and encourages you to develop a decision orientation. This kind of active learning is simply more sticky: factual knowledge decays rapidly, but the skills of defining and solving problems can last a lifetime. Through case method, you will better understand that marketing analytics is just one input to a business decision. Effective business decisions often rely on both rigorous statistical analyses and sound judgment. Remember the three pillars of effective marketing—analytics, experimentation, and evidence-based intuition. Case method, like work in the field, combines all three.

Each chapter begins with a technical section that introduces a marketing analytical tool (sometimes with hypothetical cases as examples), followed by a real-life case that calls for that tool. The case method provides the opportunity for you to apply the skills you have learned in the technical part of the chapter to a situation as close as possible to real life. Bridging these two parts is a section entitled "Concept Application," which includes guidelines or markers to consider while working through the case study; these communicate our expectations of the main features of the case on which you should focus. Of course, the real-life case studies in this book also include nuances about the industry and context that might be helpful.

Many readers of this book will encounter it in the context of a class, in which your instructor will facilitate the case discussion and you will work through the chapters with your instructor and peers. The book is also designed for independent learners, and if you are a self-learning practitioner, we recommend that you find a study group to discuss and solve the case studies. The ideas are deep, and the data analyses can be better performed by discussing the steps together as a group. Whether in a class or on your own, when you are forming your learning group, consider whether the members of the group are committed to learning, and make sure to plan ahead and allocate sufficient time for the group to fully immerse in the case analyses.

Most of the cases in this book are accompanied by data sets, to which you can apply the marketing analytics tools to obtain insights that help with decisions in the case studies. The data sets are available online at http://store.darden.virginia.edu/marketing-analytics-supplements. The supplement also includes how-to videos on using particular software to perform marketing analytics, as well as links to an interactive Forio simulation on media attribution, along with instructions. The simulation offers an opportunity to practice descriptive, predictive, and prescriptive analytics in the context of planning campaigns and media allocation plans for a fitness watch and app; it also provides real-time results and consequences to the users' decisions. Like any class or learning opportunity, this book is only as useful as the work you put into it. The more hands-on practice you do, the better you will understand these techniques and how to apply them to optimize your own marketing initiatives.

Remember that effective marketing is not just application of analytical tools, but also wise decisions as to when and how to apply those tools; in other words, managerial intuition. While the best way to build that intuition is through experience in the business world, practicing the cases in this book will get you well on your way to developing a wider, informed, and grounded marketing perspective.

1

Resource Allocation

magine you need to decide how much of your budget to spend on online versus television advertising in a certain market, or which product to make the focus of your new campaign. How much will you invest in which marketing activities to optimize your investment? In other words, how will you allocate your marketing resources? Ideal **resource allocation** is the optimal level a company spends on each of its marketing levers (campaigns, new products, and so on) to maximize success. Figuring out how to do this depends on a range of variables, and which of those variables you choose to focus on is the crux of marketing analytics and the essence of managerial intuition.

Resource allocation is the endgame of marketing analytics, a framework that ties together the various tools and techniques to serve a firm's strategic decisions. As such, it is important to keep in mind throughout this chapter and the rest of this book. The chapters that follow this one will delve much more deeply into tools and scenarios, but for now we focus on the four main steps in resource allocation. As we do so, we present ways to make the resource-allocation process more data driven.

Please note that in this chapter, we've included hypothetical cases and examples to familiarize you with the case method and our approach. In the first hypothetical case, about a pharmaceutical company, you are guided through the problem-solving process. In later cases in this book, both hypothetical and real, the steps may not be as explicit, giving you the opportunity to choose how to solve the problem, including which metrics and which analytics technique to use, enabling you to build your business intuition as you hone your analytical skills.

RESOURCE ALLOCATION: FOUR STEPS

1. Determine the objective metric that captures the business outcome of interest.
2. Develop a function that connects marketing inputs to the objective metric.
3. Using historical data on marketing inputs and the objective metric, employ marketing analytics to estimate the unknown values or parameters of the function identified in step 2.
4. Now reverse the process: keep the parameters identified in step 3 fixed, and find the optimal marketing input levels that would maximize the objective metric to determine the best resource allocation.

Step 1: Determine the Objective Metric

The first step of resource allocation is to determine the objective metric. The company needs to set a goal—such as maximizing profits or improving brand awareness—and then choose a metric to measure its progress toward that goal. Metrics often used for this include: paid search click-through rates, conversion rates from website visits, net profits, customer lifetime value, near-term sales lift, new buyers, repeat sales, market share, or customer retention rates.

Step 2: Develop a Function that Connects Marketing Inputs to the Objective Metric

The second step is to connect the firm's marketing inputs to its resource-allocation objective metric. Managerial intuition is of paramount importance in this stage, as it allows the marketer to correctly decompose a metric. If a company is examining gross profits, for example, what components of the business contribute to those profits? Unit sales is a function of price, advertising, salesforce, and trade promotions. Advertising, salesforce, and trade promotions also incur marketing costs. Gross profit is sales minus unit costs, and net profit is gross profits minus marketing costs. Thus manipulating marketing inputs can improve sales, but the different inputs are also cost centers.

Once the marketing inputs are mapped to the objective metric, the marketing manager must determine which relationships between components that contribute to the metric are computational and which are empirical.

Computational relationships, also called **accounting identities**, can be calculated directly using known quantities. An example of an accounting identity is net profit: if both gross profit and marketing costs are known, net profit is simply gross profit minus marketing costs.

Empirical relationships are more complex, and driven by unknowns. They are functions, or transformations, that reflect analysis of historical data. An example of an empirical relationship is the relationship between marketing costs and unit sales. Unit sales cannot be obtained by a direct sum of the investments in marketing (as mentioned, these include price, advertising, salesforce, and trade promotions). The relationship is termed empirical because it is based in observation: the manager must analyze historical data to develop a function that transforms the marketing inputs into unit sales. For example, the manager could analyze the historical data on price and unit sales and develop a function that describes their relationship. The transformation function ideally yields a weight that translates a product's price into unit sales; in other words, the **weight** is the amount that unit sales would be expected to change with every unit change in price. These weights do not provide perfect transformations: they are best guesses based on historical data, wherein several factors—not just price—affect unit sales.

The main difference between an empirical relationship and an identity relationship is that an empirical relationship implies a best guess or prediction, while an identity is certain.

Step 3: Estimate the Parameters of the Function Identified in Step 2

The third step in the resource-allocation process is to estimate the best values for the unknown weights of the empirical relationships identified in the second step. A common method for identifying these weights is to build an econometric, or regression, model. For example, consider a problem where unit sales is the objective metric and price is the marketing input. Let's say in step 2, we specified the function connecting price and unit sales as: unit sales = $a + b \times$ price. We don't know a and b because unit sales and price have an empirical relationship. In step 3, we collect historical data and use marketing analytics to find the values of a and b in the context we are analyzing. This process of finding the values of a and b is called **parameter estimation**.

In this model, the independent variables are what we have been calling the marketing inputs: in the current example, this is price. The dependent variables are the potential metrics that a business can use to assess its resource-allocation efforts: in the example, this is unit sales. The aim of the model is to identify which marketing inputs of interest (price, advertising, sales calls, and so on) should be considered as having an effect on the dependent variable.

Once the unknown values in the empirical relationship between marketing inputs and objective metrics are estimated, the marketing manager can begin to predict the objective metric at different levels of the marketing input. This is the mathematical model that describes the relationship between the independent variables (price, advertising, sales calls, and so on) and the dependent variable (market share, profits, customer lifetime value, and so on).

Step 4: Reverse the Process

The last step of the resource-allocation process is to keep the parameters identified in step 3 fixed, and reverse steps 1–3 to identify the optimal value of the marketing inputs and maximize the objective metric to determine the best resource allocation. Let's revisit the example about unit sales and price. In step 3, we estimated the values of the unknown weights, a and b; now in step 4, we fix the values of a and b to the estimated numbers, and then vary the price values to find the optimal price that maximizes the predicted unit sales. This will inform a manager's decisions as to how the company should allocate its resources, or in other words, what the company's precise marketing spend should be to maximize the objective metric.

HYPOTHETICAL CASE: MARKETING A PHARMACEUTICAL

Imagine you are the marketing manager of a pharmaceutical company. Your task is to determine the effects of sales calls (to physicians) on the profits the company makes per customer (customers in this case are physicians). Your first step is to determine the objective metric: here, the goal is to maximize profits, and the metric that measures progress toward that goal is profit per customer.

Your second step in the resource-allocation process for your company is to connect marketing inputs to this objective metric. In **figure 1.1**, profits are broken down into number of new prescriptions and probability of new prescriptions. One of the marketing levers available to managers in this industry is number of sales calls. Number of sales calls is empirically related to number of new prescriptions and to probability of new prescriptions.

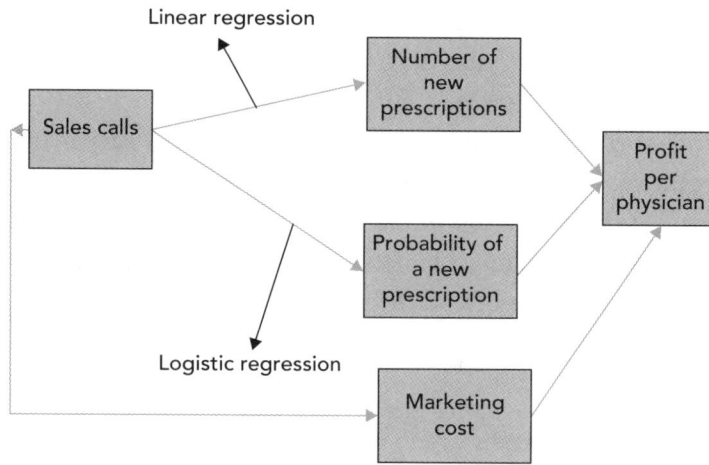

FIGURE 1.1. An example of the system of metrics in the pharmaceutical industry

In the third step of the resource-allocation process, you will estimate weights for the relationships between number of sales calls and each of the two outcome components—number of new prescriptions and probability of a new prescription—through regression analysis. To do this, you need access to historical information about the number of sales calls allocated to each physician every month and the number of prescriptions written by the physician every month. This type of information is collected by typical customer relationship management software; in this particular industry, the number of prescriptions written by physicians is collected by a federally mandated agency called IMS Health.

Each of these two components can be expressed as a function of sales calls, although the first (number of new prescriptions) would be a linear regression, since it includes a range of values, and the second (probability of a new prescription) would be a logistic regression, since it is an either/or situation (see chapter 4 for more on linear regression, and chapter 9 for logistic regression).

Because sales calls also represent a marketing cost, your goal is to balance their effect on the top line (revenues) and bottom line (costs) to maximize profits. You can mathematically express the relationship between sales calls and profits as follows. Profit for each prescribing physician is a function of the components you have identified: the number of new prescriptions times the probability (p) of a new prescription (multiplied by gross margin percentage), minus marketing costs. **Gross margin**

percentage is the amount the pharmaceutical firm makes from the sale of a single prescription of the drug, minus the variable costs.

Profit per physician = new prescriptions × p(new prescriptions)
$$\times \text{gross margin percentage} - \text{number of sales calls}$$
$$\times \text{unit cost of sales calls.}$$

Then, you need to predict the number of new prescriptions and probability of a new prescription. The first, the number of new prescriptions as a function of sales calls, is a linear regression:

Number of new prescriptions = $a + b1 \times Ln$(number of sales calls).

The terms a and $b1$ are the parameters, or weights, and are unknown. They connect the marketing inputs to the outcome metrics such as number of new prescriptions. The second function, the probability of a new prescription, is a logistic regression:

p(new prescriptions) = $\exp(u) \div [1 + \exp(u)]$,

where $u = c + d1 \times Ln$(number of sales calls).

The terms c and $d1$ are also unknown parameters. Performing the regression analyses on historical data will determine the values of a, $b1$, c, and $d1$, giving you a mathematical way to value sales calls with respect to their ability to increase the number of prescriptions written by physicians and the probability of a new prescription. And because sales calls are a cost center and are instrumental in driving sales, the pharmaceutical company would need to find the number of its sales calls that maximizes profits, subject to spending limits determined by the firm's budget (**figure 1.2**).

The figure plots the number of sales calls on the x axis, and the predicted profits, based on the function in step 2 and weights estimated in step 3, on the y axis. Notice that the relationship is shaped like an inverted "U." This is because in the equation for profits, number of sales calls affects the number of prescriptions and the probability of new prescriptions (the terms that determine the revenue), as well as the costs. The optimal number of sales calls is the level at which the benefit from the sales calls is the maximum, even after considering their cost contribution. Before the optimal number

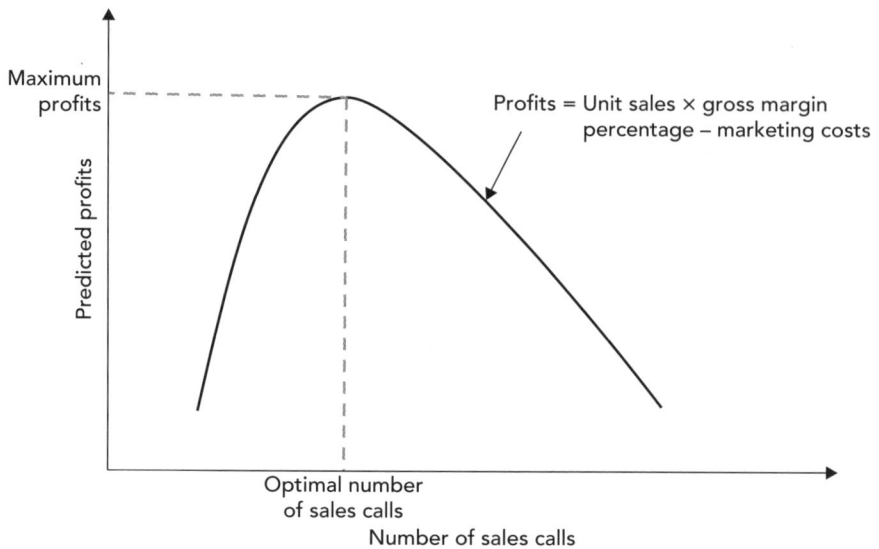

FIGURE 1.2. Optimal allocation of marketing spend

of sales calls, the benefit from the sales calls is higher than the cost contribution of the sales calls, and beyond the optimal number of sales calls, the costs contribution of sales calls is higher than the optimal number.

In the final step of resource allocation, you will identify the optimal number of sales calls to get the most prescriptions.

Say your regression analyses gave you the following values: $a = 0.05$; $b1 = 1.5$; $c = 0.006$; and $d1 = 1.2$. **Table 1.1** provides hypothetical data describing the effects of sales calls on profits per physician.

The price of a unit (one prescription) is $300, and the cost of a single sales call is $50. The drug company currently calls its physicians twice a month, on average. This example has a time period of one month, so the number of sales calls is two. Based on the estimated weights for each unknown in the described relationships $(a, b1, c, \text{and } d1)$, this strategy yields a profit of $181.65. If the company were to increase sales calls to six per month, the expected profits would be $268.74. Increasing sales calls beyond six per month, however, makes the cost of the sales calls higher than their incremental benefits, meaning profits start declining for monthly sales calls of seven and above. Six is the optimal level of sales calls because it maximizes the expected profit from each physician.

As the example illustrates, the optimal number of sales calls that maximizes profits is critically dependent on the unknown weights of the empirical relationship. Through

TABLE 1.1. Numeric example of optimal allocation of marketing spend

a	b1	c	d1	Price	Cost of sales calls
0.05	1.5	0.006	1.2	$300	$50

Sales calls	Unit sales	u	p(Unit sales)	Profit	
1	1.09	0.84	0.70	$109.73	
2	1.70	1.32	0.79	$181.65	Current
3	2.13	1.67	0.84	$226.31	
4	2.46	1.94	0.87	$252.30	
5	2.74	2.16	0.90	$265.25	
6	2.97	2.34	0.91	$268.74	Optimal
7	3.17	2.50	0.92	$265.10	
8	3.35	2.64	0.93	$255.94	
9	3.50	2.77	0.94	$242.39	
10	3.65	2.88	0.95	$225.27	

regression analysis using historical data, you can find those parameters and use them to recommend that your sales representatives increase the number of calls they make to six, and then offer a concrete prediction of increased profit as a result.

RESOURCE ALLOCATION AND NEW PRODUCT PERFORMANCE

Let's consider another example of the function that connects marketing inputs to objective metrics in the consumer-goods industry. This example provides a more realistic example of a function that would be used in practice.

Figure 1.3 shows a decomposition commonly used by consumer-goods companies to forecast the performance of new products. Using this function, a company can study, for example, how advertising leads to awareness, and how the salesforce leads to availability. Once the company understands the empirical relationships mathematically, it can calculate expected sales using simple arithmetic.

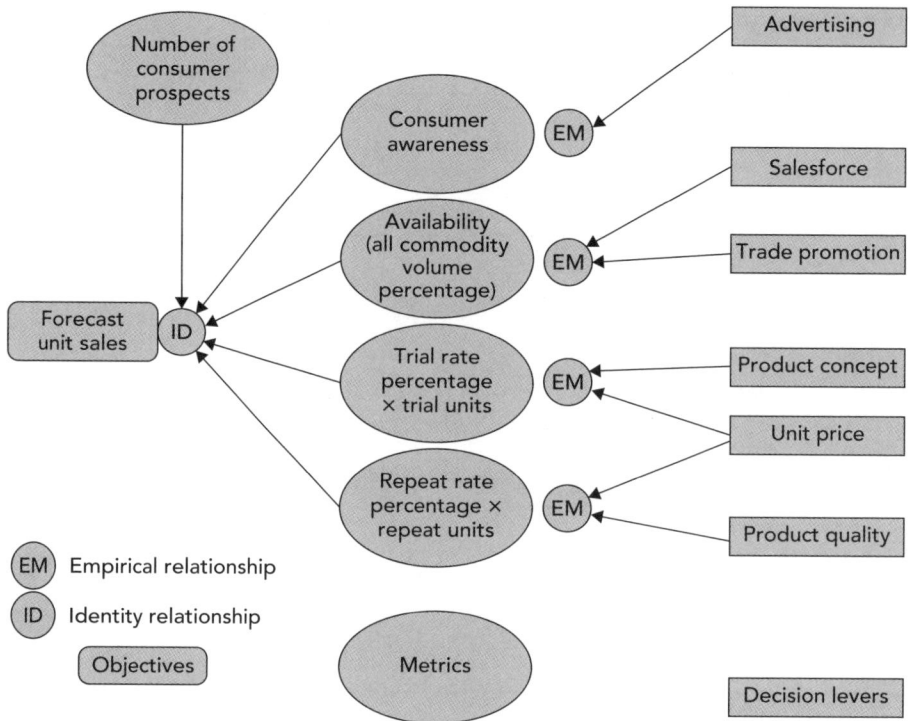

FIGURE 1.3. System of metrics to forecast new product sales

MEASURING ROI: DID THE RESOURCE ALLOCATION WORK?

Remember that the goal of marketing analytics is to determine the effectiveness of a company's various marketing strategies, or its marketing mix. For each strategy, the company wants to assess its return on investment (ROI). But which kind of ROI? What is the best way to evaluate resource allocation?

Financial ROI is equal to profit over investment value; it is a yearly average rate, comparable to rate of return.

Marketing ROI (ROMI), or marginal ROI, is equal to profits related to marketing measures divided by the value of the marketing investment—which is actually money risked, not invested:

$$\text{ROMI} = [\text{Incremental sales} \times \text{Gross margin} - \text{Marketing investment}]/$$
$$\text{Marketing investment}.$$

Incremental sales refers to an increase in sales as a result of marketing measures. Determining ROMI is simple arithmetic; it is more difficult to determine how marketing leads to incremental sales.

A major decision regarding resource-allocation decisions and assessments concerns the choice between financial (average) ROI and ROMI. Financial ROI represents the returns for any given level of marketing investment. If an executive is interested in how total returns to marketing spending have changed over the previous two years, financial ROI is the right measure. ROMI, on the other hand, means incremental return, the return for an additional dollar spent on marketing relative to existing investment levels. For example, ROMI can be used to understand the incremental returns from increases in advertising from $1 million per month to $1.2 million per month. The choice between ROMI and financial ROI relies to a large extent on whether a marketing measure such as advertising spending may yield diminishing returns. For linear models, average and incremental returns are the same, because regardless of the current level of spending, the returns will be identical (**figure 1.4**, top panel). However, the current level of investment matters when calculating incremental returns in the presence of diminishing returns (**figure 1.4**, bottom panel).

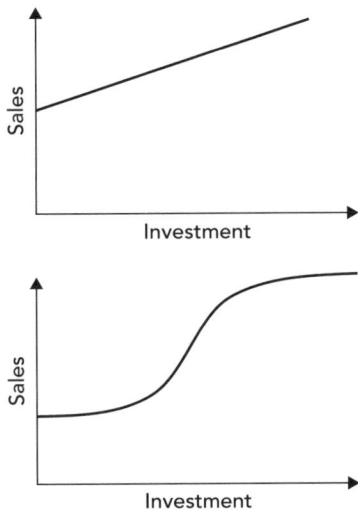

FIGURE 1.4. Sales response curves: Linear (*top*) and with diminishing returns (*bottom*)

HYPOTHETICAL CASE: POWERFUL POWERTOOLS

Imagine that in 2012, Powerful Powertools spent $2 million on search engine marketing and generated $10 million in incremental sales, with marketing contribution margins of 50%. The company would determine its ROMI as follows:

$$ROMI = (\$10 \text{ million} \times 0.5 - \$2 \text{ million}) \div \$2 \text{ million} = 1.5.$$

A marketing manager or CFO would have therefore determined that the company's return was 150% on the marketing investment. But the manager likely still had questions. Would the investment in 2012 also pay dividends in 2013 (i.e., should some new customer acquisitions in 2013 be attributed to the investment in 2012)? How was incremental gross margin determined? What was the baseline profit without the search engine marketing? Would doubling the investment to $4 million in 2013 double the returns to $20 million in incremental sales, or are there diminishing returns to marketing? What are the longer-term effects, and what is the lifetime value of the customers acquired through this campaign? The goal of analytics is to clarify these nuances of marketing's influence on sales, so that the estimate of incremental sales necessary for calculating ROMI is an accurate reflection of reality.

CASE EXAMPLE: IBM'S CLV-BASED RESOURCE ALLOCATION

To improve marketing success, companies must consistently make good decisions about which customers to target, what level of resources to allocate to the selected customers, and how to nurture the selected customers to increase future profitability.

In this real-life example, IBM changes the metric it uses to target customers (small to medium businesses as well as large companies) and allocate resources.[1] Previously, IBM targeted and allocated resources to customers based on their customer spending scores, which it defined as the total revenue it could expect from a customer in the following year. Now, the company is abandoning that method because customer spending scores focused only on revenues, not costs. Instead, IBM has chosen a new objective metric: customer lifetime value (CLV; see also chapter 5). IBM uses this metric to reflect the goal of increased long-term customer-level profits. Based on CLV, it chooses which customers to target through sales calls, telesales, emails, and catalogs,

TABLE 1.2. IBM's resource allocation

Process	Purpose
Determine the objective metric: CLV.	Obtain a measure of the potential value of IBM customers.
Develop the function that connects marketing inputs to CLV.	Allow managers to influence CLV.
Estimate the unknown parameters of the function using historical data.	Understand the relationship between marketing contacts and customer lifetime value.
Determine optimal level of marketing contacts for each customer, given the estimated parameters of the function connecting marketing inputs to CLV that would maximize that customer's CLV.	Guide managers about the level of investment required for each customer.
Develop propensity models to predict what product(s) a customer is likely to purchase.	Develop a product message when contacting a customer.
Reallocate marketing contacts from low-CLV customers to high-CLV customers.	Maximize marketing productivity.

Source: Adapted from V. Kumar, Rajkumar Venkatesan, Tim Bohling, and Denise Beckmann, "The Power of CLV: Managing Customer Lifetime Value at IBM," *Marketing Science* 27, no. 4 (July–August 2008), 585–99.

and then optimally allocates sales calls to maximize CLV. An overview of the CLV management framework in terms of resource allocation is shown in **table 1.2**.

In a pilot study of 35,000 midmarket customers, a CLV model included three aspects, which were inherently correlated with each other: customer characteristics, past purchasing behavior by that customer, and past level of marketing resources that IBM allocated to the customer. Using this model, IBM could connect the level of marketing contacts directed toward a customer to that customer's CLV. Model parameters were estimated using 54 months of past data, and then actual CLV scores were computed for each customer, enabling IBM to determine the optimal level of marketing contacts and, crucially, to reallocate resources from low-CLV to high-CLV customers.

IBM found that CLV was a much more effective objective metric than customer spending scores. In the pilot study of 35,000 midmarket customers, this approach led

Status quo: Using customer spending scores

Recommended: Using CLV

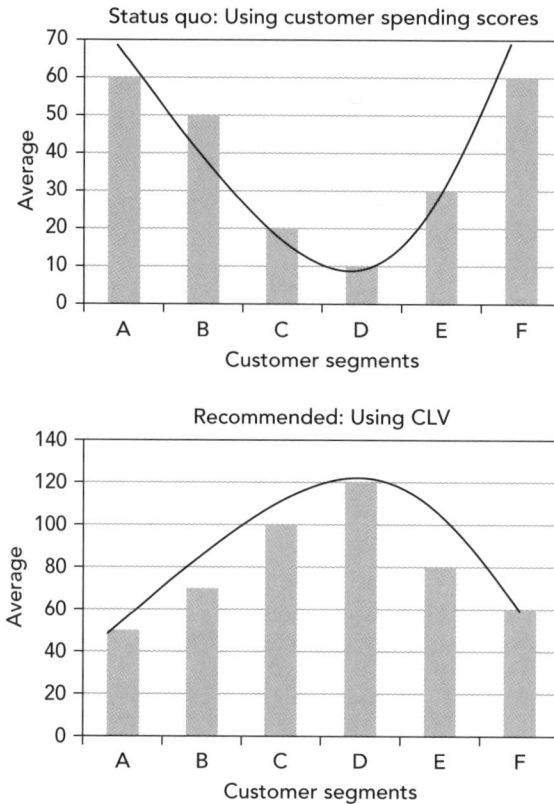

FIGURE 1.5. Benefits of CLV-based resource allocation

to reallocation of resources for about 14% of the customers (**figure 1.5**). Without any changes in the level of marketing investment, IBM's CLV-based resource reallocation led to a tenfold increase in revenue, amounting to about $20 million.

CONCLUSION

Managers must understand their marketing efforts as precisely as possible in order to determine how much to spend on each marketing media channel, which could be, for example, sales calls, television advertising, or display advertising. If paid search advertising is the most effective way to get a firm's message in front of the right customers, why would the company spend more on print advertising? If sales calls are profitable only up to a point, the marketing manager must determine what that point is, so that the calls don't start costing the company money instead of making it.

The only way to measure the effects of marketing efforts on profitability is through the best-guess relationships revealed through marketing analytics. By using statistical analysis techniques, firms can use past customer behaviors to predict how customers will react to different marketing channels in order to optimize spending on each channel. Using ROMI, managers can then assess the effectiveness and incremental returns obtained from adopting the optimal spending decisions recommended by marketing analytics.

2

Cluster Analysis

I f resource allocation is the cornerstone of marketing analytics, a key question is how to optimize it by targeting the right customers. A good marketing manager needs to find, and define, the customers on whom to focus, as well as determine how to customize marketing strategies to them in order to maximize return on marketing investment. The question, in other words, is how to do the work involved in segmentation, the first of the three main strategic aspects of marketing.

We all understand that consumers are not all alike. This complicates the development and marketing of profitable products and services. Not every offering will be right for every customer, nor will every customer be equally responsive to your marketing efforts. **Segmentation** is a way of organizing customers into groups with similar traits, product preferences, or expectations. Once segments are identified, resources can be allocated accordingly: marketing messages—in many cases even products—can be customized for each segment. The better the segmentation, the more accurate an organization's identification of its target segment and the needs of the customers in that segment. This will translate into more successful marketing efforts that appeal to the target segment, and better performance for the organization.

Since its introduction in the late 1950s, market segmentation has become a central concept of marketing practice. Exploiting customer heterogeneity and differences across segments is a key characteristic of good resource-allocation strategy. To optimize its marketing investment, a firm will often conduct a market segmentation exercise to identify target segments before employing analytics techniques discussed later in this book for each of those customer groups.

Customers are grouped into **segments**, or **clusters**, based on their (a) demographic characteristics, (b) psychographics (classification by psychological factors, like attitudes or values), (c) desired benefits from products/services, and (d) past-purchase and product-use behaviors. These days, most firms possess rich information about customers' actual purchase behaviors, geodemographics, and psychographics. When firms do not have detailed information about each customer, they often do have access to information from surveys of a representative sample of the customers, which they can use instead as the basis for segmentation. Which customer information you choose to focus on is key to the success of your segmentation; again, these choices are based on your marketing goals, which you decide using your managerial intuition and knowledge of your company and its context.

HYPOTHETICAL CASE: GEICO

Imagine you are a marketing manager at Geico. The car insurance company is planning on customizing its offerings, and your task is to figure out what customers view as important in their insurance provider. You design a survey that asks current Geico customers to rate how important the following two attributes are to them when considering the type of auto insurance they would use:

- Savings on premium
- Existence of a neighborhood agent

Attribute importance is measured using a seven-point Likert-type scale, where a rating of one represents *not important* and seven represents *very important*. Unless every respondent gives identical ratings, your data will contain variations that you can use to cluster or group respondents together. Customers are most similar to each other if they are part of the same segment, and they are most different from each other if they are part of different segments. Actions aimed toward customers in the same segment should lead to similar responses, and actions aimed toward customers in different segments should lead to different responses.

In the case of Geico, then, the aspects of auto insurance that are important to any given customer in one segment will also be important to other customers in the same segment. Furthermore, the aspects that are important to that customer will be different from those that are important to a customer in a different segment. **Figure 2.1** shows what the analysis in this example might look like.

Your analysis shows three distinct segments. The majority of Geico customers (Segment A, 49%) prefer savings on their premium and have no preference as to a

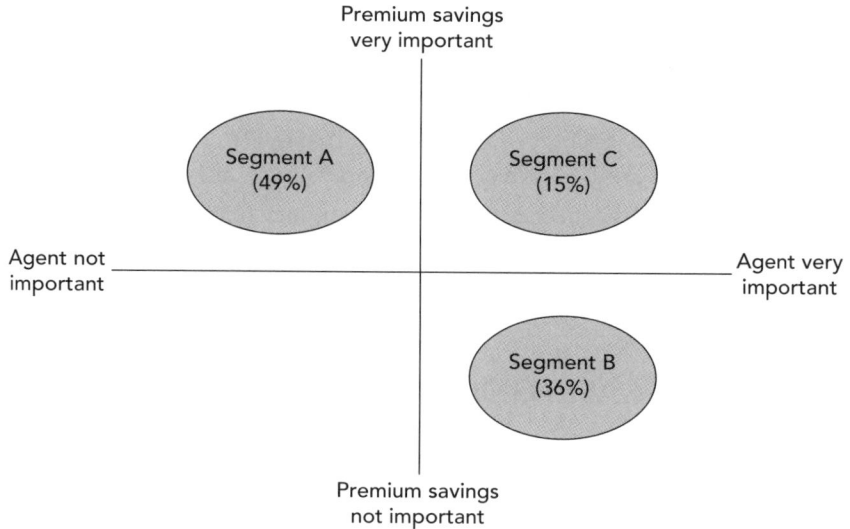

FIGURE 2.1. Segmentation of Geico customers

neighborhood agent. Customers in Segment B (36%) prefer having a neighborhood agent and don't care very much about premium savings. Some customers (Segment C, 15%) prefer both the savings on their premium and a neighborhood agent. This analysis shows that Geico can benefit by adding an offline channel (i.e., developing a network of neighborhood agents) to serve Segment B and also charge a higher premium to them for providing this convenience. Of course, the risk is increased competition with other insurance providers, such as Allstate and State Farm, which already provide this service.

CLUSTER ANALYSIS

Cluster analysis is a class of statistical techniques that sort data that exhibit natural groupings, in order to organize them into clusters, or relatively homogeneous groups. Cluster analysis makes no distinction between dependent and independent variables. The entire set of interdependent relationships is examined. Customers who belong to the same cluster are similar to each other and dissimilar to customers outside the cluster, particularly customers in other clusters. The primary inputs for cluster analysis are measures of similarity between customers, such as (a) correlation coefficients and (b) distance measures.

Correlation coefficients measure the association between two variables. They range from −1, which indicates a negative association like that between sales and price (when prices go up, sales go down, and vice versa), to 1, which indicates a positive association like that between sales and advertising (when advertising goes up, so do sales—at least, that's the intention). Zero implies no linear association between the variables. **Distance measures** are measures of the difference between two customers on the variables used for segmentation.

The basic steps involved in cluster analysis are as follows:

1. Formulate the problem.
2. Compute distance between customers along the selected variables.
3. Apply the clustering procedure to the distance measures.
4. Decide on the number of clusters.
5. Profile clusters.

Step 1: Formulate the Problem

The first step is to select the variables that you wish to use as the basis for clustering. Those variables determine how well your segmentation works in terms of marketing.

Criteria frequently used to evaluate the effectiveness of a segmentation scheme include: *identifiability, sustainability, accessibility,* and *actionability.*[1] **Identifiability** refers to the extent to which managers can recognize segments in the marketplace. In the Geico example, when demographics are included in the segmentation analysis, Geico would be able to *identify* different target segments—based solely on their demographic information—and reach out to these segments with customized messages and marketing campaigns, for example about customer service or premium savings. PRIZM and ACORN are popular databases that provide geodemographic information that can be used for segmentation as well as profiling. The **sustainability** criterion is satisfied if the segments represent a large enough portion of the market to ensure that marketing programs can be customized profitably. The extent to which managers can reach the identified segments through marketing campaigns is captured by the **accessibility** criterion. Finally, **actionability** refers to whether customers in a certain segment and the marketing mix necessary to satisfy their needs are consistent with the goals and core competencies of the firm. For example, if a certain segment can be reached only through chatbots on Facebook Messenger, and the firm is capable of developing and delivering compelling chatbots, then the firm is capable of taking action to satisfy the customer's needs, and the actionability criteria are satisfied.

When choosing variables on which to base the cluster analysis, it is important to keep these four criteria in mind: marketing goals and feasibility must be paramount. The success of any segmentation process therefore requires not only accurate data and appropriate data analysis, but also managerial intuition and careful judgment.

Step 2: Compute Distance

The main input into any cluster-analysis procedure is a measure of distance between individuals who are being clustered. The objective of a distance measure is to quantify the difference between two individuals on the variables you are using for the segmentation. A shorter distance between two individuals implies that they have similar preferences on the segmentation variables, and may be in the same cluster; conversely, a longer distance implies that they have dissimilar preferences and may be in different clusters. Distance between two individuals is obtained through a measure called **Euclidean distance**. If two individuals, Joe and Sam, are being clustered on the basis of n variables, then the Euclidean distance between Joe and Sam is represented as

$$Euclidean\ distance(Joe,\ Sam) = \sqrt{(x_{Joe,\ 1} - x_{Sam,\ 1})^2 + \cdots + (x_{Joe,\ n} - x_{Sam,\ n})^2},$$

where

$x_{Joe,1}$ = the value of Joe along variable *1*, and

$x_{Sam,1}$ = the value of Sam along variable *1*.

A pairwise distance matrix among individuals being clustered can be created using the Euclidean distance measure. Extending this example, consider three individuals, Joe, Sam, and Sara, who are being clustered based on their preferences for (a) Premium Savings, and (b) a Neighborhood Agent. The importance ratings on these two attributes given by Joe, Sam, and Sara are provided in **table 2.1**.

TABLE 2.1. Sample data for cluster analysis

	Importance score	
Individual name	Premium savings	Neighborhood agent
Joe	4	7
Sam	3	4
Sara	5	3

TABLE 2.2. Pairwise distance matrix

	Joe	Sam	Sara
Joe	0	3.2	4.1
Sam		0	2.2
Sara			0

The Euclidean distance between Joe and Sam is obtained as

$$Euclidean\ distance(Joe,\ Sam)=\sqrt{(4-3)^2+(7-4)^2}=3.2.$$

The first term in the Euclidean distance measure is the squared difference between Joe and Sam on the importance score for Premium Savings, and the second term is the squared difference between them on the importance score for Neighborhood Agent. The Euclidean distances are then computed for each pairwise combination of the three individuals being clustered to obtain a pairwise distance matrix. The pairwise distance matrix for Joe, Sam, and Sara is provided in **table 2.2**.

The distance between Joe and Sam is provided in the second row and third column of **table 2.2**. This pairwise distance matrix can then be input to a clustering algorithm.

Step 3: Apply the Clustering Procedure

Because of its simplicity and speed, **K-means clustering** is one of the more popular algorithms used for clustering, and it is gaining even more popularity with the growth of machine learning. It belongs to the **nonhierarchical** class of clustering algorithms, meaning the clustering algorithm does not impose a hierarchical structure on the variables used for the segmentation. It is also considered to be more robust to different types of variables, more appropriate for large data sets that are common in marketing, and less sensitive to outliers (customers extremely different from others).

For K-means clustering, the manager has to specify the **number of clusters, k,** required before starting the clustering algorithm. The basic algorithm for K-means clustering is as follows:

- Choose the number of clusters, k.
- Generate k random points as cluster centroids.
- Assign each point to the nearest cluster centroid.
- Recompute the new cluster centroid.
- Repeat the two previous steps until some convergence criterion is met. Usually the convergence criterion is met when the assignment of customers to clusters has not changed over multiple iterations.

A **cluster center**, or **centroid**, is simply the average of all the points in that cluster. Its coordinates are the arithmetic mean for each dimension separately over all the points in the cluster. Consider again the example of Joe, Sam, and Sara. Let us represent them based on their importance ratings on Premium Savings and Neighborhood Agent as: Joe = {4,7}, Sam = {3,4}, Sara = {5,3}. If we assume that they belong to the same cluster, then the center for their cluster is obtained as:

$$\text{Cluster centroid } Z = (z_1, z_2) = \left\{ \frac{(4+3+5)}{3}, \frac{(7+4+3)}{3} \right\}.$$

z_1 is measured as the average of the ratings of Joe, Sam, and Sara on Premium Savings. Similarly, z_2 is measured as the average of their ratings on Neighborhood Agent. **Figure 2.2** provides a visual representation of K-means clustering.

In **figure 2.2**, the x axis represents ratings for Premium Savings, and the y axis represents those for Neighborhood Agent; the diamonds are the coordinates for each customer's ratings of the importance of these two factors. The analyst's first step is to make two arbitrary decisions: the number of clusters (k) and placement of the original cluster seeds. In this example, $k = 2$, and the cluster seeds are the two circles in the top panel. In the next step, each set of ratings is assigned to the cluster seed it is most similar to, creating two clusters (panel two). The randomly chosen cluster seeds are not the cluster means, so the third step is to find the means of each of the clusters, creating new cluster centroids, the two new circles in the third panel. Next, using these

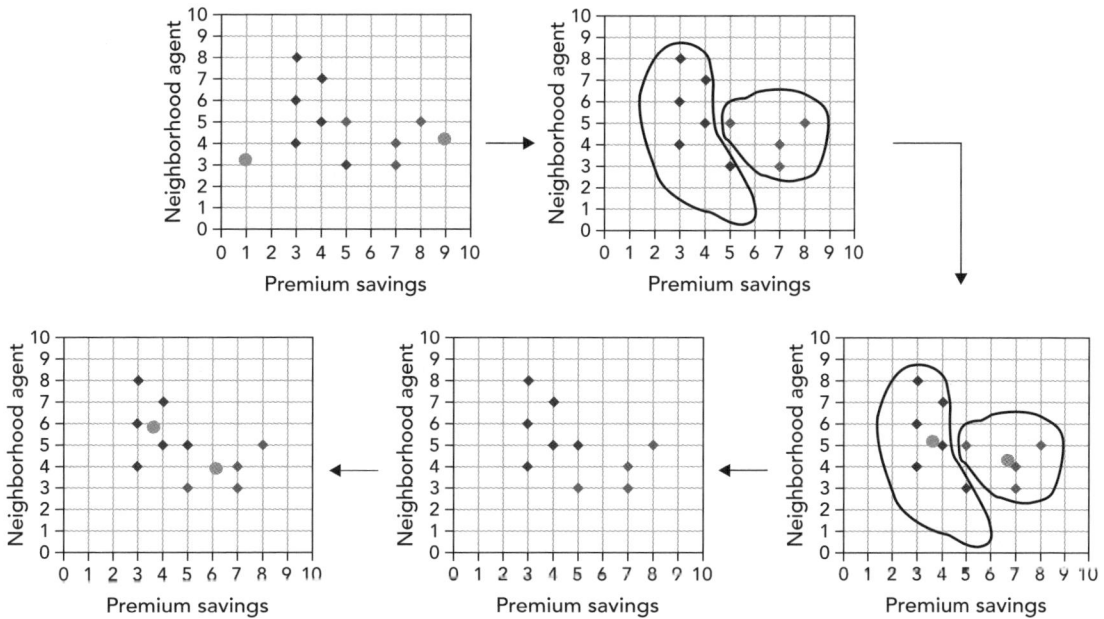

FIGURE 2.2. Visual representation of K-means clustering

new centroids, the analyst must reevaluate the ratings in terms of similarity to those centroids, reassigning them as in the fourth panel. Now with two new clusters, the procedure is repeated. As in the third step, the analyst calculates the means of the new clusters to find new centroids: these are the two circles in the fifth panel. This process—calculating coordinates' similarity to cluster centroids, reassigning coordinates to clusters, calculating new cluster centroids, and repeating—keeps iterating until the analyst is satisfied with the number of clusters and the distances between them. Once the clusters no longer change, and centroids are stable, the process starts all over again, this time with $k = 3$ and three arbitrary centroids.

Step 4: Decide on Number of Clusters

One of the main issues with K-means clustering is that it does not provide an esti-mate of the number of clusters in the data. Decision trees, introduced in chapter 11, may be one way to get around this problem. Otherwise, the K-means clustering algo-rithm has to be repeated several times with different ks to determine the number of clusters that is appropriate for the data. A commonly used method to determine the optimal k is the "elbow criterion."

The **elbow criterion** means finding a number of clusters such that adding another cluster does not add sufficient information. In other words, this is the point at which another cluster would add complexity to the marketing process that is not justified by the returns from customizing marketing to the additional segment. The elbow is identified by plotting the ratio of within-cluster variance to between-cluster variance against the number of clusters. **Within-cluster variance** is an estimate of the average variance in the variables used as a basis for segmentation among customers who belong to a particular cluster; in the Geico example, within-cluster variance captures the differences in ratings of Premium Savings and Neighborhood Agent among customers in the same cluster. **Between-cluster variance** is an estimate of the variance in the segmentation basis variables among customers who belong to different segments; in the Geico example, between-cluster variance captures the differences in those ratings among customers from different clusters.

The objective of cluster analysis is to minimize within-cluster variance and maximize between-cluster variance. As the number of clusters increases, the ratio of within-cluster variance to between-cluster variance will keep decreasing. But at some point, the marginal gain from an additional cluster will drop, giving an angle in the graph: this is the elbow. In **figure 2.3**, the elbow is indicated by the circle. The number of clusters chosen should therefore be 4.

Sometimes there is not a clear elbow in the graph. This can happen when the means of the variables chosen for segmentation are not different enough, so that between-cluster variance is not very different from within-cluster variance. When this happens, you should try the analysis again using different variables; often this is as simple as choosing from a smaller, or different, subset of survey questions.

It is important to note that the initial assignment of cluster seeds has a bearing on the final model performance. Some common methods for ensuring the stability of the results obtained from K-means clustering include:

- Running the algorithm multiple times with different starting values. When using random starting points, running the algorithm multiple times will ensure a different starting point each time.
- Splitting the data randomly into two halves and running the cluster analysis separately on each half. The results are robust and stable if the number of clusters and the size of different clusters are similar in both halves.

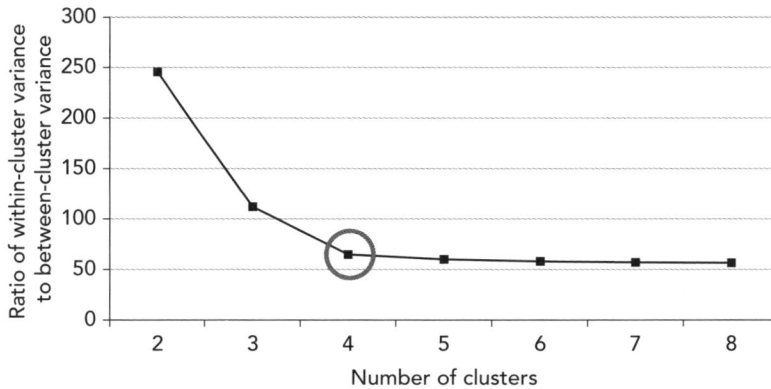

FIGURE 2.3. Elbow plot for determining number of clusters

Step 5: Profile Clusters

Managers use cluster analysis to customize marketing strategy for each segment. It is not enough just to identify the clusters; in order to use them to customize marketing, clusters need to be profiled. **Profiling clusters** means describing them in terms of the variables used for clustering—or in terms of additional data, such as demographics. This way, a company can extrapolate from data on its own customers to find the most likely potential customers. One way to illustrate clusters is through a perceptual map, as shown in **figure 2.1** in the Geico example. There is also a variety of cluster-analysis software, including SPSS, SAS, XLSTAT, and R, that provides information as to which cluster a customer belongs.

In the Geico example, it is useful to investigate whether the segments also differ with respect to demographic variables such as age and annual income. In **table 2.3**, let us consider the distribution of age and income for Segments A, B, and C as provided in **figure 2.1**.

Means and ranges of demographic variables can be used to profile each cluster, or segment. **Mean** represents the average age and income of customers belonging to a particular segment. **Range** represents the minimum and maximum values of age and income for customers in a segment. While the mean is useful for identifying the central tendency of a segment, the range helps in evaluating whether the segments overlap with regard to the profile variable.

Interpreting the cluster analysis leads to customer insights that can inform customization of marketing strategies to different segments. Using **table 2.3**, we see that

TABLE 2.3. Age and income distribution for segments

Segment	Mean		Range	
	Age	Income	Age	Income
A	21	$15,000	16–25	$0–$25,000
B	45	$120,000	33–55	$75,000–$215,000
C	39	$40,000	39–54	$24,000–$60,000

Segment A customers, who prefer high premium savings and do not care about having a neighborhood agent, tend to be younger and have lower incomes. These could be college students or recent graduates who are more comfortable transacting online. Customers who belong to Segment B, on the other hand, are older and have higher incomes. It would be interesting to evaluate if these customers also tend to be married with kids. The security of having a neighborhood agent who can help in case of an accident or emergency is very important to them, and they do not mind paying a high price for this sense of security. These customers may also not be comfortable in transacting (or providing personal information) online.

Finally, while Segment C customers are as old as Segment B customers and also prefer to have a neighborhood agent, they tend to have lower incomes and prioritize premium savings. Matching the segments with demographic characteristics enables a marketer to target each segment in terms of products offered, as well as to customize marketing communications by segment. For example, if Geico decides to develop a network of neighborhood agents, it can first focus on neighborhoods (identified through their zip codes) that match the demographic profile of Segment B customers.

CONCEPT APPLICATION

In the following case study, the owners of Sticks Kebob Shop (Sticks), a quick-service restaurant headquartered in Charlottesville, Virginia, are expanding their business and deciding where to put a new restaurant. How can cluster analysis help them?

As you read the case, keep in mind the five steps of cluster analysis. Focusing on the first—formulating the problem and choosing the variables that will define how consumers are grouped—consider the structure of the challenge for Sticks.

- What are the informative characteristics of people and place in choosing a restaurant location?

- How do people choose a quick-service restaurant?
- What is important to them: location, price, cuisine, or something else?
- Do the owners have an accurate impression of their customers before the survey?
- Which data would be enough to adequately segment customers?
- Which restaurants are Sticks' competition, and what are some pros and cons to locations near those competitors?
- Which variables the restaurant owners choose will determine how useful their segmentation scheme is. Remember that effectiveness is evaluated by *identifiability*, *sustainability*, *accessibility*, and *actionability*. How might these criteria manifest in the process of exploring new markets?

After you finish reading the case, use the survey data given in the online data set (http://store.darden.virginia.edu/marketing-analytics-supplements) to perform your own cluster analysis.

- Which of the survey questions might help you identify informative segments?
- How many clusters do you find?
- Profile the clusters you have found. How well do they predict a preference for Sticks? In other words, who wants Sticks, and why?
- Finally, using the chart of possible locations given in **table 2.8**, where do you think the new location should be?
- How would you present your analysis to Sticks management, and what marketing strategy would you recommend?

CASE: STICKS KEBOB SHOPS

Sticks had a problem. But it was a good problem to have.

A restaurant chain in a fast-growing segment of the food-service industry, Sticks expected to add about one restaurant to its portfolio every year or two starting in 2014. Its challenge was in picking the right markets to enter, and then deciding on (and waiting for) the right location.

Since opening its first quick-service restaurant (QSR) in 2001 in Charlottesville, Sticks had added another store in town (**figure 2.4**), as well as one each in Richmond, Virginia, and Williamsburg, Virginia. Because Richmond was a larger city, the Sticks executive team—composed of Chris DuBois, Ty Austin, Ingmar Leliveld, and Bill Hamilton—was interested in opening a second location there. They had narrowed

FIGURE 2.4. Sticks Charlottesville location

their search to four specific targets, but before selecting the optimal site, the team wanted to gain a better sense of who Sticks' customers were, which location would attract the best customers, and how to best connect with customers.

The restaurant-industry veterans had a rough idea of their customer base from anecdotal evidence. An opportunity to gather survey data to confirm their hypotheses presented itself. Would the demographic and psychographic assumptions they had formed by talking to people in stores align with the survey answers? And what would the data tell them about where to locate their new store and what marketing channels and messages would be most effective in promoting it?

The Sticks Story

While working at Hamiltons' at First & Main, a fine-dining restaurant in Charlottesville, DuBois and Austin realized they needed a good place to grab a good bite to eat before going into work for the night shift. When Bill Hamilton, who owned Hamiltons' at First & Main with his wife, approached the pair about going into business together, the trio decided to pursue a concept that could deliver a good meal without much fuss. "We went out for some beers and decided we were going to do it," DuBois said. "We had not settled on a concept for the restaurant at the time."[2]

The team finally settled on kebobs after kicking around food ideas ranging from barbecue to curry. In 2001, the idea of the fast-casual restaurant—essentially the QSR segment minus traditional fast food—was still in its infancy: Chipotle had just begun to expand outside its home state of Colorado. The idea was to offer high-quality, healthy food in a less stuffy environment, and to deliver it quickly. According to the Sticks website, the group wanted to "create a safe haven for fellow foodies, busy families, and health-conscious diners." It was a niche the team members thought Charlottesville lacked, and one they decided they could satisfy effectively.

The Sticks chain had learned a lot about its customer base over the years; for example, executives had increased their focus on the healthy food angle. But Sticks also made sure that its cuisine remained accessible to a broader audience. Sticks didn't claim to be authentic Middle Eastern food. For example, instead of using the original term baba ganouj for one of its menu items, Sticks called it roasted eggplant salad.

The menu was very customizable. A Sticks customer began by choosing a sandwich, salad, or platter, then had the opportunity to "Pick-A-Stick" from a list of seven kebobs, along with sides. A sandwich was a kebob and sauce in grilled flatbread with lettuce and tomato; a salad was fresh vegetables topped with a kebob, croutons, and dressing; and a platter was a kebob, sauce, side dish, basmati rice, and grilled flatbread. Kebobs offered were chicken breast with fresh herbs, chili-spiked beef sirloin, rosemary-rubbed leg of lamb, pork loin with African spices, housemade kibbeh (vegetarian), mixed garden vegetables with basil oil, and falafel. Sides included hummus, roasted eggplant salad, sesame green beans, cucumber salad, marinated grilled veggies, tabbouleh, french fries, onion rings, and pita chips. Finally, a meal could be topped with an additional kebob; garnishes including feta cheese, olives, and grilled onions; and homemade sauces like cucumber-yogurt, fire-roasted red pepper, and creamy cilantro-lime. The cost of a Sticks meal could range from a soup and half salad for $4.99 at the low end, to a platter with two lamb kebobs, two additional toppings, and limeade for $17.94.

Planning for Expansion

According to DuBois, Sticks' long-term expansion plan focused on the I-64 corridor that ran across Virginia. Richmond was the primary immediate target because the brand had already been established there, and a second store would lend efficiencies in marketing, labor, and the like. Beyond that, the company planned to look in Virginia at Newport News, Hampton Roads, Virginia Beach, Norfolk, Harrisonburg, Lynchburg, and Fredericksburg. The eventual goal was to grow from four stores in 2014 to eight in 2020, at which point the company would reassess and consider moving into the Northern Virginia and Washington, DC, areas, which would require a multiple-store launch.

In addition to adding restaurants, Sticks expected to expand in two other ways. It was in the process of launching a packaged version of its signature hummus for sale in retail outlets, and planning to purchase a food trailer to increase its off-site vending, including at an outdoor concert series in Richmond.

The Sticks growth plan had been tempered slightly in the past several years, as the Richmond location was growing more slowly than the company would have liked. The restaurant had opened right on the cusp of the 2008 recession and improved sales by about 10% every year, but the baseline had been lower than expected. See **table 2.4** for Sticks location addresses as of 2014.

The customer survey was an opportunity to ensure that the next Richmond store would be a strong fit with its market. DuBois said the goal was to gather data that

TABLE 2.4. **Sticks locations, 2014**

Store name	Address
Preston Avenue, Charlottesville	917 Preston Avenue Charlottesville, VA 22903
Pantops, Charlottesville	1820 Abbey Road Charlottesville, VA 22911
Willow Lawn, Richmond	1700 Willow Lawn Dr. Willow Lawn Plaza Richmond, VA 23221
Courthouse Commons, Williamsburg	5223 Monticello Avenue Williamsburg, VA 23188

could assist in identifying real estate options, improve on the team's knowledge of customer demographics and psychographics, and provide insight into how customers perceived Sticks relative to other restaurants they frequented in terms of value for the money and other attributes.

DuBois and Austin described the typical Sticks customers—based on knowledge gained while working as managers in the two Charlottesville stores—as people "in their 30s who have a smartphone and want food that's both healthful and satisfying." The base skewed more toward women making dining decisions for their families, but the restaurant also did well with single people in their mid-20s to mid-40s, and with professionals on their lunch break. More recently, Sticks had identified growing interest in its Mediterranean-inspired menu from an older demographic that valued active lifestyles and healthy eating.

"It may sound like a cliché, but a lot of our customers are soccer moms," DuBois said. "Soccer is a big thing in the area. We have proven to be a good fit for people who are involved in sports—either for themselves or for their kids."

When its first restaurant had opened in 2001, the Sticks team knew that offering a quick, healthy meal option would be a big part of its appeal, but the team members had debated about how heavily to market that attribute, since at the time most people associated health food with unsatisfying food. The team also wanted to combat the idea that the restaurant was exotic and unfamiliar, so it could appeal to customers who generally selected more familiar options, such as Applebee's, Arby's, or Ruby Tuesday.

DuBois and Austin said they consistently heard from customers that they appreciated the variety of the Sticks menu and its filling but nutritious food, well-priced selections, and fast service. Management considered other fast-casual restaurants such as Chipotle and Panera to be competitors, as the restaurant tended to attract most of its customers on weekday afternoons. The volume of visits during nights and weekends was generally lower.

"The challenge is not expecting people to behave in a way you want them to, but instead letting them do more of what they already want to do themselves," Austin said. "We have to remind ourselves to work from and gradually expand people's given behaviors. We try to keep hurdles low for new customers, yet offer enough options for novelty for existing customers."

The Fast-Food Industry

Fast-casual QSRs typically aimed to deliver food quickly, but they operated outside the traditional fast-food market by offering carefully selected ingredients and healthier options overall. For Sticks, that also meant avoiding being pigeonholed as a health-food restaurant or a college-town niche, and striving to become a national brand. Sticks wanted its customers to leave the restaurant feeling full and satisfied and as if they had made a smart dining choice.

From 2010 to 2012, the fast-casual industry was one of the fastest-growing segments of the restaurant business, according to *QSR* magazine, and Panera was the clear leader (**table 2.5**). According to food-industry analyst Technomic, Inc., several other fast-casual restaurants were among the fastest-growing QSRs in the country (**table 2.6**).

Sticks also fell into another fast-growing segment of restaurants: ethnic food. Although the Mexican segment was the clear ethnic food leader, DuBois said Mediterranean restaurants were also growing quickly. They were part of a group (specialty fast-casual restaurants) that made up 9% of all fast-casual restaurants (**table 2.7**).

Sticks was somewhat unique, however, in that it marketed itself without referring to ethnicity. The goal of the restaurant's owners was to make the food as accessible as possible and not intimidate customers. Sticks did not expect to attract adventurous

TABLE 2.5. Top 10 fast-casual restaurants

Fast-casual rank	Chain	2012 sales	Total units, 2012	Change in units from 2011
1	Panera	$3,861.0 million	1,652	111
2	Chipotle	$2,731.2 million	1,410	180
3	Jimmy John's	$1,262.8 million	1,560	229
4	Zaxby's	$979.3 million	565	25
5	Steak 'n Shake	$857.5 million	501	10
6	Qdoba	$583.2 million	627	44
7	Jason's Deli	$578.9 million	245	10
8	El Pollo Loco	$563.0 million	397	3
9	Boston Market	$559.0 million	469	(12)
10	Moe's	$452.0 million	482	43

Source: Data from Sam Oches, "The *QSR* 50," *QSR*, August 2013, http://www.qsrmagazine.com/reports/qsr50 -2013-top-50-chart (accessed Feb. 24, 2014).

CLUSTER ANALYSIS | 39

TABLE 2.6. Fastest-growing QSR chains (more than $200 million in annual sales)

Rank	Chain	2011 US sales	2010 US sales	Percentage change	Change
1	Five Guys	$950.63 million	$716.11 million	32.8%	$234.53 million
2	Chipotle	$2.26 billion	$1.83 billion	23.4%	$428.63 million
3	Jimmy John's	$895.00 million*	$735.00 million*	21.8%	$160.00 million
4	Firehouse Subs	$284.58 million	$235.00 million	21.1%	$49.58 million
5	Raising Cane's	$206.30 million	$174.61 million	18.2%	$31.69 million
6	Little Caesars	$1.48 billion*	$1.25 billion*	18.1%	$227.00 million
7	Noodles & Company	$300.00 million	$261.00 million	14.9%	$39.00 million
8	Wingstop	$381.66 million	$332.61 million	14.7%	$49.05 million
9	Chick-Fil-A	$4.05 billion	$3.58 billion	13.1%	$467.99 million
10	Qdoba	$531.00 million*	$475.00 million*	11.8%	$56.00 million

Source: Data from "Fastest Growing Limited-Service Chains > $200 Million," Technomic, Inc., 2012, https://www
.technomic.com/Resources/Industry_Facts/dyn_10_limited_sales.php (accessed Feb. 24, 2014).
Note: Sales numbers are rounded.
* Technomic estimate.

TABLE 2.7. Menu composition within the fast-casual segment

Rank	Category	Market share
1	Mexican	20%
2	Bakery/café/bagel	18%
3	Other sandwich	16%
4	Hamburger	11%
5	Chicken	9%
6	Specialty*	9%
7	Pizza	7%
8	Asian	6%

Source: Data from "Menu Composition within the Fast-Casual Seg-
ment," https://www.technomic.com/Resources/Industry_Facts/dyn_Menu
_Composition_within_the_fast_casual.php (accessed Jan. 6, 2014).
* Barbecue, healthy, Italian, other ethnic (including Mediterranean), and soup.

diners seeking out authentic ethnic food; it tried to position itself as a menu alternative alongside Panera and Chipotle, rather than local Middle Eastern restaurants.

Still, Austin and DuBois watched the growth of other Mediterranean restaurants
closely. They saw a larger chain from Alabama called Zoë's Kitchen move into Charlottesville and Richmond in 2014, and Taziki's, another growing chain from the South

operating a similar concept, open in Richmond. In addition to those, Austin said Roti out of Chicago and Garbanzo out of Denver were Mediterranean QSR brands worth following—both chains had high-quality management and were well funded. Despite others entering Sticks' local markets, the team didn't see competition as all bad.

"Most importantly, these larger chains help validate the concept for us," DuBois said. "They also help generate new interest in our category, which is a net benefit. But at the same time, we have to be dynamic and keep creating and emphasizing our unique points of differentiation. We are well aware of direct competition but don't want that to distract us from succeeding on our own terms."

Sticks' Existing Marketing Initiatives

Since its launch in 2001, Sticks had made a concerted effort to better understand its customer base. Over the years, the team had changed its message in subtle ways in response to what it had learned, including switching from Styrofoam containers to reusable plates and silverware and honing its marketing message.

Sticks had used simple, brand recognition–focused advertising campaigns in the Charlottesville area to reinforce its existing reputation. In its other markets, it had focused on more extensive campaigns and made product samples available to introduce what it offered to new audiences. Its most extensive television campaign featured animated spots that didn't show the restaurant's food, but were geared more toward general brand recognition, DuBois said. The spots were used extensively on the Charlottesville broadcast stations, where brand recognition was most powerful for Sticks; however, the team also used the campaign in Richmond and reported some success.

Sticks had also tried to expand its existing customer base through television. The company televised an announcement of a weekend discount on its popular chicken platter, and saw a spike in traffic for what was otherwise a slower time of the week.

The team had used print advertisements primarily in the Richmond market, where it was looking to expand. In that city, the team determined that customers enjoyed reading the alternative newspaper *Style Weekly*; advertisements in the weekly proved to be an inexpensive way to reach a desired audience. Sticks regularly enlisted local marketing experts to fine-tune decisions about how to reach the Richmond audience.

Sticks had found partnerships to be particularly beneficial in Charlottesville, both in a community service capacity and through the restaurant's ongoing advertising campaign with the University of Virginia (UVA) sports properties. In 2013, the brand was in its second year with UVA and had expanded its campaign on the strength of the first year, which featured coupons in the men's basketball, baseball, and soccer team game programs. Austin and DuBois said they considered the coupons a success, particularly those offered during the men's basketball team's ACC home games. Also in 2013, Sticks added several UVA women's sports to the campaign.

The impetus behind the partnership with UVA was largely the university's own demographic and psychographic breakdown of its audience. UVA's sports fans were active, particularly in tennis and golf, dined in various fast-casual restaurants, enjoyed artisanal beverages, and skewed toward higher household incomes. In addition to offering the chance to stay in front of a crowd of people similar to those Sticks believed were its customer base, the campaign also allowed it to build its brand among UVA students.

"The gravy is to attract students as well," DuBois said. "But our main focus is the family and the long-term local resident, rather than the mostly transient students. We looked at that, and it seems to match up with who we already feel are our loyal core customers, so it lets us serve them better."

DuBois and Austin also said Sticks considered its two alternative growth strategies, retail sales and off-site vending, to be promising marketing avenues. Finally, Sticks began offering a successful mobile application that enabled advance ordering and faster pickup in the store in an effort to align it with its technologically savvy base.

Implementing the Survey

Sticks was relatively certain it had a good handle on its customer base—active people making choices for their families, and working professionals looking for a quick, healthy lunch—but the team wanted to confirm that hypothesis. So management worked with an outside consultant to prepare and distribute a survey to both customers and noncustomers. The consultant took the following steps:

1. Create a small but in-depth survey of 5 to 10 existing customers to better inform suggestions for the questionnaires and desired outputs from the study.
2. Prepare the customer and noncustomer surveys for distribution.
3. Sample 200 existing customers, primarily from the Richmond market, using Surveymonkey.com.
4. Utilize a third-party vendor to sample 200 noncustomers online.

1. How many times in the last week did you do the following?
   a. Made and ate lunch at home
   b. Brought own lunch to work
   c. Bought lunch at workplace (e.g., cafeteria)
   d. Bought lunch at restaurant/food court/food truck
   e. Skipped lunch and ate a small snack item
   f. Other
2. Please specify the top five restaurants you have visited in the last six months in order of visit frequency.
3. Have you ever visited Sticks Kebob Shop?
   a. Yes
   b. No
4. How did you first find out about Sticks?
   a. Heard from friend or colleague
   b. Saw in media (print or online—FB, blog, review)
   c. Direct marketing (e.g., Valpak or Groupon)
   d. Noticed from driving or walking by store
   e. Noticed from catering at work (e.g., menu stack)
   f. Noticed at outdoor event/food festival
   g. Other
5. Have you eaten at Sticks in the past three months?
   a. Yes
   b. No
6. In the last month, how often have you visited Sticks for the following occasions?
   a. Weekday lunch
   b. Weekday dinner
   c. Weekend lunch
   d. Weekend dinner
   e. Sticks event (catering at work, food festival)
   f. After-school snack or after-sports practice snack
   g. Other
7. Please indicate how important the following factors are when you visit a restaurant:
   a. Convenient place to eat
   b. Variety of menu options
   c. Good value for the money
   d. Healthy menu options
   e. Food taste and satisfaction
   f. Friendly staff
   g. Pleasant ambiance
   h. Consistency/reliability
   i. Part of community
   j. Other
8. Please indicate how you rate Sticks in comparison to similar restaurants that you visit regularly on the following:
   a. Convenient place to eat
   b. Variety of menu options
   c. Good value for money
   d. Healthy menu options
   e. Food taste and satisfaction
   f. Friendly staff
   g. Pleasant ambiance
   h. Consistency/reliability
   i. Part of community
   j. Other
9. What is your gender?
10. What is your age?
11. What is your approximate average annual household income?
12. How would you best describe your household type?
13. How many children, by age, currently live in your household?
14. In what zip code is your home located?
15. In what zip code is your work located?
16. Please indicate your best answers to the following:
    a. I tend to plan things very carefully
    b. I sometimes have trouble controlling my spending
    c. I think it is important to purchase products that are made locally
    d. I carefully consider the health benefits of what I eat
17. What is your profession?
18. If you have children living at home, in what activities do they participate?
19. In what activities or hobbies do you participate yourself?
20. In the last month, how many times have you used coupons when you visited a restaurant?
21. How do you find restaurant coupons?

FIGURE 2.5. Sticks customer survey questions. (Survey courtesy of Sticks Kebob Shop)

TABLE 2.8. Demographic information

Location	Population	Median age	Median income	Consumer spend	Major customer profiles
A	29,321	39.1	$92,700	$722 million	Blue Blood Estates; Brite Lites, Li'l City; Executive Suites; Upward Bound; Winner's Circle
B	34,183	32.5	$31,900	$482 million	City Startups; Family Thrifts; Hometown Retired; New Beginnings; Sunset City Blues
C	42,913	32.5	$55,700	$754 million	Brite Lites, Li'l City; Family Thrifts; Up-and-Comers; Upward Bound; White Picket Fences
D	57,509	34.8	$75,500	$1,184 million	Brite Lites, Li'l City; Country Squires; Up-and-Comers; Upward Bound; White Picket Fences

Source: Data from PRIZM clusters, Claritas PRIZM Premier, https://www.claritas.com/prizmr-premier (accessed July 2015), courtesy of Sticks Kebob Shop.

The survey questions (see **figure 2.5**) were designed based on the Sticks team's hypotheses about its customers. The Sticks team was particularly interested in responses to question 16, which it hoped would uphold many of its hypotheses about its customers.

DuBois and Austin next wanted to identify segments among its customer base and find the unique preferences of each group. The profile descriptions in **table 2.8** are based on data from PRIZM clusters, developed by marketing analytics firm Claritas; the data about people's behaviors as separated by zip codes are derived from census data and other proprietary sources. DuBois and Austin wanted to use the segmentation information to drive their search for real estate in Richmond and to determine how they should tweak their existing marketing strategy.

CONCLUSION

Many of the hypotheses held by the Sticks executives were upheld. But several of their assumptions proved to be wrong. For the first time, Sticks recognized the importance of its white-collar lunch crowd, and where it had once considered other fast-casual chains such as Panera and Chipotle to be rivals, it now saw that it could become part of customers' regular lunch rotation along with those restaurants. Could Sticks focus on building the loyalty of those customers and making them dinner and weekend customers as well?

The difficulty for the team was examining its value proposition and customer profile and mapping this data to a demographics-based real estate model. While the data the team had collected certainly lent insight into just who Sticks customers were, would it lead it to picking the correct location for the next Sticks Richmond store? Was it even the right data needed to make the decision?

3

Conjoint Analysis

C luster analysis and conjoint analysis are both marketing research techniques whose goal is matching customers with appropriate products and marketing strategies. However, they differ in their focus, their place in the marketing process, and the tools involved. Conjoint analysis is a marketing research technique designed to help managers determine the preferences of customers and potential customers—not to profile customers, but to analyze the product itself. In terms of the marketing process, cluster analysis is a key strategic element, while conjoint analysis is tactical, having to do specifically with product design.

Conjoint analysis seeks to determine how consumers value the different attributes that make up a product and the trade-offs they are willing to make among those different attributes or features. As such, it is best suited for products that have very tangible attributes that can be easily described or quantified. Through conjoint analysis, managers learn which brands and products, or product features, can increase demand and thereby increase the company's ROMI and help optimize its resource-allocation efforts.

While the history of conjoint analysis can be traced to early work in mathematical psychology, its popularity has grown tremendously over the last few years, as access to easy-to-use software has allowed its widespread implementation. There have been probably hundreds of applications of conjoint analysis in industrial settings. Many of these are variants of trade-off analysis, market share forecasting, and attribute importance, the three very common applications presented in this chapter. The increasingly widespread availability of conjoint analysis software—both PC and web-enabled—points to its continued growth as a marketing decision aid.

Some of the important issues that can be solved using modern conjoint analysis are the following:

1. Predicting the market share of a proposed new product, given the current offerings of competitors.
2. Predicting the impact of a new competitive product on the market share of any given product in the marketplace.
3. Determining consumers' willingness to pay for a proposed new product.
4. Quantifying the trade-offs customers or potential customers are willing to make among the various attributes or features that are under consideration in the new product design.

THE ANATOMY OF A CONJOINT ANALYSIS

Literally, **conjoint analysis** means an analysis of features considered jointly. The idea is that, while it is difficult for consumers to tell us directly how much each feature of a product is worth to them, we can infer the value of an individual feature by experimentally manipulating various combinations of features and observing consumers' ratings for products with those combinations.

To fix your intuition here, consider the simple example of a sports car. It would be difficult for the average consumer to tell a market researcher exactly how much they value a car with 240 horsepower relative to one with 220. It is possible that a consumer might be able to come up with some dollar value, but that value may not reflect the way they would act in a real marketplace situation. Instead, marketers have found that they get more accurate results when they present individuals from the target market with a series of cars, described not only by their horsepower but by other attributes as well (color, price, standard/automatic transmission, and so on), and then ask them to rate each of the cars on a numerical scale. Another useful alternative is to present several competing cars with different attributes and ask the consumer to choose one. Then, by repeatedly asking the potential customers to rate the cars or choose a car from a competing set, the researcher can infer the value of each individual attribute. This is the essence of a conjoint analysis: replacing the relatively inaccurate method of asking about each attribute in isolation with a model that allows the attributes' values to be inferred from a series of ratings or choices.

The three main steps of a conjoint analysis are the basis of any experimental process.

1. Design the experiment.
2. Collect data.
3. Interpret results, to understand the basic output.

Step 1: Experimental Design

Conjoint analysis begins with a survey-based experimental design. As with cluster analysis, this experimental design does not involve independent and dependent variables. Instead, this design includes all product features, called attributes in conjoint analysis. Conjoint analysis distinguishes between attributes and what are generally called levels. An **attribute** is a feature in the abstract, like price, color, horsepower, upholstery material, or presence of a sunroof; a **level** is the specific kind or realization of an attribute. For example, a color attribute might have levels "red," "blue," and "yellow," while a sunroof presence attribute would have levels "yes" and "no." Before a researcher begins to collect data, it is important that all the levels of each attribute to be tested are written down. Commercially available conjoint analysis software packages—one popular option is Sawtooth—require that the analyst provide these as input. Once the attributes and levels are determined, the researcher can write survey questions that ask respondents to compare and/or place a value on particular combinations of those levels.

Continuing with our car example, an experimental design might include the information presented in **table 3.1**.

This is a very simple design that contains a total of 15 attribute levels. Real designs often contain more attributes and levels than are presented here.

TABLE 3.1. **Example of experimental design**

Attribute	Price	Brand	Horsepower	Upholstery	Sunroof
Level	$23,000	Toyota	220	Cloth	Yes
	$25,000	Volkswagen	250	Leather	No
	$27,000	Saturn	280		
	$29,000	Kia			

When constructing an experiment, the following points are important to keep in mind:

1. The more tangible and understandable the levels of each attribute are to the respondents, the more valid the results of the research will be. For example, attribute levels such as "really roomy" are vague, mean different things to different people, and should be avoided.
2. The greater the number of attribute levels to be tested, the more data will be needed to achieve the same degree of output accuracy.
3. For attributes that are quantitative variables, the greater the distance between any two consecutive levels, the harder it will be to get a good idea of how a consumer might evaluate something in between the two. For example, given the levels of the quantitative attribute price in **table 3.1**, it would be hard to know how a consumer would evaluate a level of $24,000.
4. For a given attribute, the levels should span the entire range of possible values for that attribute in order to get accurate and realistic data. For example, the price attribute in the car experiment should have levels that cover the entire range of possible prices for car brands that are tested.
5. The population surveyed may have particular characteristics that must be kept in mind when drawing conclusions from the data.

Just as the success and applicability to marketing of cluster analysis depends on the choice of variables on which the segmentation is based, in conjoint analysis, the choice of attributes and granularity of levels determines marketing success. Managerial intuition and familiarity with the statistical tools are key.

Step 2: Data Collection

Collecting data for a conjoint analysis has been made relatively simple by the advent of dedicated off-the-shelf software. The exact nature of the data collected will be dictated by the type of conjoint analysis that is used. Conjoint analysis is a general approach: for a good discussion of the benefits and drawbacks of each of the many different types of conjoint analysis now in use, see Orme (2013).[1]

The state of the art in conjoint data collection involves using personal computers or web-based software to create hypothetical product profiles based on the experimental design provided by the researcher, then guide respondents through an interactive conjoint survey. Participant ratings of those profiles, or choices among profiles, are the raw data; the same software then estimates the attribute-level utilities based on those data.

Step 3: Interpreting Conjoint Results

Statistical analysis of consumer preferences for various combinations yields estimated **utilities**, or part-worths in terms of value to customers, for each individual level. Keeping with the example in **table 3.1**, conjoint output might look like **table 3.2**.

The estimated utilities correspond to average consumer preferences for the level of any given attribute. Within a given attribute, the estimated utilities are generally scaled in such a way that they add up to zero. So a negative number does not mean that a given level has "negative utility"; it means instead that this level is on average less preferred than a level with an estimated utility that is positive. Since the utilities add to zero, conjoint analysis never gives the absolute utility of any level, only its utility relative to the other levels tested. As such, the estimated utility of any particular

TABLE 3.2. Conjoint analysis output

Attribute	Level	Utility (part-worth)	t-value
Price	$23,000	2.10	14.00
	$25,000	1.15	7.67
	$27,000	−1.56	10.40
	$29,000	−1.69	11.27
Brand	Toyota	0.75	5.00
	Volkswagen	0.65	4.33
	Saturn	−0.13	0.87
	Kia	−1.27	8.47
Horsepower	220	−2.24	14.93
	250	1.06	7.07
	280	1.18	7.87
Upholstery	Cloth	−1.60	10.67
	Leather	1.60	10.67
Sunroof	Yes	0.68	4.53
	No	−0.68	4.53

level of any attribute will be sensitive to the number of levels specified and the description of those levels.

Conjoint analysis output is also often accompanied by **t-values**. A standard metric for evaluating statistical significance, a **t-test** measures the probability that the true value of a parameter is not different from zero. Because of the way conjoint utilities are scaled, the standard interpretation of t-values can yield misleading results. For example, the level "Saturn" of the brand attribute has a t-value of 0.87. In general, a t-value of this magnitude would fail a test of statistical significance; however, this t-value is generated because within the brand attribute, the level "Saturn" has neither a very high nor very low relative preference. It is basically in the middle in terms of overall preference. Because of the scaling, more moderate levels of preference within a given attribute are likely to have estimated utilities close to zero, which will tend to produce very low t-values.

Rather than individual t-values, a better way to think about statistical significance in this context is to examine the t-values of the levels within a given attribute with the highest and lowest preference. According to common practice, if the sum of the absolute value of these two statistics is greater than three, then that attribute is significant in the overall choice process of consumers. In practice, it is rare that an attribute will not be significant. When it is, it means that respondents are not considering that attribute's information when they make choices, and that the attribute probably should not have been included in the experimental design in the first place. For more on determining attribute importance, see the next section, Conjoint Analysis Applications.

CONJOINT ANALYSIS APPLICATIONS

As mentioned previously, there are many different possible applications of conjoint analysis. We will focus on three very common applications: trade-off analysis, predicting market share, and determining overall attribute importance. Each of these applications involves different ways of manipulating the basic output of a conjoint analysis to obtain insights relevant for marketing.

Trade-Off Analysis

In a **trade-off analysis**, a researcher compares the overall value a consumer obtains—the utilities—from two competing products to discover what an average customer would be willing to give up, in terms of one attribute, to gain improvements in another. This is called "trade-off" because it often means asking how much more an average customer would be willing to pay (in other words, give up in terms of price) for an upgrade to a product.

The utility of any given product can be easily computed by simply summing the utilities of its attribute levels. For example, a Toyota with 280 horsepower, leather interior, no sunroof, and a price of $23,000 has a utility of 0.75 + 1.18 + 1.60 − 0.68 + 2.10 = 4.95. If a car with the same basic specifications were a Volkswagen, the overall utility would drop to 0.65 + 1.18 + 1.60 − 0.68 + 2.10 = 4.85, a drop of 0.10. This drop can be seen directly by noticing that the difference between the utility for the brands Toyota (0.75) and Volkswagen (0.65) is 0.10: because nothing else in the profile of the car has changed, this is the exact utility difference between the two cars.

A natural consequence of this observation is that comparing utilities will show what average consumers would be willing to give up on one particular attribute to gain improvements in another. For example, how much money would they be willing to give up if a sunroof was added to the vehicle? We will now look directly at this issue of the hypothetical car detailed in the previous paragraph. Adding a sunroof to the Toyota would yield an overall utility of 0.75 + 1.18 + 1.60 + 0.68 + 2.10 = 6.31. This represents an increase in utility of 6.31 − 4.95 = 1.36 over the identical car without a sunroof.

This information directly implies that we can reduce the utility of price by 1.36, and average consumers would be just as happy as before the sunroof was installed. To find out how much the price can be raised to maintain the same level of utility, we must convert the change in utility with a change in price. We do this by first noting how much the original car costs ($23,000) and the utility associated with that figure (2.10). We know that we can reduce the price utility by 1.36. This is equivalent to saying that we can reduce the price utility to 2.10 − 1.36 = 0.74. By referring to **table 3.2**, we can immediately see that this implies a price between $25,000 and $27,000, because −1.56 < 0.74 < 1.15.

In fact, if we assume a linear relationship between price and utility in the range between $25,000 and $27,000, we can solve for the exact price by performing a linear interpolation within this range. **Linear interpolation** is a common way to approximate the relationship between the value of the attribute and its utility, for attribute values that were not directly tested by the conjoint analysis. The closer the tested levels are to each other, the more accurate this approximation will be. Note that this interpolation can be performed only for quantitative attributes, such as price. Interpolating between qualitative attributes, such as brand, is nonsensical.

Returning to our example, linear interpolation to find the price customers would pay for a Toyota with a sunroof, all else equal, yields

$$\$25,000+\frac{(1.15-0.74)}{(1.15-[-1.56])}\times\$2,000=\$25,302.58.$$

Here, the key part of the calculation is within the brackets. The numerator, $(1.15-0.74)$, is the utility spread between utility at \$25,000 and the target utility, and the denominator, $(1.15-[-1.56])$, is the utility spread between the two tested price points (\$25,000 and \$27,000). We multiply this number by \$2,000, because that is the difference between \$27,000 and \$25,000, and add that result to \$25,000.

This implies that, if the sunroof is added, the willingness to pay for the average respondent rises from \$23,000 to about \$25,300. Qualitatively, it shows that the value of a sunroof to consumers is substantial. Note that this does not imply that the company marketing this particular vehicle could raise the market price by \$2,300 if a sunroof is added. While a well-constructed conjoint analysis can provide useful insights into consumers' willingness to pay, it does not account for product costs or competitive price responses, both of which are important determinants of price in real-world markets.

This same kind of analysis can be performed for other attributes. For example, we could compare the utilities of horsepower and upholstery by asking how much additional horsepower would make a car with cloth upholstery of equivalent value to one with leather. This particular question does present a problem, however. Because the vehicle under consideration has the maximum amount of horsepower tested by the conjoint analysis (280), it will be impossible to determine how much consumers will value additional horsepower. This leads to an important consideration when designing the conjoint analysis survey. That is, if the output is to be used for trade-off analysis, it is important that the range of the levels tested within each attribute span the entire range of that attribute. The goal of trade-off analysis is a new target optimal design (perhaps a car with 300 horsepower and cloth interior); management would consider this new design as a realistic design alternative only if the analysis covers the entire range of levels. If the experimental design covers the complete range, we can perform trade-off analysis between any two attributes in the design.

Market Share Forecasting

Another common application of conjoint analysis is forecasting market share. In order to use conjoint output for this kind of prediction, two conditions must be satisfied:

1. The company must know the other products, besides its own offering, that a consumer is likely to consider when making a selection in the category.
2. Each of these competitive products' important features must be included in the experimental design. In other words, the company must be able to calculate the utility of not only its own product offering, but also that of the competition.

Market share prediction relies on the use of a multinomial logistic regression (logit) model. A good marketing reference to learn about the basics of the logit model is Lilien and Rangaswamy, *Marketing Engineering: Computer-Assisted Marketing Analysis and Planning* (2002); most econometrics textbooks will also have information on logit models. The basic form of the logit model is

$$\text{Share}_i = \frac{e^{U_i}}{\sum_{j=1}^{n} e^{U_j}},$$

where

U_i is the estimated utility of product i,

U_j is the estimated utility of product j, and

n is the total number of products in the competitive set, including product i.

Consider the following example. Suppose we are interested in predicting the market share of a car with the following profile: Saturn; $23,000; 220 horsepower; cloth interior; no sunroof. We believe that when consumers consider our car, they will also consider purchasing cars that are currently on the market with the following profiles:

1. Toyota; $27,000; 250 horsepower; cloth interior; no sunroof
2. Volkswagen; $29,000; 280 horsepower; leather interior; no sunroof
3. Kia; $23,000; 220 horsepower; cloth interior; no sunroof

For the Saturn and its associated product profile, the estimated utility is

$$2.10 - 0.13 - 2.24 - 1.60 - 0.68 = -2.55.$$

Similarly, the utilities of the three competing products can be calculated as follows:

1. $-1.56 + 0.75 + 1.06 - 1.60 - 0.68 = -2.03$
2. $-1.69 + 0.65 + 1.18 + 1.60 - 0.68 = 1.06$
3. $2.10 - 1.27 - 2.24 - 1.60 - 0.68 = -3.69$

With these utilities in hand, we can now directly apply the logit model to forecast market share for the Saturn. This is given by the following:

$$\text{Share}_{\text{Saturn}} = \frac{e^{-2.55}}{e^{-2.55} + e^{-2.03} + e^{1.06} + e^{-3.69}} = 0.025 \text{ or } 2.5\%.$$

This implies that this particular Saturn vehicle will achieve a 2.5% market share within the specified competitive set. The market share of any vehicle can be found in a similar manner, when both it and a set of competitive vehicles can be described by the experimental design. As we've seen before, the input choices have a huge effect on output: the competitive set is decided by the experimenter, so the market share prediction will necessarily reflect only the share within that experimentally defined set. Here again, managerial intuition and understanding of the competition is key.

Determining Attribute Importance

A researcher may also be interested in determining the importance of any individual attribute in consumer decision processes. Quantifying these attribute importances using the conjoint output is straightforward and can provide interesting and useful insights into consumer behavior.

Intuitively, you have an understanding of the importance of an attribute in the choice process based on the variance of the estimated utilities within a given attribute. Take, for example, the sunroof and upholstery attributes, both of which have only two levels. It should be reasonably clear that upholstery is a more important attribute than sunroof, because the utility difference between having and not having a sunroof ($2 \times 0.68 = 1.36$) is smaller than the utility difference between a leather interior and a cloth interior ($2 \times 1.60 = 3.20$).

The common metric used to measure attribute importances is

$$I_i = \frac{\bar{U}_i - \underline{U}_i}{\sum_{j=1}^{n} \bar{U}_j - \underline{U}_j},$$

where

I_i = the importance of any given attribute i,

$\bar{U}$ = the highest utility level within a given attribute (subscripts indicate which attribute), and

$\underline{U}$ = the lowest utility level within a given attribute.

This equation is really quite intuitive. In order to calculate the importance of any given attribute, you take the difference between the highest and lowest utility level of that attribute and divide this by the sum of the differences between the highest and lowest utility level for all attributes (including the one in question). The resulting number will always lie between zero and one, and is generally interpreted as the percentage decision weight of an attribute in the overall choice process.

It also should be clear at this point that this estimated attribute importance depends critically on your experimental design. If you add or delete attributes, or change the number of levels of a given attribute, the estimated attribute importances will likely change. In addition, if you increase the distance between the most extreme levels of any given attribute, you will almost certainly increase the overall attribute importance. For example, if the tested price range was $21,000 to $31,000 instead of $23,000 to $29,000 (**table 3.1**), the estimated attribute importance of price would very likely increase.

Let's now consider a concrete example using the horsepower attribute. The importance of this attribute is calculated as follows:

$$I_{Horsepower} = \frac{1.18 + 2.24}{\left((2.10 + 1.69) + (0.75 + 1.27) + (1.18 + 2.24) + (1.60 + 1.60) + (0.68 + 0.68)\right)}$$

$$= 0.25.$$

In our example, 25% of the overall decision weight is assigned to horsepower. The reader may verify through analogous calculations that the decision weight for price is about 27%; for brand, about 15%; for sunroof, about 10%; and for upholstery, about 23%. The numbers provide a very intuitive metric for thinking about the importance of each attribute in the decision process.

ADVANCES IN CONJOINT ANALYSIS

The analysis presented here is what is generally known as "aggregate-level" conjoint analysis. That is, all the respondents are pooled into one group, and a single set of attribute-level utilities is estimated from the ratings or choices provided by the people in this group. Recent advances in conjoint analysis have enabled researchers to estimate different utilities for different groups of respondents and even, in some cases, for individual respondents. Although the mathematics necessary for this procedure is sometimes quite complex, it is now possible to estimate the attribute-level utilities and to compute trade-off analyses for *each individual respondent*. This has some significant advantages over aggregate-level analysis, particularly when considering marketing segmentation issues and analysis of differences in individual consumers' willingness to pay for specific product designs. Either way, the data collection and the basic interpretation of the output remain the same.

Although there is currently no textbook that can provide answers to all the questions that might arise when applying this technique in a business setting, there is, as of this writing, a very good and surprisingly comprehensive collection of technical papers located on the site of a company that markets conjoint analysis software (http://www.sawtoothsoftware.com/techpap.shtml). These papers provide answers to many of the practical implementation questions a user may face.

CONCEPT APPLICATION

In the case that follows, the management of a struggling basketball team faces the challenge of boosting regular-season game attendance irrespective of the team's on-court performance. The management hires a research firm to administer fan surveys about season ticket passes and then analyzes the results using conjoint analysis to determine the right balance between seat prices and free gifts, like hot dogs or team jerseys.

As you read about the team's context and fans, and as you learn about the potential components of season ticket passes, consider the following questions and perform calculations as needed using the case data (http://store.darden.virginia.edu/marketing -analytics-supplements):

- Which attribute does the analysis indicate will be most important to a fan's overall purchase decision?
- What other information can you glean from the analysis?
- Are the results of the analysis useful in deciding how to price the packages, which promotional item (if any) to include, and what size ticket package to offer?
- What recommendations (about these or other aspects of the package) should the research firm offer to the team management?
- Is there anything you would change about the survey?

CASE: PORTLAND TRAIL BLAZERS, A TEAM IN UPHEAVAL

The Trail Blazers had a monopoly on the professional sports market in Portland, Oregon. Without a dominant university sports program affiliated with the city, the team competed only with minor-league baseball and hockey for its share of the city's sporting dollars. At just under two million people in the metro area, Portland was the fourth-smallest market in the NBA.

Each year, the Trail Blazers management tracked Portland-area residents' general perception of the team (see **figure 3.1**). The historically strong relationship between the team and the city had soured over the past few seasons, with the percentage of people perceiving the team negatively having increased tenfold since 2000. Fan support had dwindled due to a number of widely publicized player transgressions including marijuana use, fights among teammates, and an incident involving animal cruelty.[2]

Less than a month after the 2005 NBA All-Star break, the Portland Trail Blazers were in upheaval. On the court, they had just fired their coach of the previous four seasons and had a win–loss record of 22–36; they were in danger of playing one of the worst seasons in franchise history. Off the court, the Blazers organization was facing considerable challenges as well. The team's home arena, the Rose Garden, had filed for Chapter 11 bankruptcy and was being run by the building's creditors.

The arena, a virtual lock to sell out just three seasons before, had seen attendance numbers fall more than 15% since the 2003 season (**figure 3.2**). During the same

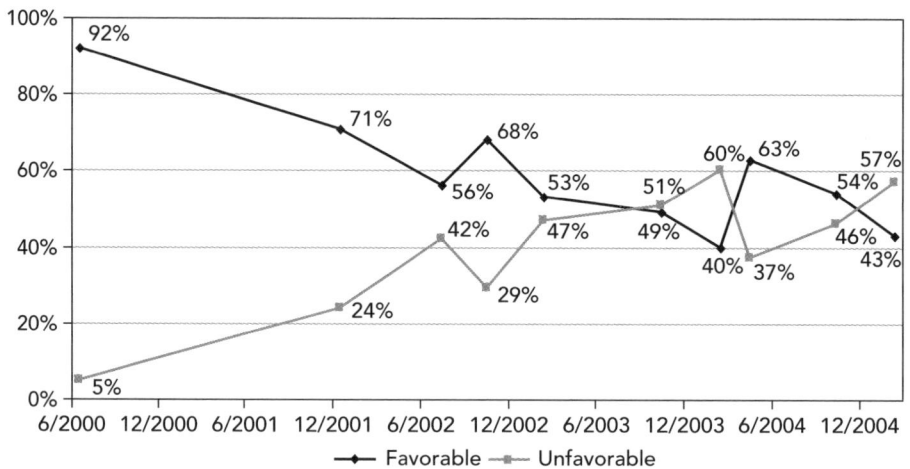

FIGURE 3.1. Portland-area residents' general perceptions of the Portland Trail Blazers. (Data courtesy of the Portland Trail Blazers)

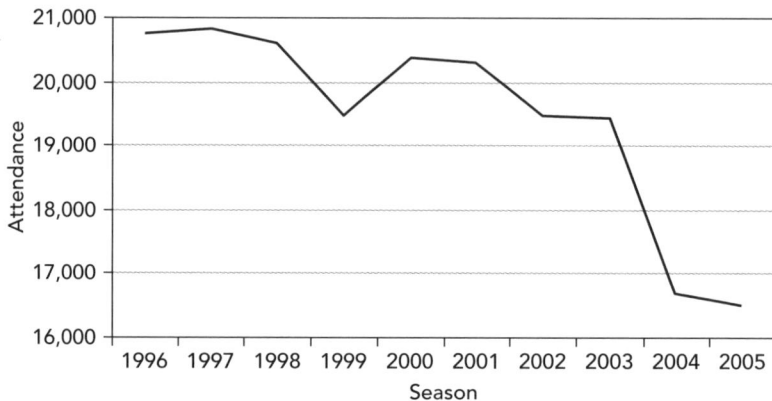

FIGURE 3.2. Average home attendance, 1996–2005. (Data courtesy of the Portland Trail Blazers)

time, the organization had been successful in renewing only 9 of the 46 luxury-suite contracts that came due in 2005; 42 of the 70 total luxury suites sat empty during the season.[3] Television interest also declined, with a Portland-area Nielsen share of just 5% when the Blazers played the Minneapolis Timberwolves (weather coverage generally received up to 20%).[4]

A similar story was occurring in the sale of the team's "club seats"—special seats for Blazers games that were sold on a multiyear contract and came with club perks. Of 1,800 club seats, 700 remained available in 2005, most of them because subscribers had dropped their contracts during the previous season.

Multigame Ticket Packages

One of the more successful Blazers promotions during the past few seasons had been multigame ticket packages. This program allowed fans to purchase tickets for a number of games at once, and usually included at least one game with a marquee opponent, for which individual tickets were difficult to find. Trail Blazers' management saw this program as an effective tool to:

1. Increase ticket sales for less popular games, which were typically bundled in the package with tickets for hard-to-find games;
2. Increase overall ticket sales: the multigame packages acted as an effective incentive for those who planned on attending only one or two games during the season to increase the number of games they attended; and
3. Develop more of an ongoing relationship with fans who could potentially become season ticket holders.

Despite the program's relative success, management wanted to explore all potential packages and better understand which options were most popular with fans. The program's goal was to offer a multigame ticket package that had a high appeal to fans, while being profitable to the team and not undermining current pricing policies.

Designing the Research Study

The Trail Blazers management team hired Acuity Market Research, a Portland-based research firm, to help design the multigame package study. Together, they determined that there were six aspects of the multigame ticket packages that drove a customer's decision to purchase:

1. The team the Blazers played
2. The day of the week the game was played

3. The number of games included in the package
4. The location of the seats
5. The price (per seat) of the package
6. The promotional item included in the package

The project team designed a conjoint analysis study to ascertain the importance of the individual attributes, as well as the likely response of the market to specific multi-game ticket packages. Some things were givens: (1) there was a high number of teams in the NBA (30 including the Blazers); and (2) the dates of the games included in the package could not be changed. Those attributes would not be included as part of the conjoint products. Instead, questions pertaining to favorite teams and days to watch a game were asked individually, after the conjoint portion of the survey.

An email went out from the Blazers' director of database and internet marketing to 960 fans who had purchased multigame ticket packages or season tickets in the past but were not current season ticket holders. The project team decided it was more important to get feedback from people who had already expressed some level of commitment to purchasing Blazers tickets, rather than from general fans, and the team knew it had current email addresses for this group. Although new fans did purchase multigame or season ticket packages, Blazers management believed past purchasers were likely the best prospects for new multigame packages.

The initial email explained the purpose of the study and asked fans to participate. One week later, a reminder email was sent in hopes of increasing the overall response rate of the study. Both emails contained a link to an online conjoint-based survey, which included 20 different conjoint choice tasks (an example is included in **figure 3.3**), Blazers-specific questions, and a battery of demographic questions. Most respondents took 10 to 15 minutes to complete the survey.

As an incentive to complete the survey, participants were told they might win free tickets to Blazers games, or autographed Blazers items such as jerseys, basketballs, and posters.

Study Findings

The email solicitations received a total of 204 valid responses (a 21% response rate). **Figures 3.4** and **3.5** include summary statistics regarding demographics and past Blazers game attendance.

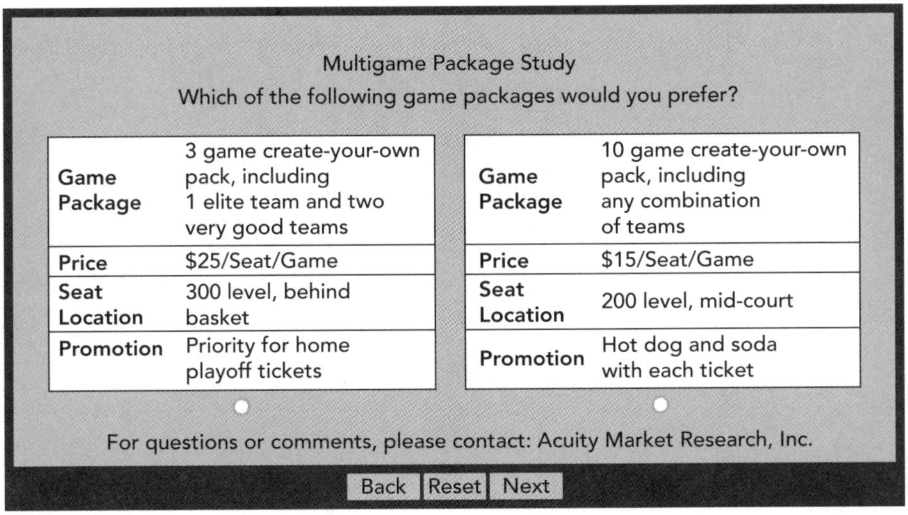

Multigame Package Study
Which of the following game packages would you prefer?

Game Package	3 game create-your-own pack, including 1 elite team and two very good teams	Game Package	10 game create-your-own pack, including any combination of teams
Price	$25/Seat/Game	Price	$15/Seat/Game
Seat Location	300 level, behind basket	Seat Location	200 level, mid-court
Promotion	Priority for home playoff tickets	Promotion	Hot dog and soda with each ticket

For questions or comments, please contact: Acuity Market Research, Inc.

Back | Reset | Next

FIGURE 3.3. Online conjoint survey. (Survey screenshot courtesy of the Portland Trail Blazers)

Acuity began its analysis of the multigame packages by computing the attribute-level utility scores to better understand the individual attribute levels. **Table 3.3** shows the utility score data.

While the conjoint study allowed all the attributes and levels to be randomly assigned, in reality the Blazers management was unwilling to allow certain price and seating combinations—no matter how well received they were—due to the cost structure of the arena. Management disallowed: (1) 200-level seats for less than $60; and (2) 300-level, midcourt seats for less than $25.

Costs of Multigame Packages

While the fan preference was extremely important to Blazers management, any multigame packages the group designed had to be financially attractive and align with the organization's strategic goals. Each of the multigame ticket package attributes had associated costs and strategic implications. These attributes included number of games, seat location, and promotional items.

In terms of number of games in a package, the Blazers preferred the 6-game package because it offered the capability of pairing the most popular teams with games

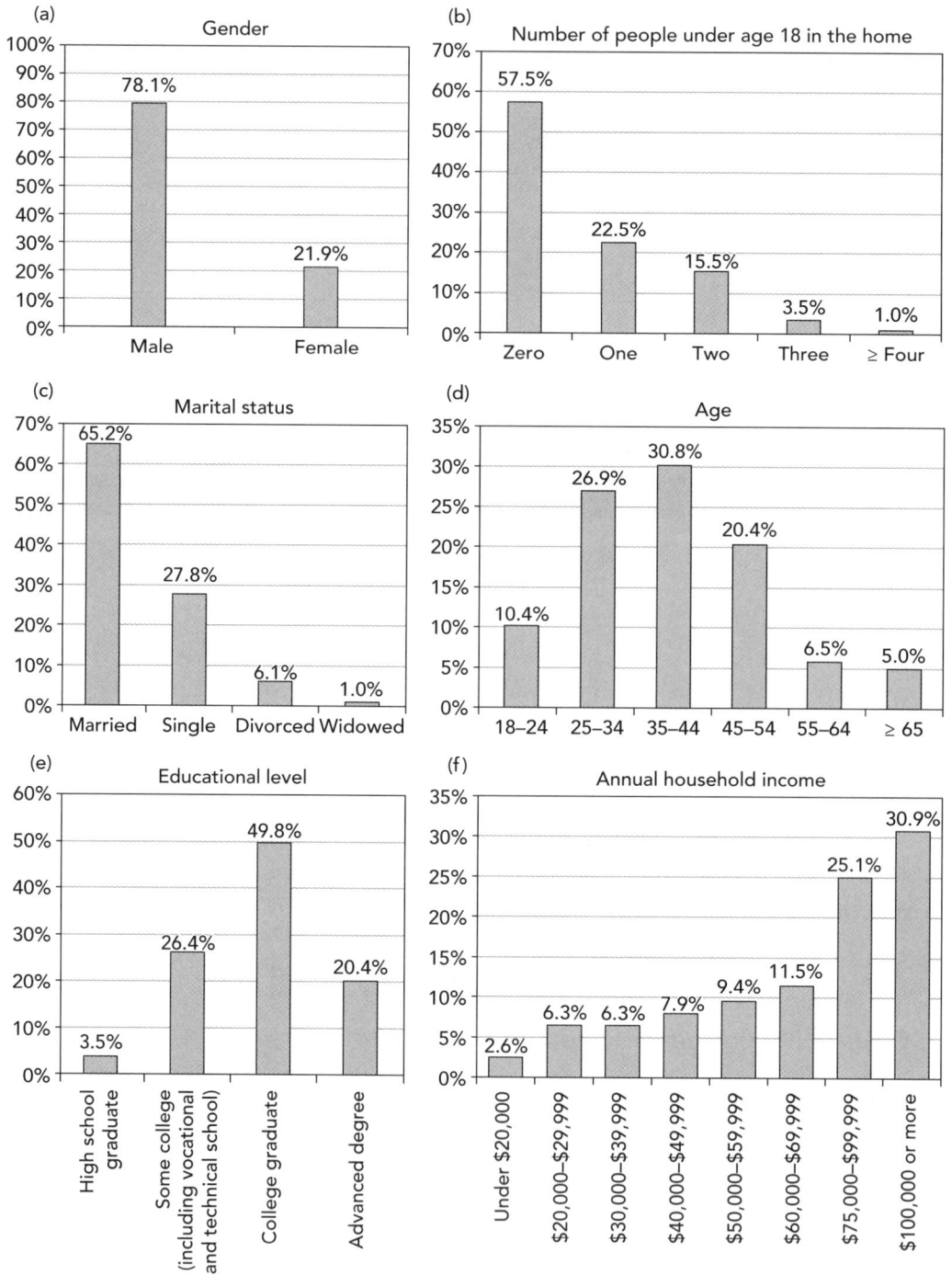

FIGURE 3.4. **Study demographics. (Data courtesy of the Portland Trail Blazers)**

(a)

(b)

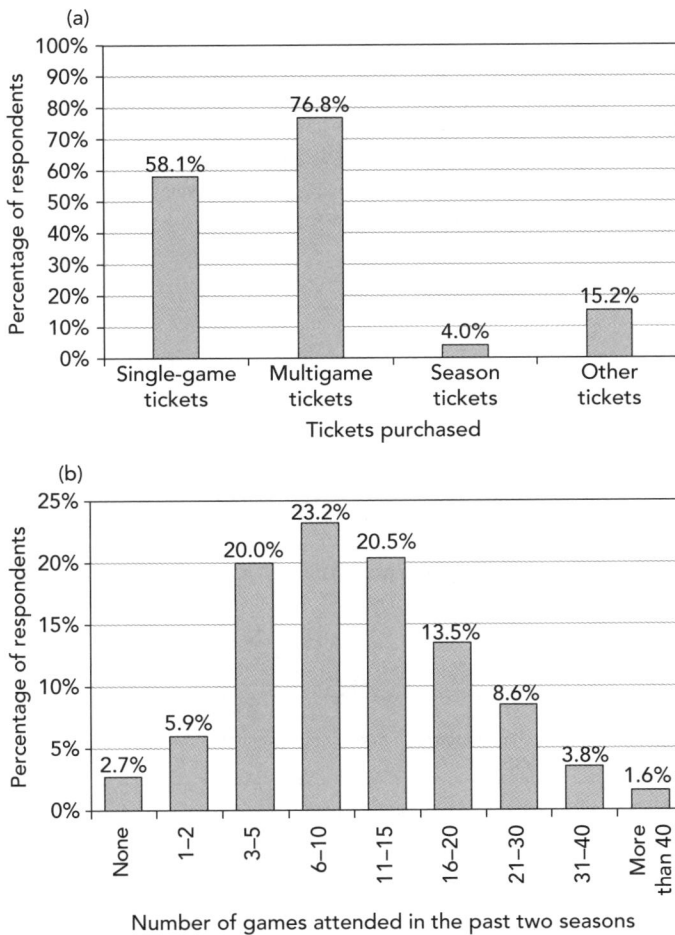

FIGURE 3.5. Game attendance behavior. (Data courtesy of the Portland Trail Blazers)

that were more difficult to sell tickets to (weekday games, less competitive teams, and so on). Its next preference was a 10-game package, because it allowed the team to efficiently sell a large number of the remaining games to a single fan.

As for seat locations, although nearly all the Blazers' stadium costs were fixed expenses, the organization still applied a cost to each of the seat locations in the stadium. This cost structure had to be met, at a minimum, for any tickets that were sold, and differed based on seat location. **Table 3.4** shows the minimum seat pricing, and **figure 3.6** shows a seating chart, for reference.

TABLE 3.3. Utility score data

Utility	Number of games
0.03257	3-game create-your-own pack, including 1 elite team and 2 very good teams
0.24383	6-game create-your-own pack, including 2 elite teams and 4 very good teams
−0.2764	10-game create-your-own pack, including any combination of teams

Utility	Ticket price
0.65646	$15 per seat per game
0.22011	$25 per seat per game
0.126	$35 per seat per game
−1.00257	$60 per seat per game

Utility	Ticket location
−0.73169	300 level, behind the baskets
−0.43716	300 level, on the corners
0.15736	300 level, midcourt
1.01148	200 level, midcourt

Utility	Promotional item
0.12511	Priority for home playoff tickets
0.17428	Hot dog and soda with each ticket
0.00158	Trail Blazers apparel (hat, jersey, etc.)
0.01689	$20 gift certificate for popular local restaurant
−0.31786	No promotional item

Source: Data courtesy of the Portland Trail Blazers.

A direct cost was also associated with each of the promotional items the Blazers might offer fans. For example, if the Blazers were to offer a hot dog and soda with each ticket, they would have to pay the Rose Garden's vendor services a negotiated price of $3.25 per package. The $20 gift certificate to a popular restaurant was purchased for a negotiated price of $10. The restaurateur deeply discounted the gift certificates in exchange for the marketing exposure.

The only promotional item without a direct cost was priority for home playoff tickets, given that the tickets were still sold at full retail price and multigame ticket

TABLE 3.4. Fixed costs based on seat location

Seat location	Fixed cost
300 level, behind the baskets	$10.00
300 level, on the corners	$12.00
300 level, midcourt	$18.00
200 level, midcourt	$40.00

Source: Data courtesy of the Portland Trail Blazers.

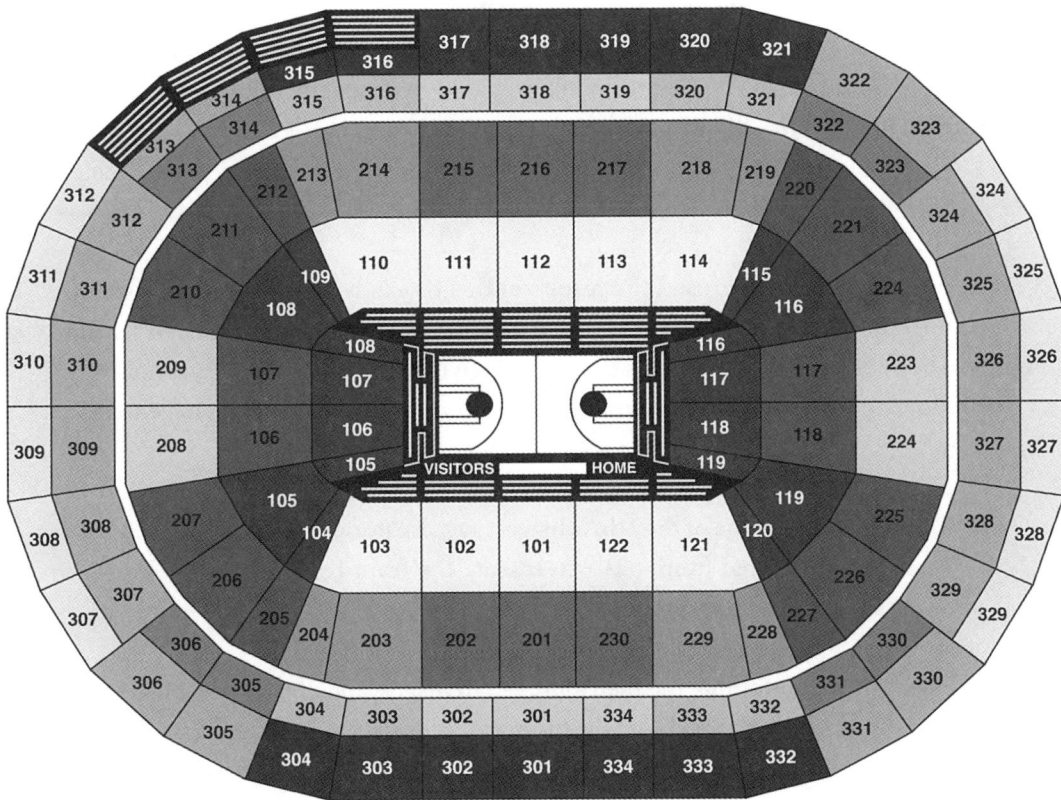

FIGURE 3.6. Rose Garden seating chart. (Courtesy of the Portland Trail Blazers)

TABLE 3.5. **Cost of promotional items**

Promotional item	Cost
Priority for playoff tickets	$0.00
Hot dog and soda with each ticket	$3.25
Trail Blazers apparel (hat, jersey, etc.)	$12.00
$20 gift certificate to a popular restaurant	$10.00

Source: Data courtesy of the Portland Trail Blazers.

holders just received priority in purchasing available tickets. **Table 3.5** presents the unit cost of each of the potential promotional items.

Utilizing the conjoint information, in addition to the other data available from the survey, the Blazers management team felt prepared to design the multigame package it believed the fans would most prefer.

CONCLUSION

The Portland Trail Blazers used the results of this research to implement a more robust program of promotional items. The real story, though, is how the team has improved both its performance and its image—which no doubt helped to draw more fans. The following is an excerpt of an email update from the Trail Blazers management:

> Four years after the completion of the conjoint analysis and case study, the Portland Trail Blazers are one of the NBA's biggest success stories.
>
> Three years removed from a 21-win season, the team is on a pace to win 50 games and reach the postseason for the first time since 2003, despite [being] one of the NBA's youngest teams.
>
> Players more notorious for their off-court transgressions than their on-court contributions were jettisoned, and the team was reconstructed with young, socially conscious and community-minded players who happily answer the team's call to "Make It Better" in the Portland community.
>
> No longer in bankruptcy, the Rose Garden is rocking. The building has hosted 55 consecutive sellouts [through February 2009], and is one of the NBA's loudest and best-attended arenas.
>
> In 2008, the Trail Blazers won the University of Massachusetts esteemed PRISM award for "Best Sports Team."

4

Linear Regression

Wﾐ e've examined some ways in which a marketing manager can profitably analyze data about customer characteristics, and about customer preferences for product characteristics; now we turn from customers and product to the promotion itself. Regression analyses can help marketing managers discover which marketing-mix elements have the greatest effect on demand. Models of elasticity of demand describe consumer responsiveness to changes in price or advertising, helping marketing managers determine the effects on demand of those changes and therefore to choose the changes in which to invest marketing funds. For this reason, elasticity can be considered the workhorse of resource allocation.

This chapter begins with an overview of linear regression, beginning with single-variable and progressing to multivariable models. While single-variable models are an important and useful starting point, multivariable models are more reflective of the real world. Indeed, a fundamental premise of marketing-mix analytics is that multiple mix elements, such as price and promotion, affect customer behavior simultaneously.

Models that estimate elasticity should also reflect this notion, and it is necessary to consider the joint effect of the marketing mix on customer behavior. After an overview of linear regression, the chapter explores specific linear regression models of price elasticity and advertising elasticity. It goes through applications and effects of price elasticity and advertising elasticity, presents the log-log linear model framework for estimating elasticity, lists the control variables that marketing-mix models must include in order to avoid biased elasticity estimates, and discusses omitted-variable bias and statistical versus economic significance.

MULTIPLE REGRESSION IN MARKETING-MIX MODELS

Moneyball has a lot to teach us about optimizing marketing mix. In the movie, the management of the Oakland Athletics discovers that the baseball team can get ahead of its competitors by rethinking player data.

The A's know most major-league teams use batting average (hits over real opportunities) as the prevailing metric for determining the worth of a hitter. Traditional wisdom says, "you hit more, you win more." So the players who have more hits per at bat are generally the most sought after and are paid the most money. But by examining the outcome of decades of baseball games, the A's find a variable they believe to be more predictive of success. Hits are not the only contributors to a win; walks count too. Getting on base and not making outs is more closely correlated with winning games than hits alone.

The team's management uses its analysis to buy undervalued players—those who don't necessarily have the highest batting averages but who do have high on-base percentages. For a small-market team such as the A's, which has less money than other franchises to spend on players, this strategy changes the game.

Moneyball is about baseball, but the idea also works in the context of business marketing. While management often makes assumptions, a business can better understand how to succeed by actually analyzing the data. And if a business can find an important variable before others do, it can build its strategy around that variable to gain an advantage.

Regression analysis helps marketing managers find those important variables, by illuminating the relationship between two or more variables or concepts. Typically, a company will use historical sales data or data generated through experiments to identify factors that most affect a brand's sales; the company can then manipulate those factors to increase profits.

Hypothetical Case: No More Germs

Single-Variable Regressions for Marketing

Single-variable regression analyses enable us to predict outcomes using one variable. While such analyses are often oversimplifications of real-world marketing problems, it is necessary to understand them before moving on to more illustrative multivari-

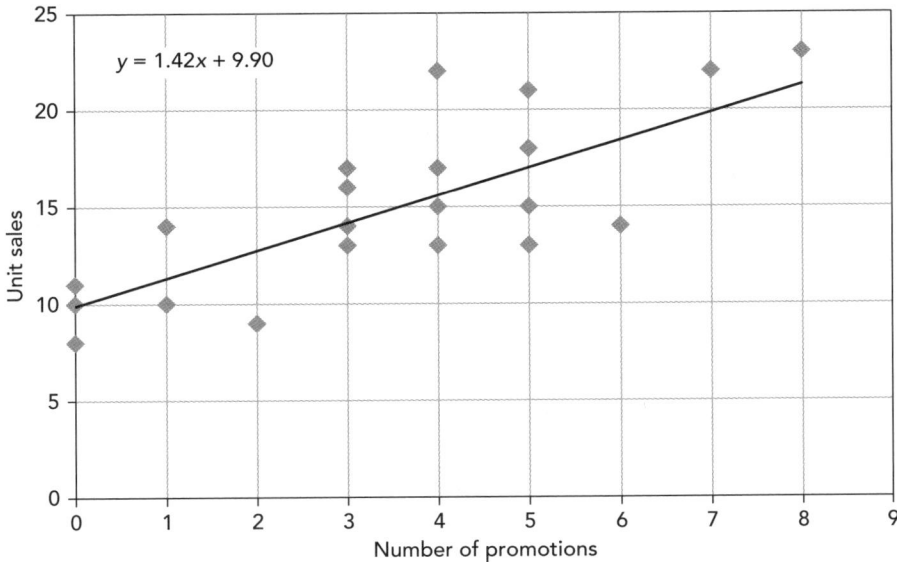

FIGURE 4.1. Illustration of single-variable regression

able analyses. It is important to remember that linear regressions, whether single- or multivariable, assume a bell-curve (normal) distribution of outcomes, from negative infinity to infinity; if the outcome can be only 1 or 0, the appropriate analysis is logistic rather than linear regression. For more on logistic regression, see chapter 9.

Consider the marketing mix for a hypothetical company, No More Germs, which sells toothpaste. In order to determine the relationship between the number of promotions the company does and the number of units it sells, the company plots its known data on an x–y plane (**figure 4.1**). On the x axis, the company plots the number of promotions (i.e., price reductions) it could have in a month. On the y axis, No More Germs plots the number of purchases made by customers for each given number of promotions.

In this example, No More Germs has data covering a time period of 29 weeks, promotions ranging between 0 and 9, and corresponding unit sales from 10 to 23. A linear, single-variable regression analysis can be run on those data with the aid of computer software (for more on this, including hands-on applications for you to practice, see the online supplement at http://store.darden.virginia.edu/marketing-analytics-supplements). The analysis will help No More Germs see the relationship between the number of promotions and the level of customer spending, by producing a function that describes the relationship. The objective is to draw a line that at each point represents the number of unit sales that are likely for any given number of promotions. In this case, the independent variable, x, is the number of promotions. The dependent variable, y (known as dependent because it depends on x), is units sold.

The function produced by the regression is intended to cover as many of the known data points as possible and/or reduce the distance between the line and the points as much as possible; this is sometimes known as the **line of best fit**, or the **trend line**. The function the line represents will allow the data analyst to accurately predict sales, given the number of promotions in other sample sets of data (in this case, if data from other weeks are used). The equation from the regression analysis for the best-fit straight line for No More Germs is $y = 1.42x + 9.9$.

The most critical outputs of a regression for the marketing manager are two coefficients: the intercept (where the line crosses the y axis) and the line's slope. The **intercept** represents the number of unit sales that are likely when promotions are 0: in this example, the intercept is equal to 9.9. The **slope** of the line describes the relationship between unit sales (y, the dependent variable) and promotions (x, the independent variable) by stating the ratio of the change in y to a unit change in x. In our example, the number of unit sales increases by 1.42 for every one-unit increase in promotions (**figure 4.2**). The slope (often referred to as "rise over run") is therefore $1.42 \div 1$, or 1.42.

The slope of the line can mean one of three things: (1) If the slope is positive, the relationship between the two variables is positive, meaning as the independent variable increases, so does the dependent variable. (2) If the slope is 0, no changes are observed in the dependent variable as the independent variable changes (in other words, the variables are not correlated). Or (3) if the slope is negative, a change in the independent variable will produce the opposite effect in the dependent variable (i.e., unit sales would decrease if promotions increased).

Remember that while in this example, the relationship between promotions and unit sales is obvious, most regression analyses show a relationship between variables that is not as clear. For example, what if No More Germs wanted to know the effect of web advertising on sales of its products? The company's marketing manager might not know how effective web ads are compared with print ads, for example, and use the regression to decide where to put the company's advertising dollars.

The output of No More Germs's sample regression is shown in **table 4.1**: this is a typical report. In most cases, marketing managers do not run the analyses themselves,

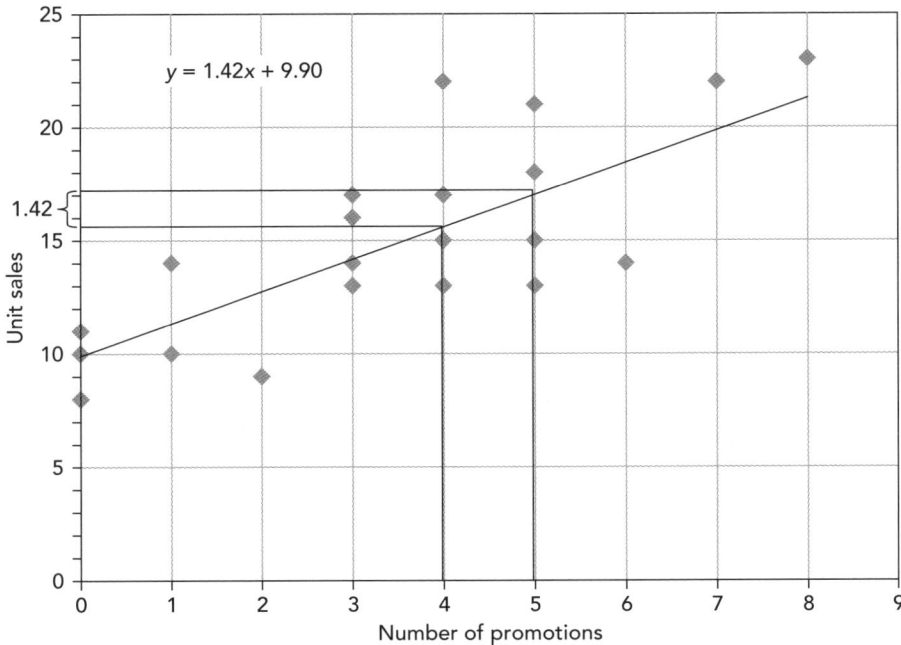

FIGURE 4.2. Illustration of slope in a single-variable regression

but they do need to be smart consumers of regression outputs, so they need to understand which outputs are most important and what they mean. While the analysis yields multiple statistics, the most critical for marketing analysts are r squared and p-value. **R squared** indicates how accurate the function is within the current sample of data. In this example, r squared is 60%, meaning the line described by this function can explain 60% of the data points. This is a hypothetical and simplified case; in the real world, a typical marketing-focused regression would have an r squared of about 20% to 30%, as numerous factors that affect sales—such as competition, weather, and so on—would be unknown before running the analysis.

To better understand the meaning of r squared, imagine your regression output indicates an r squared of 0. The resulting plot will look like a disorderly scattering of data (**figure 4.3**). A line cannot be produced that will explain any of the data.

Now imagine r squared is 100%. In this case, all of the data points (dots) will be on a line (**figure 4.4**). The line accounts for all of the points in the data set. All regression analyses will result in lines with accuracy somewhere between these extremes.

TABLE 4.1. Illustration of output from single-variable regression analysis

	Regression statistics
Multiple r	0.775
R squared	0.601
Adjusted r squared	0.586
Standard error	2.566
Observations	29

ANOVA

	Degrees of freedom	Sum of squares	Mean square	F statistic	Significance of F statistic
Regression	1	267.28	267.28	40.60	0.00
Residual	27	177.75	6.58		
Total	28	445.03			

	Coefficients	Standard error	T-stat	P-value
Intercept	9.90	0.85	11.60	0.00
Number of promotions	1.42	0.22	6.37	0.00

P-value describes the significance of the findings given the sample size. But what does significant mean? In this population sample, 29 observations are used. Since this is a regression analysis of a small sample, we want to know whether we will still see the resulting coefficients if we include another 29 observations, or another 29,000. Will the slope of the line be 1.42, or will it be 0 or negative? Here, the p-value indicates there is a 0% chance the coefficients will change beyond the standard error given the addition of more data points or different samples. Most important, it indicates a 0% chance the slope will become negative. In other words, **significance** means that, regardless of how many times the data are sampled, the relationship will hold.

In addition to these critical outputs of a regression analysis, statisticians refer to another value. In this linear regression example, **t-stat** is a reflection of p-value; however, in logistic regression, a **chi-square** test is used instead of the t-stat. P-value, on the other hand, will always be referred to in the same way regardless of the analytics technique used. Particularly for marketing managers, who need to be smart consumers

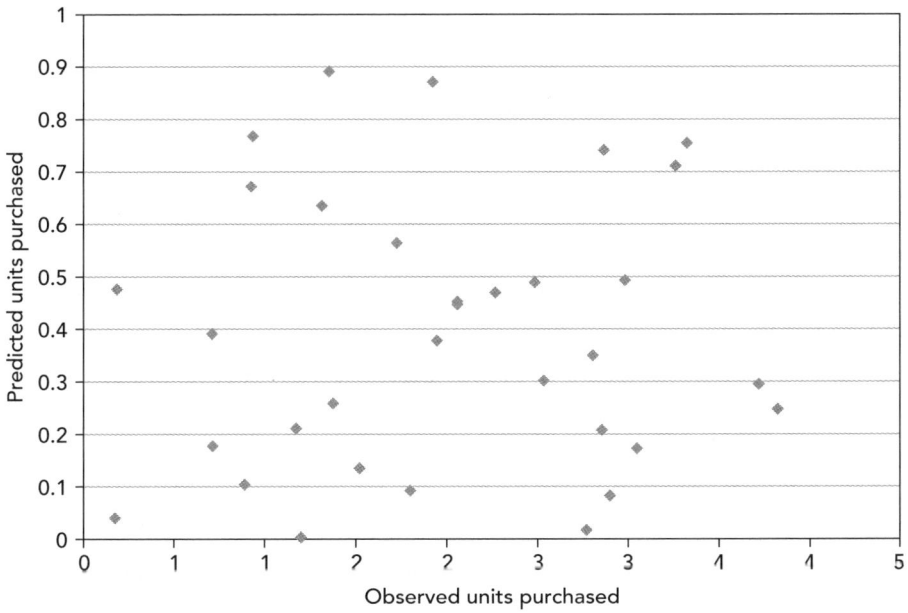

FIGURE 4.3. Illustration of r squared = 0%

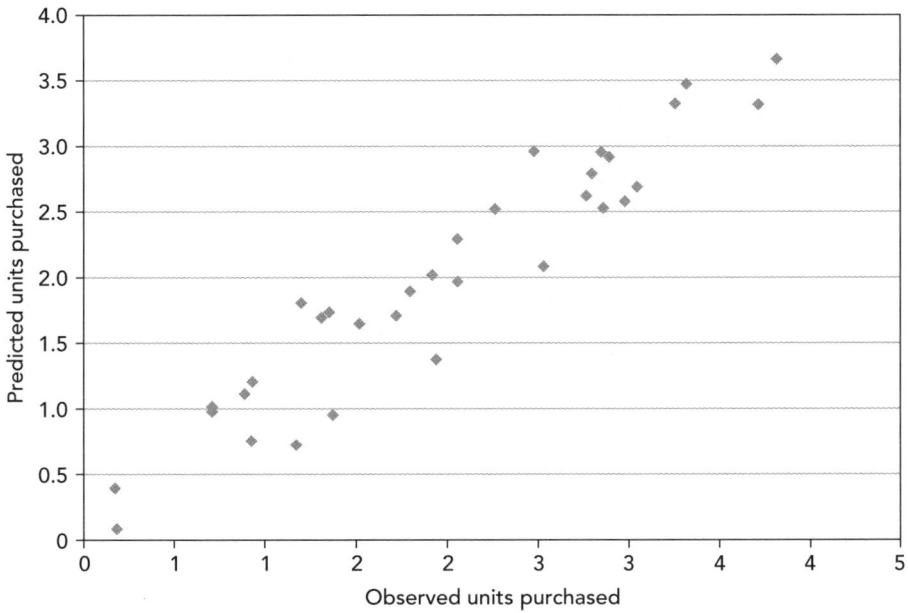

FIGURE 4.4. Illustration of r squared = 100%

of regression outputs, p-value will provide adequate information about the significance of the findings.

Adding Variables to the Regression

Single-variable regressions are by nature oversimplified, and they cannot explain most real-world marketing situations.

So, let us consider an analysis of the effects of multiple variables on the number of No More Germs units purchased by hypothetical consumers. When marketing managers work through a problem, they have to gather data in order to find a solution. To illustrate **multivariable regression**, we are going to start with a solution (i.e., a true model) and use only data that we know are a part of that model to explore how regression predicts outcomes based on a group of independent variables.

The data shown in **table 4.2** reflect an analysis of three variables: price paid, whether the unit was on feature (highlighted in a mailer or other promotion, but not necessarily at a reduced price), and whether the unit was on a store display (on an endcap or stand-alone cardboard cutout). Because we created the model, we can fix the coefficients—a is the intercept; b_1 is the coefficient of price paid; b_2 is the coefficient of feature; and b_3 is the coefficient of display—and we know the true effect of each of these variables on the outcome. Feature and display are both coded as either 1 (yes) or 0 (no).

Because this is a hypothetical situation, the data are known to coincide with the true model (**table 4.3**), in which the intercept is 6.22, the price coefficient is −2.28 (meaning the slope is downward and, as price increases, unit sales decrease), the feature coefficient is 0.38, and the display coefficient is 0.22 (meaning the slope is upward and, as feature and display increase, unit sales increase). Also, because this is the true model, r squared is 0.99, indicating an extremely low chance of error (the 1% error is inserted randomly in the true model we created).

Omitted-Variable Bias

Imagine you are a marketing manager for No More Germs. Since no one can know the true model in any real-world situation, you must approximate it as closely as possible by looking only at the data. Imagine now that you don't think price is important in your model, and consider only feature and display. As shown in **table 4.3**, the

TABLE 4.2. Hypothetical data on sales of No More Germs toothpaste

Customer	Price paid	Feature	Display	Units purchased*
1	$1.50	0	0	3
1	$2.56	1	1	1
1	$1.62	1	0	3
2	$2.41	1	0	1
2	$2.37	0	1	1
2	$2.23	0	1	1
2	$2.65	0	0	0
2	$2.06	1	0	2
2	$2.12	1	1	2
3	$2.31	0	1	1
3	$1.69	1	1	3
3	$1.37	1	1	4
3	$1.82	0	0	2
3	$1.54	0	1	3
3	$1.29	1	1	4
3	$1.96	1	0	2
3	$2.20	0	0	1
3	$1.55	1	0	3
3	$2.01	0	1	2
4	$2.07	0	1	2
4	$2.79	1	0	0
4	$2.15	0	0	1
4	$2.50	1	0	1

* Units purchased = $a + b_1 \times$ price paid + $b_2 \times$ feature + $b_3 \times$ display + error.

TABLE 4.3. Model estimates using hypothetical data

	True model	Estimated model
Intercept	6.22	1.14
Price	−2.28	—
Feature	0.38	0.892
Display	0.22	0.758
R squared	0.99	0.305

coefficients describing those variables' effects on units purchased are higher in your estimated model than in the true model.

How would the results of your estimated model influence your decisions as a manager? You would expect that feature and display would be more effective than they actually are and invest more heavily in those marketing strategies. As shown in the true model, however, price has a great effect on units purchased, and the effects of feature and display are therefore overstated in your estimated model.

To correct such a bias, intuition and experience come into play. When you create a model, it is crucial that you think critically about which variables you include and which you omit. Once you consider that you have omitted price, you should know from experience that price has a significant effect on units purchased. You should also know that when items are on feature and display, they tend to come with a reduced price. In other words, price and feature/display tend to be negatively correlated.

By omitting price from your model, you have introduced what is known as **omitted-variable bias**: the estimated model has not taken into account a variable that has a significant effect on what is being measured. While such biases may not always be as obvious as in this example, they are common in multivariable regression analyses: this is the main point of differentiation when moving away from single-variable analyses.

To ensure that a bias is not detrimental to the findings of a regression analysis, we must examine the direction of the bias in the coefficients of the variables, such as feature and display, that are included in the estimated model. In this case, the bias is positive because feature and display have a higher coefficient in the estimated model than in the true model; in other words, the effects of feature and of display in the estimated model are greater than they would be if price were also included. But how do we know the direction of the bias if we do not know the true model? Again, intuition and experience are necessary. We know from experience that price and unit sales have a negative correlation, and that there are negative correlations between price and feature and between price and display. The direction of the bias when price is the omitted variable is the product of the sign of the correlation between price and units purchased and the sign of the correlation between price and feature and display. Since the product of a negative and a negative is a positive, the bias is positive (**table 4.4**).

In general terms, the direction of the omitted-variable bias is the product of the signs of the correlations between the omitted variable and each of the other variables. **Figure 4.5** illustrates this rule. Here, x and y are shown with respect to some omitted

TABLE 4.4. Correlation between independent and dependent variables

	Price	Feature	Display	Units purchased
Price	1	(0.25)	(0.24)	(0.98)
Feature		1	(0.09)	0.45
Display			1	0.32
Units purchased				1

		Price	Bias
Direction of bias in feature =	Units	–	
(sign of correlation between price and units) ×	Feature	–	+
(sign of correlation between price and feature)	Display	–	+

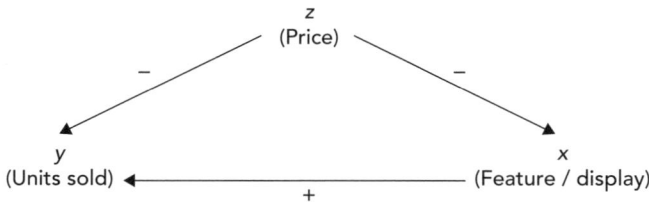

FIGURE 4.5. Illustration of omitted-variable bias

variable, z. By examining the relationships among these variables, the marketing manager can determine the direction of the bias created by omitting z.

Note that an omitted variable is a problem only when it affects both the other independent variables included in the model and the dependent variable. If it is not correlated with other independent variables in the model, removing it will reduce r squared, but will not affect the coefficient of the variables included in the model. If the changes in one variable do not affect another, variation in the dependent variable will still reflect reality. For example, weather can have a profound effect on sales (imagine a hurricane that keeps buyers in Florida from making it to stores for an extended period), without affecting the feature or display plans for a brand. If weather and feature and display plans are not correlated, then inclusion of weather is not necessary to obtain accurate estimates of feature or display. However, in the case of the estimated model for No More Germs, the omitted variable, price, is a problem because it affects the dependent variable, unit sales, and is correlated with the other independent variables, feature and display. The variation in units is being assigned to feature and display, when in fact it should be assigned to price.

In this example, we have what is known as an **optimistic model**: the bias in the coefficients of feature and display is positive, leading marketing managers to attribute a higher effectiveness to these variables than they really have. When presenting such results to decision-makers, the findings will be overstated because a significant variable—price—was omitted. While you cannot include everything in your model, it is important to know whether the results are conservative or optimistic. Typically, it is better to have a **conservative model**, which has a negative bias, meaning the variables are likely less effective in the model than in reality. Investing in a marketing channel shown to be effective by a conservative model may still represent lost opportunity if the amount of the investment is low, but it will not represent an outright mistake in resource allocation, as might be the consequence of acting on an optimistic model.

When do you know if you have the true model? You can never know for sure, but examining the four Ps (product, price, place, and promotion) is a good place to start. The results of a regression analysis are only hypotheses, and they should be tested in field experiments in order to ensure their validity.

It is worth repeating that the value of a regression model is only as good as the variables selected to be in the model. Strong managerial intuition is required to identify variables (price, feature, and display, among others) that are most closely related to unit sales. For best results, managers should also have some insight into how these variables actually relate in the real world, so they can determine whether the results of a regression might be conservative or overly optimistic. This intuition—the creative side of analytics—is necessary to move a regression beyond a statistical exercise and turn it into something of value to a business.

Economic Significance: Acting on Regression Outputs

There are two types of significance: statistical and economic. **Statistical significance** is expressed by the p-value, which indicates whether the relationship observed in a sample is likely to be observed in the population as well. A p-value under 0.1 is typically considered statistically significant.

But how do you know when it makes economic sense to invest in the findings of a regression? As a marketing manager, you must ask yourself if the benefit of a marketing intervention (i.e., the size of the coefficient, or, in other words, the slope of the line of best fit) justifies the expense. This is what is known as **economic significance**.

Consider the single-variable regression example in which we examined promotions versus purchases. The benefit provided from one promotion was found to be an increase in number of unit sales of 1.42. This was found to be statistically significant. To determine economic significance, you must weigh this benefit against the cost of doing a promotion, taking into account the gross profit from the sale of a single unit.

Let us assume that the gross profit per unit is $5.00 and the cost of a promotion is $0.50. Therefore,

Profit = (units purchased × gross profit) − (cost of promotion
        × number of promotions), or,

Profit = 1.42 × 5 − 0.50 × 1 = 7.1 − 0.5 = 6.6.

In this example, the company will make $6.60 per promotion. But if the cost of the promotion increases, or the company makes less gross profit per unit, the economic significance of the promotion could quickly be lost. In other words, even if your regression findings are significant and identify marketing-mix elements that are closely related to unit sales, you should act on the results of the regression only if the profit/loss calculation indicates economic significance.

ELASTICITY MODELS

Elasticity models are a specific kind of linear regression model, using natural logarithms of the dependent and independent variables. **Elasticity of demand**—a measure of the responsiveness of consumer demand to changes in price or advertising—is an important contributor to a manager's profit/loss calculations, and as such is key to determining the economic significance of marketing initiatives. A product's profit depends on its price, and as a marketing manager, you need to understand how responsive consumers will be to changes in price: this is the **price elasticity of demand (PED)**. To maximize product sales, you'll also need to understand how responsive consumers will be to changes in advertising: this is the **advertising elasticity of demand (AED)**. Thus elasticity models will help you determine which marketing-mix elements are most important, in terms of both statistical and economic significance.

Hypothetical Case: Belvedere Vodka

Belvedere Vodka traced its roots back to the Warsaw suburb of Żyrardów, Poland, and its production process went back more than 600 years. It was introduced in the United States in 1996, and barely 15 years later, its overall share of the vodka market had begun to decline. The company suspected the cause to be new market entrants that were capturing market share with effective advertising. To sustain its growth rate and defend its share from the competition, Belvedere was considering two options: increasing its advertising expenditure and/or reducing its prices. Such a choice is very common for brands during the various stages of their brand (or product) life cycles. The first step toward making this decision is to estimate the elasticity of a brand to its price and advertising.

Price Elasticity of Demand

Pricing is one of the most critical variables for marketers. Common sense suggests that consumers buy more of a product as its price goes down and less as its price goes up. This observation is described by PED: a measure of the responsiveness of consumer demand for a good or service to a change in its price. Higher price elasticity means that consumers respond more to a change in price. A product might have high price elasticity if people can easily find a substitute for it (if apples are more expensive, people buy more pears) or if people can simply decide not to buy it (if cars go up in price, people decide to keep their current cars longer). On the other hand, lower price elasticity means consumers don't respond much to a change in price. A product might have low price elasticity if people are attached to a particular brand, regardless of its price; if people are addicted to a certain product; or if the product is a necessary accessory, like car parts or gas.

PED gives the percentage change in quantity demanded in response to a 1% change in price. The illustration in **figure 4.6** is an oversimplification that holds constant all the other variables in the marketing mix (a situation that is essentially never the case in the real world, as we'll see later on in this chapter). A product with price elasticity whose absolute value is above 1 is said to be **elastic**, as changes in demand are relatively large compared with changes in price. Correspondingly, a product whose absolute value of price elasticity goes below 1 is deemed **inelastic**.

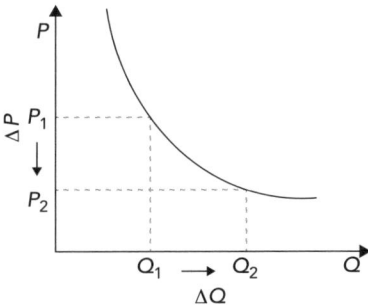

FIGURE 4.6. Price elasticity of demand

Q is quantity demanded, or unit sales. P is price. PED can be calculated using the following equation:

$$\text{PED} = \left(\frac{\text{Change in unit sales}}{\text{Change in price}} \right) \times \left(\frac{\text{Initial price}}{\text{Initial unit sales}} \right) = \left(\frac{\Delta Q}{\Delta P} \right) \times \left(\frac{P_1}{Q_1} \right).$$

Let us suppose that the price in period 1 was \$1 and total units sold were 200. Then in period 2, the price increased to \$1.25 and the total units sold were 100. Here, a price increase of \$0.25 resulted in a sales decrease of 100 units. So,

$$\text{PED} = \left(\frac{-100}{\$0.25} \right) \times \left(\frac{\$1.00}{200} \right) = -2.$$

In other words, a 1% increase in price results in a 2% decrease in sales.

As discussed in the first part of this chapter, if we have a sample of historical sales and price data, then we can regress the sales against price. The coefficient of this regression will give price elasticity, as shown in the next equation. Note that the regression coefficient and price elasticity are by definition not the same, but they are very closely related to each other, and in most cases, the coefficient is a close proxy for the elasticity.

PED = Coefficient of price when Ln(unit sales) is regressed on Ln(price).

Here, we are assuming that the **Ln-Ln model**—here, a *log-log* model in which dependent Ln(unit sales) is regressed on independent Ln(price)—is more accurate than a linear model, because it captures the shape of the relationship between price and unit sales better, and the coefficient directly provides elasticity. Historically, this has been the case with most models, such as that in the equation for Ln(unit sales):

$$Ln(\text{unit sales}) = \alpha_1 + \beta_1 \times Ln(\text{price}) + \varepsilon_1,$$

where β_1 represents the price elasticity, α_1 is the intercept, and ε_1 is the random error term drawn from a normal distribution (the standard assumption in a linear regression model).

Assuming consumers are rational and reasonably informed, the coefficient (and hence the price elasticity) should be negative. The sign of elasticity simply means whether demand rises (positive elasticity) or falls (negative elasticity); it doesn't mean the degree of elasticity, which is expressed as the absolute value of elasticity. In other words, PED can be both very elastic and negative. The phrase "greater price sensitivity" means more negative price elasticity, and similarly "lower price sensitivity" means less negative price elasticity.

Recall that Belvedere Vodka is considering reducing its prices in order to increase sales. To estimate the PED, Belvedere runs a regression on its unit sales and price data. Those regression results are shown in **table 4.5** and **figure 4.7**.

With a regression coefficient of −1.259, we can say that price elasticity of sales for Belvedere is high (meaning its customers are fairly price sensitive). Reducing price may have a positive impact on unit sales. This model suggests that a price decrease of 1% may result in a 1.259% sales increase of 9-liter cases of Belvedere Vodka.

Advertising Elasticity of Demand

Along with the option of reducing prices, Belvedere is also considering increasing its advertising. To compare the likely results, in terms of unit sales, to each of those changes, the company also needs to estimate the AED for its vodka. The AED is a measure of the responsiveness of consumer demand for a product or service to changes in the level of advertising. It can be calculated using the following equation:

$$AED = \left(\frac{\text{Change in unit sales}}{\text{Change in advertising}}\right) \times \left(\frac{\text{Initial advertising}}{\text{Initial unit sales}}\right) = \left(\frac{\Delta Q}{\Delta A}\right) \times \left(\frac{A_1}{Q_1}\right).$$

TABLE 4.5. Regression of *Ln*(unit sales) versus *Ln*(price) for Belvedere Vodka

Year	Unit sales (thousands of units)	*Ln*(unit sales)	Price	*Ln*(price)
2007	410	6.016	$215.44	$5.373
2006	381	5.943	$211.45	$5.354
2005	365	5.900	$207.45	$5.335
2004	369	5.911	$240.87	$5.484
2003	339	5.826	$241.33	$5.486
2002	306	5.724	$247.55	$5.512
2001	273	5.609	$240.48	$5.483

Regression statistics

Multiple r	0.67536
R squared	0.45611
Adjusted r squared	0.34733
Standard error	0.11269
Observations	7

	Coefficients	Standard error	T-stat	P-value
Intercept	12.686	3.340	3.798	0.013
Ln(price)	−1.259	0.615	−2.048	0.096

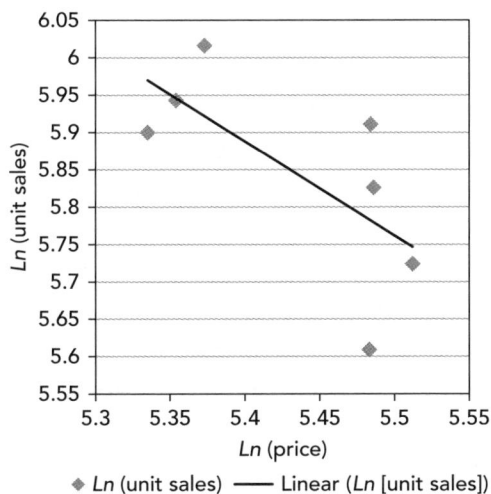

FIGURE 4.7. Visualization of regression of *Ln*(unit sales) versus *Ln*(price) for Belvedere Vodka

Let us suppose that the total advertising expenditure in period 1 was $100 and total units sold were 200. Then in period 2, the advertising was increased to $125 and the total sales were 300 units. Here, an advertising spend increase of $25 resulted in a sales increase of 100 units. So,

$$AED = \left(\frac{100}{\$25}\right) \times \left(\frac{\$100}{200}\right) = 2.$$

In other words, a 1% increase in advertising results in a 2% increase in unit sales.

Similar to the procedure for price elasticity, the basic formulation to estimate advertising elasticity is to run a regression of log of unit sales (or market share) on log of advertising. β_2, the coefficient of the log of advertising, will be the estimate of advertising elasticity:

$$Ln(\text{unit sales}) = \alpha_2 + \beta_2 \times Ln(\text{advertising}) + \varepsilon_2.$$

Again, α_2 is the intercept and ε_2 is the random error term drawn from a normal distribution.

All other factors remaining equal, an increase in advertising is expected to result in a positive shift in demand, indicating a positive advertising elasticity. A firm can utilize AED to make sure its advertising expenses are in line; an increase in demand may not be the only desired outcome of advertising.

To find AED for its vodka, Belvedere runs another regression, this time on its unit sales and advertising data; see the results in **table 4.6** and **figure 4.8**.

A regression coefficient of −0.013 and low t-stat value—and therefore high p-value—suggest that changing advertising expenses may have no impact on Belvedere's sales, or that the change cannot be predicted. Therefore, since the PED results were more promising, the marketing manager obtains the insight that Belvedere customers are more sensitive to price than to advertising. The decision of the optimal price and advertising levels would be made using an optimization routine (using the steps discussed in chapter 1, on resource allocation) after considering other strategic factors such as the effects of reduced price on a firm's **brand equity**, the value contained in the name of a brand.

Elasticities (or sensitivities) can be used for short-term advertising effects. Remember that in elasticity models, which are *Ln-Ln* models, the coefficients are elasticities.

TABLE 4.6. Regression of *Ln*(unit sales) versus *Ln*(advertising) for Belvedere Vodka

Year	Unit sales (thousands of units)	*Ln*(unit sales)	Advertising (in thousands)	*Ln*(advertising)
2007	410	6.016	$20,486.1	$9.93
2006	381	5.943	$2,923.5	$7.98
2005	365	5.900	$4,826.3	$8.48
2004	369	5.911	$13,726.6	$9.53
2003	339	5.826	$10,330.2	$9.24
2002	306	5.724	$13,473.6	$9.51
2001	273	5.609	$9,264.6	$9.13

Regression statistics

Multiple r	0.06102
R squared	0.00372
Adjusted r squared	−0.19553
Standard error	0.15252
Observations	7

	Coefficients	Standard error	T-stat	P-value
Intercept	5.963	0.850	7.018	0.001
Ln(advertising)	−0.013	0.093	−0.137	0.897

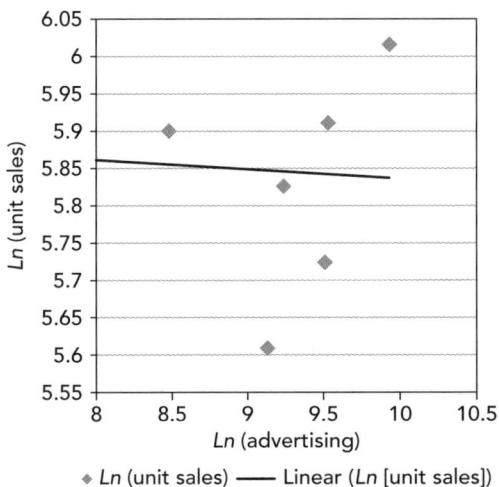

FIGURE 4.8. Visualization of regression of *Ln*(unit sales) versus *Ln*(advertising) for Belvedere Vodka

To obtain elasticities from linear models, one needs to estimate the linear model, take the coefficient, and then multiply it by the ratio of the means of the dependent variable and the advertising measure (often, unit sales and price). Thus, the linear model equation remains the same, but its coefficient must be transformed to calculate elasticity. Values of elasticities less than 0 imply negative returns to advertising, and values greater than 1 imply the firm is underadvertising. So the value should range from 0 to 1. In our simple regression model, we took advertising expenditure as one simple independent variable by combining expenditures for all possible media. But different media (e.g., print, display, in-store, television) may have varied impact on the demand for a product based on its characteristics. More analysis is required to study the impact of different media, and if required, more than one variable should be incorporated in the regression model to get a better-fitting model and help the marketing manager decide on the advertising expenditure—both the total amount and its distribution across different media.

Building a Comprehensive Model

If both PED and AED are statistically significant, the regression model should include both price and advertising as independent variables:

$$Ln(\text{unit sales}) = \alpha + \beta_1 \times Ln(\text{price}) + \beta_2 \times Ln(\text{advertising}) + \varepsilon.$$

As before, α is the intercept, β_1 is price elasticity, β_2 is advertising elasticity, and ε is the random error term.

As with multivariable linear regressions, elasticity models are vulnerable to problems of bias. **Bias** occurs when there are systematic differences between the estimated elasticity (due to errors in estimation, not environmental differences) and the true elasticity in the market. As discussed, bias may be caused by omission of variables that are correlated with those included in the equation; the decision to include or omit certain variables in the model other than price and advertising depends on their correlations with the dependent variable and the other independent variables.

Recall that a higher absolute value of price elasticity means consumers react more to changes in price, and that usually PED is negative, since sales increase when prices decrease and vice versa. In terms of bias, if the price elasticity as estimated by a regression model is higher (that is, more negative) than it is in the true model (meaning that based on the model, consumers are expected to buy more of a product when its price decreases than they actually would in reality), the bias is positive and the model is optimistic. Likewise, if price elasticity is less negative in the model than in reality, the bias is negative and the model is conservative.

Advertising elasticity is the mirror image. Higher advertising elasticity means consumers react more to changes in advertising, and usually AED is positive, since sales increase when advertising increases and vice versa. In terms of bias, if advertising elasticity in the model is higher (that is, more positive) than in the true model (meaning consumers are expected to buy more in response to more advertising than they actually do), then the bias is said to be positive and the model optimistic. If the modeled AED is less positive than the true value, then the bias is called negative and the model conservative.

Imagine the true model is as follows:

$$Ln(Y) = a^{\text{true}} + \beta_1^{\text{true}} \times Ln(\text{price}) + \beta_2^{\text{true}} \times Z + \varepsilon,$$

where Y is unit sales, a is the intercept, β_1 is the coefficient of price elasticity, β_2 is the coefficient of the omitted variable, Z is the omitted variable, and ε is the error term.

However, we estimate the model to be

$$Ln(Y) = a + \beta_1 \times Ln(\text{price}) + \varepsilon.$$

Then the true value of coefficient β_1 will be the sum of the estimated coefficient β_1 and the bias:

$$\beta_1^{\text{true}} = \beta_1 + \text{bias}.$$

If r is the covariance between independent variables, $Ln(\text{price})$ and Z, then the direction of bias can be proven to be the product of the sign of the correlation (α_2) between the omitted variable (Z) and the dependent variable, $Ln(Y)$, and the sign of covariance of independent variables, $f(r)$:

$$\text{Bias} = \alpha_2 \times f(r).$$

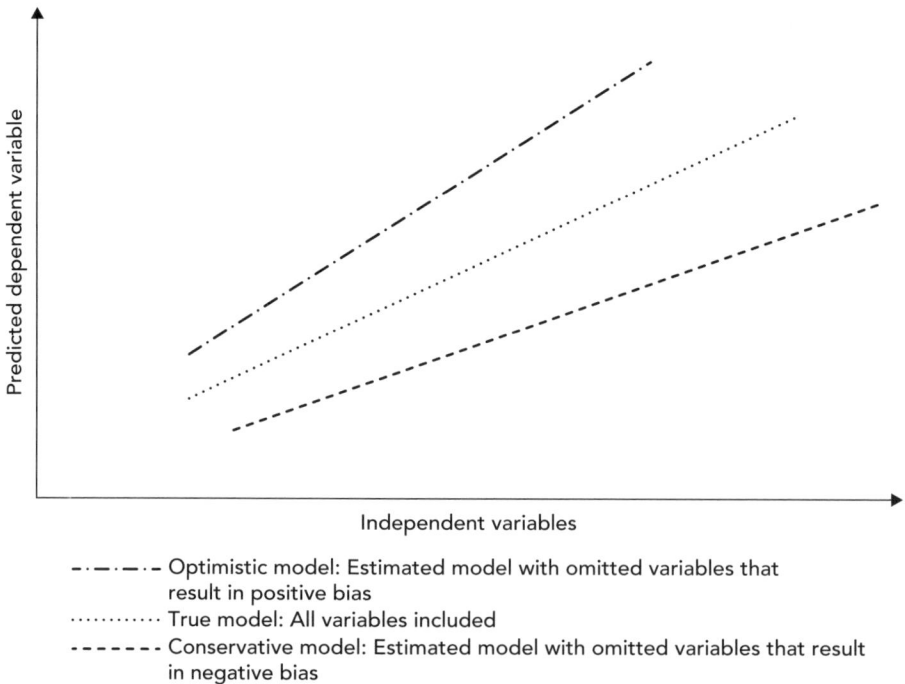

FIGURE 4.9. Linear regression models

- If the dependent variable is not related to the omitted variable, then there is no bias (bias = 0).
- If the included independent variable, $Ln(\text{price})$, is not correlated to the omitted variable (i.e., covariance is zero), then there is no bias (bias = 0).
- If α_2 and $f(r)$ are of same signs, then the bias is positive.
- If α_2 and $f(r)$ are of different signs, then the bias is negative.

The three categories of model—true, optimistic, and conservative—are illustrated in **figure 4.9**.

Variables to Include in a Comprehensive Model

A comprehensive marketing-mix model for price and advertising elasticity should include the following variables.

Product quality. If consumers are even minimally informed about the quality of products, then the better-quality product would be able to command higher prices.

With this assumption, the correlation coefficient for a regression model on price and quality will be positive. Therefore, if higher-quality products also sell more, the omission of quality from the model would lead to positive bias of price elasticity, and therefore an optimistic model. This means that the estimated price elasticity in a model without product quality would be more negative (meaning more elastic) than a model that includes product quality, and a company would assume price had a stronger effect than it actually does.

Distribution. The more widely the product is available to customers, the better the sales of that product. But the relationship between distribution and price (and between distribution and sales) is not straightforward. Firms with high-priced brands typically have selective (or exclusive) distribution channels. If this strategy holds, omitting distribution from the model would lead to less negative price elasticity. The bias would then be negative and the price elasticity model conservative, meaning a company would think customers react less to changes in price than they actually do when distribution is also considered.

Brand life cycle. As a brand matures, consumers get more familiar with that brand (in terms of, for example, deals, prices, comparability, availability) and become more price sensitive. Price elasticity tends to increase (i.e., become more negative) over the life cycle of a brand, but customer familiarity also, naturally, has an effect on unit sales. Omitting brand life cycle from a model means that higher sales in later stages in the brand's life will be attributed only to lower prices, not to the increase in customer base that occurs as the product matures; in other words, price elasticity is estimated to be higher (more negative) than it really is, resulting in a positive bias and an optimistic model.

Time-series data versus cross-sectional data. Price elasticity for a brand has two components: (1) a within-brand component, a measure of sensitivity to prices of a particular brand over time; and (2) a between-brands component, a measure of sensitivity to differences between brands. Because consumers mostly respond to prices at the point of purchase, using only a snapshot of data across brands without any time variation leaves out the within-brand component of elasticity. If the within-brand component is strong (more negative), then this sort of data aggregation over time would lead to a negative bias in price and advertising elasticity. In other words, if the model used data across brands for a single time period, omitting within-brand price sensitivity over time, then the resulting price elasticity would be less negative, advertising elasticity would be less positive, and the model would be conservative.

When prices and advertising are included over time, it is better if the frequency of the time series reflects the product's purchase cycle. For example, for consumer packaged goods, the price and advertising elasticities are more accurate if the sales, pricing, and advertising decisions are sampled every week so that they reflect consumers' typical grocery trip frequency.

Carryover effect of advertising. Advertising rarely has an immediate impact on sales. If we take into account the effect of advertising on unit sales for the current period, more often than not those effects would be in the form of spikes and would be relatively small (and therefore quite fragile) as compared with other marketing variables. Some research indicates that the current effect of price is 20 times larger than the current effect of advertising. The portion of advertising that retains its effect on consumers beyond the period of its exposure is known as the **carryover effect**. Depending on the product type, consumer segment, and firm's strategy, there could be several reasons for this carryover effect: delayed consumer response due to backup inventory, delayed exposure to the ad, shortage of retail inventory, and so on. Therefore, to account for the total effect of advertising, it is important to include both the current effect and all the carryover effect.

The **Koyck model**, a variation on a comprehensive marketing-mix linear regression model, provides a way to capture the carryover effect of advertising. It enhances the basic linear marketing-mix model by including a lagged dependent variable as an additional independent variable. A **lagged variable** means one whose value is from an earlier point in time; here, it is prior sales. So, in the enhanced model, unit sales of the current period depend on unit sales of the prior period (lagged dependent variable) and all the independent variables that caused prior sales, plus the current values of the same independent variables.

If the original model (before Koyck) was

$$Ln(Y_t) = \alpha + \delta_1 \times Ln(A_t) + \delta_2 \times B_t + \varepsilon_t,$$

then the enhanced Koyck model is:

$$Ln(Y_t) = \alpha + \boldsymbol{\lambda} \times \boldsymbol{Ln(Y_{t-1})} + \delta_1 \times Ln(A_t) + \delta_2 \times B_t + \varepsilon_t.$$

For both the original and the enhanced Koyck model, Y is unit sales; α is the intercept; A is advertising; B_t are the other independent variables included in the model; and

ε is the error term. δ_1 captures the current effect of advertising, while $\delta_1 \times \lambda/(1-\lambda)$ can be calculated to find the carryover effect of advertising. The higher the value of factor λ, the longer the effect of advertising will be. Similarly, the smaller the value of λ, the shorter the effect of advertising will be (meaning sales depend more on current advertising). The total effect of advertising is the sum of current and carryover effects; that is, $\delta_1/(1-\lambda)$.

If the advertising effects are positively correlated from one period to the next (in other words, if the last period's advertising has a positive correlation with the current period's advertising), and if the past advertising has a positive correlation with the current period's sales, then the omission of the carryover effect will result in a positive bias.

Contextual factors. Another factor that may come into play is the disposable income of consumers in the region where a product is being sold. Consumers with high disposable income may be less price sensitive. If so, then higher income would lead to lower (less negative) price elasticity. At the same time, better-informed customers (as well as those in regions with stronger regulations and antitrust laws) may lead to increased price sensitivity.

Overall, exogenous variables—gross national product (GNP) and sociodemographics such as average family income and family size—generally have a positive correlation with sales, and their exclusion could mean the model has a positive bias. Regional context may also have a correlation with advertising, due to differences in preferences, production cost structures, and restrictions, for example.

Overview of the Effects of Omitted Variables

Table 4.7 summarizes the impact of bias due to the omission of different variables from the marketing mix.

Other Factors

Other factors to consider while designing the model include:

Promotion. Promotional activities can take one of two forms: (1) increasing product awareness through displays, campaigns, demonstrations, and so forth; or (2) incentivizing consumers to try a company's products through coupons, rebates, and so on. Firms tend to run the incentive programs at the same time as they charge

TABLE 4.7. Impact of bias in price and advertising elasticity

Factor	Bias in price elasticity	Bias in advertising elasticity
Product quality	+	
Distribution	−	
Brand life cycle—early	+	
Time series	−	−
Include carryover		+
Contextual factors (income, family size, etc.)		+

higher prices, in a combination of higher prices for existing customers and rebates to acquire new customers. In such a case, prices and promotions would be positively correlated. On the other hand, the other form of promotions (increasing awareness) is generally used concurrently with lower prices. The goal is to maximize consumer awareness, and in this case, the prices and promotions would be negatively correlated. In either case, inclusion of promotion characteristics is necessary to obtain a better distinction between price effects and promotion effects on sales.

Competition. Price elasticity tends to be more sensitive if the firm compares the price of its products with that of its competitors. Consumers tend to consider relative price rather than absolute price when opting for a specific brand. Therefore, an increase in price may not negatively impact unit sales if the competition also raises prices in the same period. Following the same logic, if a firm fails to respond to a price change from its competition, the choice may affect its sales (negative for price decline by competition, and positive for price increase).

Share versus volume. If sales volume is used as a dependent variable and advertising as an independent variable, unit sales may be gained from a competitor (existing market) and/or from new customers (market expansion due to advertising). But if instead of unit sales, market share is used as a dependent variable, market expansion is eliminated as a possible reason for the effect of the independent variables (with market share as a dependent variable, the impact of advertising will appear in both numerator and denominator). As a result, the models using share instead of unit sales should normally have smaller elasticity.

Time Frame

Most generally, managers should be aware that response models assume that the market a company will face in the future would remain unchanged as compared with the past (or the time frame used to estimate the advertising and price elasticities). Price and advertising elasticities accurately reflect consumer preferences, competitor reactions, the number of brands, firm strategy, and other market factors *only during the time of data collection.*

Even if we include all the possible variables, we need to keep in mind that predictive models assume that the market conditions in the past, when the data were collected, will continue in the future. But expectations of returns from a firm's marketing-mix decisions must be informed by anticipated competitor actions and changes in the consumer preferences and competitive landscape. For this reason, it is important to periodically update the marketing-mix models and reestimate price and advertising elasticities.

CONCEPT APPLICATION

As we've seen, a marketing-mix model can be a key strategic asset for a firm. Developing a good model requires knowledge of advanced statistics, as well as a deep understanding of consumer behavior and the business context. Marketing-mix models give managers a way to assess the relative importance of their different marketing-mix options. The product line may be the most effective marketing-mix option, followed by distribution, price, and promotion.[1]

The case that follows gives you the opportunity to build marketing-mix models, as you imagine yourself as the marketing manager for another vodka company relatively new to the market: SVEDKA. The related data set (http://store.darden.virginia.edu /marketing-analytics-supplements) includes annual sales, price, and advertising spend in each channel for the major vodka brands from 1994 to 2007, in the United States. You can use the vodka data to estimate price and advertising elasticity for the entire industry and for each segment. The long time frame of the data also presents opportunities for you to consider market dynamics and competitive reactions.

After reading the case, analyze the data in the online supplement in the following ways:

1. Run a regression of the natural logarithm of unit sales on all the following: price, print marketing expenditure, outdoor marketing expenditure, broadcast marketing expenditure, and previous year's sales.
2. Run a regression of the natural logarithm of changes in unit sales on the natural logarithm of the previous period's prices, and the natural log of marketing expenditures on print, outdoor, and broadcasting.
3. To understand the influence of vodka quality, run a regression by adding the tier 1 and tier 2 dummy variables (that indicate whether a vodka brand belongs to first- or second-quality tiers) to the set of independent variables in question 2 (the previous period's prices and marketing expenditures on print, outdoor, and broadcasting).
4. To understand the influence of competition and brand power, run a regression by adding the sum of sales of all the competing brands in the previous year ("lagtotalminussales") to the independent variables in question 3.
5. To measure the sales growth of new brands compared to the existent ones, include the variable "firstintro" to the independent variable set in question 4. Firstintro is equal to 1 in the first three years after a brand is introduced, and 0 elsewhere.

Given your results, consider why the coefficients of price and advertising change in your regressions.

The variables available in the vodka industry data are as shown in **table 4.8**.

TABLE 4.8. Vodka industry data variables

Dependent variable	Independent variables
Quantity of 9-liter cases sold	Price
	Magazine advertising expenditure
	Newspaper advertising expenditure
	Broadcast advertising expenditure
	Outdoor advertising expenditure
	Tier 1
	Tier 2
	Total sales of vodkas within tier
	Total sales of vodkas outside tier
	Total sales of other brands
	Market share
	Brand introduction year

CASE: SVEDKA VODKA

A Brief History of Vodka

Associated with sophistication since James Bond first ordered a vodka martini "shaken, not stirred," vodka enjoyed tremendous success in the United States in the late twentieth century.

A flavorless spirit distilled from rye or wheat, vodka originated in the fourteenth century in either Russia or Poland. Branded vodka dated back to the late 1860s, when Smirnoff cultivated the endorsement of the tzar, engaged in comparative advertising with competitors, and paid patrons of Moscow bars to demand Smirnoff and accept no substitutes. Smirnoff was eventually produced in the United States, where it came to dominate the domestic vodka segment, capturing almost 20% of the market share by 1998. Until Absolut's launch in 1979, Smirnoff dominated the premium vodka segment with a brand name that derived authenticity from its Russian heritage.

Absolut's now-famous ad campaign helped the brand attain pop-culture status. In 1998, Absolut spent $18 million on advertising.[2] Years later, *USA Today* reported: "Absolut had pioneered selling distilled spirits on image, persuading consumers to buy prestige in a bottle for $20. But the new prestige vodkas, at $25 to $200, have become what Absolut was 20 years ago."[3] It took more than a decade after Absolut changed the vodka market for the Dutch Ketel One and American Skyy (then the only domestic vodka priced above $10) to enter it. New prestige vodkas available at high price points did indeed seem to become what Absolut once was. The success of Grey Goose, which received a score of 96 on the Beverage Testing Institute's well-regarded 100-point scale, proved that people would pay $30 for a bottle of vodka; in 1998, Grey Goose's sales increased 50% from the previous year.[4] People were becoming more discerning vodka consumers, and increasingly willing to pay more for higher quality. The *Business of Spirits* stated that the price for vodka "increased to $30 with the debut of Grey Goose, Chopin, and Belvedere in the late 1990s. Now, the debut market [was] flooded with $30 vodkas."[5]

Meanwhile, older brands of lower-priced vodka such as Popov, Gordon's, McCormick, and Barton (each priced under $10) sold the most cases and enjoyed the largest shares.[6] A significant portion of these sales was in larger-size plastic bottles.

The late 1990s were a time of huge expansion for the vodka industry. In 1998, vodka was the top-selling distilled spirits category, representing 24% of total spirit consumption in the United States, up 3.6% in volume sales from 1997; this growth in premium vodka was in stark contrast to the negative long-term trend for most other spirits.[7] SVEDKA, founded in 1998, was part of this boom.

SVEDKA

SVEDKA vodka was priced at a midpoint between the high-volume, low-priced brands like Popov, and the upscale, luxury brands like Grey Goose. In terms of quality reviews, it was closer to the latter: in 1999, *Wine Enthusiast* rated SVEDKA 93 out of 100. Classifying the vodka as a "Best Buy," the review said, "We can't remember using the word 'complex' when describing a vodka before, but this one shows a tightly knit set of characteristics that deserve applause."[8] Favorable reviews continued, and the brand won prestigious awards including gold medals at the 2002 International Wine and Spirit Competition and the 2003 World Spirit Competition.

Vodka's Marketing-Mix Elements

Product

The US vodka boom continued in the new millennium.

Between 2000 and 2007, the number of vodka brands increased from 14 to 26. Flavors and packaging were the more popular product variations introduced. Absolut was the first to introduce flavored vodka in 1986, using three types of peppers. The company called it Absolut Peppar (peh-PAR) and proclaimed it to be perfect for a Bloody Mary. Smirnoff and Absolut introduced the most flavors, and by 2007, Smirnoff's product line included 20 different flavors, while Absolut had more than 10. In 2007, Smirnoff was the highest-selling spirit brand worldwide (25.7 million cases) and in the United States (9 million cases). US vodka sales topped $7 billion in 2007, and two spots in the top five spirit brands worldwide belonged to vodka brands Smirnoff and Absolut.[9] Innovative packaging evolved, starting with Absolut's recognizable shape, inspired by a vintage Swedish apothecary bottle. By 2011, brands such as Vox and Ciroc were bottled in elegant frosted glass. SVEDKA also changed its bottle, and between 2003 and 2009, added five flavors.

Price

In 1997, Grey Goose had invented the super-premium category, marketing a 750-ml bottle of vodka priced above $30. Vodka retail prices varied across states because of taxes and the regulation of distributors. The wholesale price of a 9-liter case of vodka was above $200 for the super-premium brands such as Chopin, Belvedere, Grey Goose, and Level, whereas the prices of some value brands such as Aristocrat, McCormick, Barton, and Crystal Palace were below $35 per 9-liter case.[10]

Advertising

In 2007, the industry spent more than $200 million on advertising through various channels including outdoor, magazine, newspaper, and television.

TV advertising of alcoholic drinks had been controversial; indeed, for 48 years, liquor producers had chosen not to air commercials. In 1996, Seagram broke that trend with network spots promoting Crown Royal and Lime Twisted Gin. In spite of the public outcry that arose, other liquor brands slowly started testing cable TV spots. Eventually, cable television came to be seen as the most suitable venue for TV liquor advertising.

The print ads for vodka were very sophisticated. In 1980, Absolut began featuring its bottle's distinct silhouette, a practice it continued for more than two decades. Its innovative campaign prompted an account representative at TBWA, Absolut's ad agency, to write a book about its print campaign.[11]

SVEDKA's print ads also evolved. Its first campaign, aimed mostly at salespeople but directed toward image-conscious 21-to-30-year-old consumers, had featured two young, Nordic-looking blond women, "the SVEDKA sisters," who urged readers to "try something Swedish tonight." Following that, its first national campaign was themed "Adult Entertainment" and brought more press recognition: SVEDKA won *Impact* magazine's 2003 Hot Brand Award, and it was mentioned regularly in publications including *People*, *US Weekly*, and the *New York Post* as the vodka of choice among the young celebrity crowd. Finally, in 2005, SVEDKA rolled out its second national campaign, introducing SVEDKA_Grl as its futuristic and provocative mascot. Her sexy image appeared on the website and in advertising and buzz marketing pieces. The brand rallying cry "Voted #1 Vodka in 2033" was used in the ads to offer social commentary on hot topics of the day. SVEDKA_Grl set her own rules and delivered tongue-in-cheek messages on current events such as stem cell research and smoking bans. She appeared on billboards, bus shelters, and wallscapes in key markets such as New York, Chicago, San Francisco, and Boston.

Once again, the press responded. This time, industry associations weighed in as well. SVEDKA's ads twice drew censure from the Distilled Spirits Council (DISCUS) for using sex to sell alcohol. Although the industry's self-regulating body didn't impose a fine or require that ads be pulled, all major liquor companies in DISCUS voluntarily pulled or altered censured ads. SVEDKA was not a DISCUS member and did not retreat from its ad strategy. SVEDKA's growth rates accelerated from 35% to 40% to 60%. Perhaps just as important as the sales results, the campaign brought life and awareness to the brand. SVEDKA had a clear personality that consumers recognized across all the marketing vehicles.

Distribution

After the repeal of Prohibition in 1933, US alcohol distribution was highly regulated via a three-tier system that restricted producers from directly distributing alcohol. Producers were required to supply distributors, who then supplied retailers; consumers could purchase alcohol only from the retailers. Some states, called control states, had a monopoly over the wholesaling and/or retailing of some or all categories of alcohol. In those states, consumers could obtain alcohol only from state-run Alcoholic Beverage Control stores, and marketers could obtain distribution only by persuading each independent state liquor commission to carry their brands. By 2011, there were 19 control states.

Given that distribution was entirely under alcohol producers' control, the marketing-mix model for vodka had to focus on balancing product line, price, and advertising decisions.

CONCLUSION

After almost 10 years in the business, SVEDKA needed to further distinguish and market its already successful vodka. Historical data on US vodka sales enabled evaluation of the effects of new flavors, segment membership, and advertising. Analysis of these data might answer marketing questions about whether, and how much, consumer reactions to vodka advertising and pricing differed among the super-premium,

premium, and value segments; whether new brand entries had different price and advertising elasticities compared with the established brands; and the effect of new flavors on vodka sales. Perhaps SVEDKA could quantify the financial value of its *Wine Enthusiast* certification and 2002 and 2003 gold medals. Understanding the value generated by each of the three campaigns from 1998 through 2005 would provide a good basis for the design of future campaigns. And identifying brands that directly competed with SVEDKA would allow SVEDKA to effectively allocate marketing resources.

5

Customer Lifetime Value

In chapter 4, we discussed marketing mix and measures of elasticity, or consumer responsiveness to changes in advertising and price. In this chapter, we consider marketing mix and consumers again, now in terms of their value to a company. **Customer lifetime value (CLV)** is a way to quantify the expected value of a customer to a company in the future, and thus is a key integrating metric for customer management. Once a company can predict the value of its customers and has an idea of their purchasing behaviors, it can make informed decisions about how to market to them and how much to spend on marketing to acquire and keep them.

CLV: QUANTIFYING CUSTOMER RELATIONSHIPS

One way to quantify the value of a customer to the company and differentiate among customers is through **customer profit (CP)**, the difference between the revenues from and the costs of a customer relationship during a specified period. CP measures the past. CLV is a similar kind of measure, but it looks forward. As such, CLV can be more useful than CP in shaping managers' decisions, but it is much more difficult to quantify. Quantifying CP is a matter of carefully reporting and summarizing the results of past activity, whereas quantifying CLV involves forecasting future activity. CP is descriptive analytics, while CLV is predictive.

Conceptually, CLV is nothing more than the concept of present value applied to the cash flows of the customer relationship. The present value of any stream of future cash flows is a measure of the single lump-sum value, today, of those future cash flows. Likewise, CLV represents the single lump-sum value, today, of the future customer relationship. Even more simply, CLV is the dollar value of the customer relationship to the firm. It is an upper bound on what the firm would be willing to pay to acquire the customer relationship, as well as an upper bound on the amount the firm would be willing to pay to avoid losing the customer relationship. If we view a customer relationship as an asset of the firm, CLV would represent the dollar value of that asset.

COHORT AND INCUBATE

Assuming that customers acquired several periods ago are no better or worse (in terms of their CLV) than the ones currently acquired, a simple way to predict CLV of new customers is to use the CP of existing longer-term customers. To figure out the CP of existing, long-term customers, define a cohort as a group of customers all acquired at about the same time, then collect data on that cohort and carefully reconstruct their cash flows over some finite number of periods; this tracking and reconstruction is known as **incubation**. Then, you can discount the cash flow for each customer back to the time of acquisition to calculate that sample customer's CP. Finally, to estimate the CP of a newly acquired customer, average all sample CPs together. This method is called the **cohort-and-incubate approach**.

Equivalently, you could calculate the present value of the *total* cash flow from the cohort and divide by the number of customers to get the average CP for the cohort. If the value of customer relationships is stable across time, the average CP of the cohort sample is an appropriate estimate of the CLV of newly acquired customers.

Using this cohort-and-incubate approach, Berger, Weinberg, and Hanna (2003) followed all the customers acquired by a cruise-ship line in 1993. The 6,094 customers in the cohort of 1993 were tracked (incubated) for five years. The total net present value of the cash flows from these customers was $27,916,614. These flows included revenue from the cruises taken (the 6,094 customers took 8,660 cruises over the five-year period), variable cost of the cruises, and promotional costs. The total five-year net present value of the cohort expressed on a per-customer basis came out to $27,916,614 ÷ 6,094, or $4,581 per customer. This is the average five-year CP for the cohort, and thus the estimated CLV as well. Berger, Weinberg, and Hanna (2003) stated,

> Prior to this analysis, [cruise-line] management would never spend more than $3,314 to acquire a passenger. . . . Now, aware of CLV (both the concept and the actual numerical results), an advertisement that [resulted in a cost per acquisition of $3,000 to $4,000] was welcomed—especially since the CLV numbers are conservative (again, as noted, the CLV does not include any residual business after five years).[1]

The cohort-and-incubate approach works well when customer relationships are stationary or change slowly over time. When relationships change slowly, a company can use the value of incubated past relationships to predict the value of new relationships.

In situations where the value of customer relationships changes more rapidly, firms often use a simple model—a group of assumptions about how the customer relationship will unfold—to forecast the value of those relationships. If the model is simple enough, it can be expressed as an equation, making CLV calculations even easier. The model in the following section is perhaps the simplest model for future customer cash flows and the equation for the present value of those expected cash flows. While not the only model of future customer cash flows, this one is used the most.

CLV MODEL

The standard CLV formula[2] multiplies the per-period cash margin, M, by a factor that represents the present value of the customer relationship's expected length:

$$CLV = \$M\left(\frac{r}{1+d-r}\right),$$

where r is the per-period retention rate and d is the per-period discount rate.

In the model, CLV is a multiple of M, the per-period dollar margin (net of retention spending). The multiplicative factor (the expression in parentheses) is the **long-term multiplier**, which represents the present value of the expected length, or number of periods, of the customer relationship.

The model for customer cash flows treats the firm's customer relationships as something of a leaky bucket. In each period, a fraction (1 minus the retention rate) of the firm's customers leave and are lost for good. When $r = 0$, the customer will never be retained and the multiplicative factor is zero. When $r = 1$, the customer is always retained and the present value of the M in perpetuity is $M \div d$. For retention rates between 0 and 1, the standard CLV formula gives us the appropriate multiplier.

Hypothetical Case 1: ISP

An internet service provider charges $19.95 per month. Variable costs are about $1.50 per account per month, and marketing spending is $6.00 per year. Customer attrition is only 0.5% per month. At a monthly discount rate of 1%, what is the CLV?

$$\$M = \$19.95 - \$1.50 - \left(\frac{\$6.00}{12}\right) = \$17.95,$$

$$r = 0.995$$

$$d = 0.01$$

$$CLV = \$M\left(\frac{r}{1+d-r}\right),$$

$$CLV = \$17.95\left(\frac{0.995}{1+0.01-0.995}\right),$$

$$CLV = \$17.95 \times 66.33,$$

$$CLV = \$1,191.$$

LIMITATIONS OF THE CLV MODEL

The standard CLV model has only three parameters:

1. Constant margin (contribution after deducting variable costs including retention spending) per period (M),
2. Constant retention probability per period (r), and
3. Discount rate (d).

Each of these parameters involves assumptions, and a good marketing manager must be aware of those assumptions and of the limitations inherent in the parameters.

First, the **margin**, or contribution, M, is assumed to be constant across time. If the margin is expected to increase or decrease with the duration of the customer relationship, the simple model will not apply.

Second, r, the **retention rate**—and by extension the attrition rate—is a key driver of CLV. Very small changes can make a major difference to the lifetime value calculated. Accuracy in this parameter is vital to meaningful results. Furthermore, like the contribution, the retention rate is assumed to be constant across the life of the customer relationship. For products and services that go through a trial–conversion–loyalty progression, retention rates will increase over the lifetime of the relationship.

In those situations, the model given here might be too simple. If the firm wishes to utilize a sequence of retention rates, a predictive analytics model can be used to calculate CLV.[3]

Third, for both parameters that take into account the period—*r* as the *per-period* retention rate and *d* as the *per-period* discount rate—it is crucial to think critically about what a **period** is. The period of the model must match the period of the retention events. If retention happens monthly, for example, then a monthly model is appropriate. If retention happens every six months (as for auto insurance), then a biannual model is necessary. If cash flows are spread out within the retention period, then it is their present value that should be used in the CLV formula.

Along with the assumptions related to each of the model parameters, the CLV model that is used most widely and the one explained here assumes that a lost customer is lost for good. This assumption of the **permanence of customer loss** is appropriate for some relationships but not for others. In catalogs, for example, a small percentage of the firm's customers purchase from any given catalog. It is important to avoid confusing the percentage of customers active in a given period (relevant for the cataloger) with the retention rates in this model. If customers often return to do business with the firm after a period of inactivity, the standard CLV formula does not apply.

Model Based on Purchase-Occasion Rates

In some cases—if a company feels that its business model or market competition or customers might change beyond a certain time in the future; if the company is not a subscription business, so that purchases happen irregularly; and if the margins and retention rates of the company vary substantially—a firm might prefer to organize customer data by purchase occasion rather than by time period. In those cases, it is better to use purchase occasion–specific rates rather the constant retention rate in the standard CLV model. The CLV model using purchase occasion rather than period is:

$$\text{CLV} = \sum_{t=1}^{30} \frac{r_t M_t}{(1+i)^{(t-1)}},$$

where:

- r_t is the probability that an individual will make purchases on at least *t* occasions, given that they have made one purchase. For the first purchase occasion, $r_t = 1$.

- M_t is the dollar contribution margin of a shopping basket at purchase occasion t, adjusted for distribution costs and coupon-redemption expenses.
- i is the relevant discount rate between any two purchase occasions. This can be found by converting the annual discount rate (a) to the discount rate between two purchase occasions, using the following equation. In this example, the average time between purchases is two weeks, so there are about 26 purchase occasions in a year:

$$i = (1 + a)^{1/26} - 1.$$

Other Assumptions

Along with the three parameters and their associated limitations, the standard CLV model makes several other assumptions:

Always a customer. The model assumes that the customer goes through dormancy but is always retained and is not lost for good. This is because the model sums to 30 periods, with a decreasing retention rate that never reaches zero; therefore, in the intervals between purchases, it is assumed that the customer will eventually come back.

Initial margin at period end. The model assumes the first margin will be received (with probability equal to the retention rate) at the *end* of the first period. This assumption may also be inappropriate in some relationships, such as subscriptions to a streaming service. For these, the following formula is better:

$$CLV_{alternative} = \$M\left[\frac{1+d}{1+d-r}\right].$$

This alternative formula applies to a situation in which the initial cash flow is a certain $\$M$ received at the *beginning* of the first period. Because of this, this alternative formula always comes out to be $\$M$ higher than the original formula. It represents the value of the customer if and when acquired.

Infinite horizon. Finally, no firm actually has an **infinite horizon**, and it is important to be aware of the consequences of assuming one.

In some industries and companies, such as retailers or business-to-business (B2B) industrial goods manufacturers, it is typical to calculate four- or five-year customer values instead of using the infinite time horizon inherent in the standard CLV formula. Of course, over shorter periods, customer retention rates are less likely to be affected

TABLE 5.1. Five-year CLV as a percentage of infinite-horizon CLV

Percentage of CLV accruing in first five years

Discount rate (%)	Retention rate (%)					
	40	50	60	70	80	90
2	99	97	93	85	70	47
4	99	97	94	86	73	51
6	99	98	94	87	76	56
8	99	98	95	89	78	60
10	99	98	95	90	80	63
12	99	98	96	90	81	66
14	99	98	96	91	83	69
16	100	99	96	92	84	72
18	100	99	97	93	86	74
20	100	99	97	93	87	76

by major shifts in technology or competitive strategies, and more likely to be captured by historical retention rates. For managers, the question is, "Does it make a difference whether I use the infinite time horizon or, for example, the five-year customer value?" The answer to this question is, "Yes, sometimes it can make a difference, because the value over five years can be less than 70% of the value over an infinite horizon."

Table 5.1 calculates the percentages of (infinite-horizon) CLV accruing in the first five years. If retention rates are higher than 80% and discount rates are lower than 20%, differences in the two approaches will be substantial. Depending on the strategic risks that companies perceive, the additional complexities of using a finite horizon may be informative.

PROSPECT LIFETIME VALUE

One of the major uses of CLV is to inform prospecting decisions. A **prospect** is someone on whom the firm will spend money in an attempt to acquire as a customer. The **acquisition spending** must be compared not just with the contribution from the immediate sales it generates, but also with the future cash flows expected from the newly acquired customer relationship (the CLV). Only with a full accounting of the value of the newly acquired customer relationship will the firm be able to make informed, economic-prospecting decisions.

The expected **prospect lifetime value (PLV)** is the value expected from each prospect minus the cost of prospecting. The value expected from each prospect will be a—the expected fraction of prospects who will make a purchase and become customers—multiplied by $(\$M_0 + \text{CLV})$, where $\$M_0$ is the average margin the firm makes on the customer's initial purchases, net of any marketing spending used to attempt to retain the customer at the end of the first period. The cost will be $\$A$, the amount of acquisition spending per prospect. The formula for expected PLV is

$$PLV = a\ (\$M_0 + \text{CLV}) - \$A.$$

If PLV is positive, the acquisition spending is a wise investment. If PLV is negative, the acquisition spending should not be made.

PLV will usually be very small. While CLV is sometimes in the hundreds of dollars, PLV can come out to be only a few pennies. Just remember that PLV applies to prospects, not customers. A large number of prospects with small but positive value can add up to a considerable amount of value for a firm.

Hypothetical Case 2

Imagine that the ISP in hypothetical case 1 plans to spend $60,000 on an advertisement reaching 75,000 subscribers. If the service company expects the advertisement to convince 1.2% of the subscribers to take advantage of a special introductory offer (priced so low that the firm makes a $10 margin on this initial purchase) and the CLV of the acquired customers is $100, is the advertisement economically attractive?

Here, $\$A$ is $0.80, a is 0.012, and $\$M_0$ is $10. Using the expected PLV equation, the PLV of each of the 75,000 prospects

$$= 0.012 \times (\$10 + \$100) - \$0.80$$

$$= \$0.52.$$

The expected lifetime value of a prospect is $0.52. The total expected value of the prospecting effort will be $75,000 \times \$0.52 = \$39,000$. The proposed acquisition spending *is* economically attractive. (Note that the acquisition cost, or advertising expense, is already subtracted from the PLV formula; $\$0.80 \times 75,000 = \$60,000$.)

If we are uncertain about the 0.012 acquisition rate, we might ask what the response rate from the prospecting campaign must be in order for it to be economically successful. We can get that number using Excel's Goal Seek function to find the a value that sets PLV to zero. Or we can use a little algebra and substitute $0 for PLV and solve for a:

$$a = \frac{\$A}{\$M_0 + \text{CLV}}$$

$$= \frac{\$0.80}{(\$10 + \$100)},$$

$$= 0.007273.$$

The acquisition rate must exceed 0.7273% for the campaign to break even on a net present value basis.

ISSUES WITH PLV

Perhaps the biggest challenge in calculating PLV is estimating CLV. The other terms (acquisition spending, expected acquisition rates, and initial margin) all refer to flows or outcomes in the near future, whereas CLV requires longer-term projections.

Another challenge is the decision on when to spend money on customer acquisition. If a company decides to do so whenever PLV is positive, it is important to keep in mind that this rests on an assumption that the customers acquired would not have been acquired had the firm not spent the money. In other words, this approach gives the acquisition spending "full credit" for the subsequent customers acquired. If the firm has several simultaneous acquisition efforts, for example, dropping one of them might lead to increased acquisition rates for the others. Situations such as these, where one solicitation cannibalizes another, require a more complicated analysis.

The firm must be careful to search for the most economical way of acquiring new customers. If there are alternative prospecting approaches, the firm must be careful not to simply go with the first one that gives a positive projected PLV. Given a limited number of prospects, the approach that gives the highest expected PLV should be used.

Finally, there are other ways to perform the calculations necessary to judge the economic viability of a given prospecting effort. While these other approaches are equivalent to the one presented here, they differ with respect to what is included in CLV. Some approaches will include the initial margin as part of CLV. For the ISP example, this approach would find that CLV is $110. Another common approach includes both the initial margin and the expected acquisition cost per acquired customer as part of the CLV. For the ISP example, this CLV will equal $110 − ($60,000 ÷ 900) = $43.33. Here, 900 is the expected number of new customers, and $60,000 ÷ 900 is the expected cost per new customer. The $43.33 is the expected value of the prospecting effort expressed on a per-customer-acquired basis. If this CLV is positive, the prospecting effort is economically attractive. Notice that $43.33 times the 900 expected new customers equals $39,000, the same total net value from the campaign calculated in the original example. The two ways to do the calculations are equivalent.

RETENTION AND CLV

Reichheld and Sasser (1990)[4] helped popularize the idea that customer retention is an important driver of a firm's financial success. They reported that "reducing defections by 5% boosts profits 25% to 85%."[5] We offer three approaches for quantifying the economic benefits of increased retention for a given firm.[6]

In the first approach, the firm might build a predictive analytics model (using linear or logistic regression, for example) to forecast future company profits and cash flows as a function of a retention rate or schedule of retention rates. One could then change the retention rate or schedule of retention rates and observe what happens to profits and cash flows. These "what-if" analyses conducted using a predictive model would be one way to quantify the benefits of increased retention. If the firm thought, for example, that increased retention would reduce the need for future acquisition spending, that linkage could be built into the model and captured in the what-if analyses.

The second and third approaches ask how increased retention affects the lifetime value of the customer. Whereas the first approach projects the future stream of company profits and cash flows, CLV accounts for the dollar value of the future cash flows attributed to the customer—either a single customer or (more often) an average customer.

In the second approach, the firm might build a predictive analytics model of future cash flows associated with the customer relationship. That model might allow for margins and retention rates to increase with customer tenure. The present value of the projected future cash flows would be the estimated CLV. To quantify the economic benefits of increased retention, once again the firm could conduct what-if sensitivities using the model of customer cash flows. For example, one might multiply the schedule of retention rates by 1.01 and recalculate the CLV. The resulting number would represent the CLV if all retention rates increased by 1%.

In the third approach, the firm might assume constant margins and retention rates, and perform what-if analyses directly on the standard CLV formula.

Consider again the hypothetical case of ISP, the internet service provider with the customer relationship where $\$M = \$17.95$, $d = 0.01$, and $r = 0.995$. The calculated CLV was $1,191. Now suppose ISP expected r to increase to 0.996 as a result of initiatives to improve customer-relationship management. To quantify the benefits of the expected increased retention, we calculate CLV for $r = 0.996$ and get $1,277 (an increase of about 7.2%).

When using the CLV formula, remember the timing assumptions inherent in it. The formula applies to current customers whose next cash flow occurs in one period, in the event they are retained. This timing assumption is conservative because, in actuality, the firm's current customers will be spread throughout the renewal cycle. For some customers, the renewal event will be imminent, not a full period away.

The change in CLV for a change in retention rate is a measure of the increase in dollar value of the firm's current customer base. This dollar value does not translate directly to an equivalent increase in yearly profits, because many other factors affect firm profits. If the firm wishes to measure the impact of increased retention rate on yearly profits, a firm-level model as described in the first approach is required.

The firm should also remember that increases in retention rate affect not only the value of the firm's current customers, but also the value of the firm's current prospects, whenever the increases in retention rate are expected to also apply to customers the firm will acquire in the future. In order to make a sound investment decision, a marketing manager must compare the economic benefits of increased retention with the costs required to achieve the increased retention rates.

Most generally, regardless of model or approach, a good marketing manager must always be aware of the assumptions in the tools they choose, and must think critically about the pitfalls and limitations of those assumptions, as well as whether they match the real-life situation of the company and its customers. As always, effective marketing analytics combines data analysis with managerial intuition and common sense.

CONCEPT APPLICATION

Use of CLV as a fundamental tool in marketing is increasing. In a business situation in which individual customers make repeated transactions with a company, and you can identify the purchases of individual customers (as is common for online and direct marketing companies), CLV is an important metric to consider as you develop sound marketing strategies and evaluate the usefulness of various marketing tactics. The case in this chapter demonstrates the importance of CLV in evaluating customer acquisition strategies and analyzing promotional profitability.

The case offers opportunities for you to calculate CLV in a noncontractual setting and to evaluate various customer acquisition activities based on marketing research results. In the case, imagine yourself as part of the management of Retail Relay (Relay), a new internet-based business that sources products from local grocery stores, boutique food retailers, and local farms, then delivers customer orders to conveniently placed pickup locations. Your task is to determine the profitability of various promotional plans that Relay has piloted.

Note that the data in the online supplement to this book, http://store.darden .virginia.edu/marketing-analytics-supplements, have several important features that affect the way they should be analyzed. First, they are organized by purchase occasion rather than by time period. Thus, instead of the constant retention rate found in some models of CLV, the case includes purchase occasion–specific rates. The CLV expected from a new customer can therefore be calculated using the model for purchase-occasion rates:

$$CLV = \sum_{t=1}^{30} \frac{r_t M_t}{(1+i)^{(t-1)}}.$$

Second, it is easy to determine the probability that a customer who makes purchase number t_1 will go on to make purchase number $t + 1$, and therefore the probability that any new customer making a first purchase will continue to purchase through occasion t_n. Stated another way, these data allow you to answer the question,

- What is the probability that a new customer will make purchases from Relay on at least 10 occasions?

It should also be noted that the data provided in the Excel spreadsheet do not provide the retention rate (r_t), so some (minor) data manipulation is required.

Finally, the data set contains information on 30 potential purchase observations. While the predicted CLV might increase if there were data beyond 30 purchase occasions, 30 is sufficient to provide a reasonably accurate estimate of CLV for the purposes of this case. The case provides data for roughly a two-year CLV (30 weeks × average interpurchase time of 3 weeks = 90 weeks).

- In order to usefully analyze the customer data collected by Relay and available in the online supplement to this book, you need to understand the expected profitability of a newly acquired customer. Assuming an annual discount rate of 10%, what is the expected CLV of a newly acquired customer?
- Do you think this value is likely to increase or decrease as the company grows?
- Which of Relay's existing promotions are worth pursuing on a larger scale?
- As you work through these questions, consider carefully what goes into the margin calculation.
- Think carefully about the two studies explained in the case. Is one more useful than the other?

CASE: RETAIL RELAY

During the summer of 2007, Zach Buckner, the 31-year-old founder and CEO of Retail Relay (Relay), was again confronted with an ongoing frustration of suburban life. After his third trip to a local hardware store to get supplies for the same home improvement project, Buckner realized that a one-day project had now effectively become an all-weekend affair. He had spent more time shopping than installing new wiring in his 1930s-era house. Buckner had studied electrical and systems engineering, and he had completed many consulting assignments for companies looking to improve their business operations. He drew on that knowledge and experience to come up with the concept of Relay. And a new paradigm for online shopping was born.

Although online retailing was certainly not a new concept, Buckner's approach was unique. His overall objective was to provide a solution to a problem faced by all Americans: time wasted, inefficiencies, and costs caused by the daily need to run errands. His initial concept was to provide an online means for consumers to order and purchase goods from a variety of local retailers (i.e., grocers, hardware stores, clothiers), minimizing the burden of traveling to individual stores. Although the obvious solution was to provide convenient delivery service to customers' homes, Buckner soon realized there was no way to make this economically feasible.

Many online businesses that had entered the home-delivery market had failed. Perhaps the most spectacular of these early failures was Webvan, a grocery home-delivery service that at its height operated in 10 metropolitan areas in the United States. Webvan built a billion-dollar order-processing, warehousing, and delivery infrastructure. Its revenues and profits never came close to covering its capital outlay, however, and in 2001, it filed for bankruptcy protection.

But not all the home-delivery businesses had failed. Bolstered by substantial growth in both online retailing and the rapidly expanding market for fresh, organically produced food items (in 2009, US sales of organic foods totaled about $6.2 billion, after several years of growth rates exceeding 20% per year), Long Island food purveyor Fresh Direct had enjoyed considerable success. Founded in 1999, this online grocery business offered custom-prepared groceries and meals. By sourcing food items directly from local farms, dairies, and fisheries, and preparing meats, breads, and so on in an on-site warehouse facility, Fresh Direct was able to reduce transit time and improve the quality and freshness of its products, while also reducing costs by eliminating the need for a middleman. In that sense, Fresh Direct acted in many ways like a traditional grocery retailer, buying direct and carrying inventory. Though its delivery area was still limited mainly to Manhattan, Brooklyn, and Queens, it had plans to expand.

Buckner was determined not to repeat the mistakes of others. "The last-mile delivery cost kills most home-delivery businesses," Buckner understood. "I knew we could find a better way."[7]

To make Relay successful, it would be imperative to cut out those "last-mile delivery costs" and to minimize up-front working capital requirements. Last-mile delivery costs greatly reduced operating margins. Getting a truckload of products to a single neighborhood or workplace location was not nearly as costly as paying for drivers and trucks to bring products to individual homes. Likewise, a simple initial distribution system would not require the kind of elaborate, automated "Willy Wonka operation" that had strained the financial viability of so many other businesses. Fresh Direct had been able to make its more expensive warehouse and home-delivery system work, but it operated in a densely populated area of New York City.

Buckner wanted to find several pickup locations that were convenient for many customers, both in location and in ease of order pickup. These would be the "relay" points for the grocery items on their journey from farm or store to the customer's home. If these cost-reduction measures were successful, they would allow Relay to provide this service to customers without charge, which effectively meant customers would pay the same price for these items as if they had shopped at the stores themselves. Relay also offered a fee-based home-delivery option, but this constituted a small part of its business and was not the focus.

While the original plan was to sell much more than grocery-type items, initial sales feedback confirmed that local, natural, organic, and healthy foods and household items were by far the best-selling categories. The custom leather belts did not sell. Neither did electrical wiring. Relay soon narrowed its business concept, becoming a grocery- and farm-product retailer.

Even though the company abandoned the idea of selling nongrocery items early on, it was still important to offer customers a wide selection of grocery items. A narrow selection would not achieve the goal of reducing the amount of time customers spent grocery shopping, because they might still have to stop at a store to pick up items Relay did not offer. Customers wanted free-range chicken and freshly picked English peas, but they also wanted paper towels and laundry detergent—and if possible to avoid a supermarket trip entirely. While signing up large grocery retailers as suppliers had the advantage of quickly producing a wide available assortment, the large retailers had little to gain and potentially much to lose by acting as Relay's suppliers. Sales through Relay might cannibalize their own in-store sales. For this reason, the initial push for suppliers focused on smaller, boutique-type retailers, restaurants, and local farms. For smaller retailers and farms, Relay offered a promising new vehicle through which to reach a previously untapped consumer market, and their risk of cannibalization was small.

After sending proposals to local businesses, Relay experienced overwhelming acceptance, with a 100% positive response rate from the retailers it approached with this collaborative opportunity. Relay enlisted over 40 unique suppliers, covering a wide assortment of grocery items. Large supermarkets, such as Whole Foods, were not suppliers.

Retail Relay Operations

Relay set up initial operations in Charlottesville, Virginia, a city with a population of 50,000 and that was home to the University of Virginia as well as several other large private and government employers. Although pockets of poverty existed in Charlottesville, significantly more than the average number of residents could be described as having a high level of income and/or a high level of education. It also had an unusually high proportion of residents who were interested in local and organic food. Relay's management team believed that Charlottesville was an ideal location in which to test its concept.

The typical customer order and product pickup process followed six discrete steps:

1. Customers submitted orders and paid for them online at RetailRelay.com, selecting from what evolved into an assortment of mostly grocery and home products. Customers who wanted to pick up their orders the next day had to place them by midnight the night before.
2. Relay downloaded orders immediately after midnight and then broke them down and transmitted them to participating retailers.
3. Retailers used these orders to pack and sort bags by customer number.
4. A Relay driver picked up the bagged orders the following morning and returned to the warehouse.
5. Relay workers manually sorted orders from multiple retailers by customer and temperature zone (shelf-stable, refrigerated, frozen) and repacked them in the truck (**figures 5.1** and **5.2**). Any one customer might have bags from several retailers and multiple bags from a given retailer.
6. Finally, a driver transported orders to the customer pickup location in a Relay truck.

Although not as cost prohibitive as home delivery, the process of collecting, sorting, and delivering products to the pickup location did cost money. The first four steps were inexpensive. Because individual suppliers removed ordered products from their own shelves and had them ready for the Relay driver near the front of the store, it took drivers very little time to collect merchandise from individual suppliers. It also took very little time for the driver to move from one supplier to the next during the collection process because the community was relatively small. Overall, the costs associated with collecting merchandise from suppliers were negligible.

On the other hand, sorting and distributing products was significantly more expensive. Because the process of sorting by customer order was very labor intensive, an individual worker could sort only about $400 of product per hour. The cost of labor, both for workers who sorted and for truck drivers, was about $15 per hour. Unlike

FIGURE 5.1. A Retail Relay delivery truck, which also served as a moving billboard

product collection, distribution was not a quick process. Drivers had to drive to the pickup location and wait for three to four hours while customers came by to pick up their orders. On average, a driver would spend about five hours transporting product from the warehouse to the pickup location, setting up at the location, waiting for customers to pick up their orders, and then returning to the warehouse.

A fully loaded truck could carry about $3,200 of merchandise and made deliveries about 200 days per year. The trucks themselves were utilitarian, lacking the comforts of longer-haul vehicles. They were also inexpensive to operate. Relay estimated that the total cost of a truck, including maintenance and fuel, was about $3,000 per year.

Prices

The basic contract with suppliers stipulated that suppliers had to sell products to Relay at 15% less than their in-store shelf price. The retail price to customers was set to the current shelf price at the supplier's brick-and-mortar establishment. Suppliers

FIGURE 5.2. A Retail Relay driver waiting at a pickup location

were required to input their own product prices—using in-house-developed iPhone, BlackBerry, and Android applications—into Relay's ordering system. While it was possible for Relay to audit its system to make sure its prices were indeed the same as an individual supplier's regular shelf prices, it was difficult to know whether every deal price offered at a supplier's store was passed through to Relay customers. As a practical matter, management believed that some suppliers were more diligent than others in making sure their Relay prices matched those on their shelves.

Studies: Customer Purchasing Behavior

To decide what kind of promotions to offer, Relay undertook two studies involving purchase data from customers. The first, a small pilot study, tracked the purchase activity of 81 randomly chosen customers who had made their first purchase with Relay before June 2009. In constructing the pilot study, management wanted to be sure it could track these individuals over a period long enough to observe many purchase occasions. The company was growing very quickly, and many of its customers were new and had made only a small number of purchases. Given that the average inter-purchase interval for individuals in this sample was approximately three weeks, and that the end of the time frame for analysis was February 2010, it seemed reasonable to restrict the pilot group to those who had made their first purchase at least nine months earlier. Descriptive statistics for this pilot study are provided in **table 5.2** (and in the online supplement).

Two things stood out in the results of this pilot study. First, many people seemed to be purchasing from Relay once and not returning to make another purchase. Of the 81 customers tracked in the study, 32% never returned to make a second purchase. Second, the average size of the basket of goods purchased increased once an individual became experienced in dealing with Relay. The average size of an individual's first purchase was $49.51, whereas the average size of a regular customer's 20th purchase was $92.91. Both of these findings suggested to management that offering promotions for the second and third purchase occasion to get new customers "over the hump" might be an effective way to retain them.

Once the results of the pilot study were known, Relay conducted a more extensive study using 587 randomly selected customers, chosen regardless of when they had made their first purchase. The managers hoped this new, much larger sample size would provide more reliable results than those of the pilot study. Descriptive statistics for this study can be found in **table 5.3** (and in the online supplement).

The more extensive study showed an even larger attrition rate between the occasions of the first and second purchases—45%—a worrisome number for management. But the results of the more extensive study were not convincing to everyone on the management team. In particular, some were concerned that using a sample that contained many individuals who had only recently become customers would bias the analysis, because management would not be able to observe anything other than their first few purchase occasions. Whether the pilot study or the larger study provided a more accurate depiction of customers' purchase patterns was an open question.

Promotions

Using the results of the two studies, Relay engaged in a limited amount of price promotional activity. New customers generally received a coupon for 10% off their next purchase, printed on the receipt of their first purchase. On the second purchase, they

TABLE 5.2. Descriptive statistics of customer purchases conditioned on how many times an individual ordered from Retail Relay (pilot study)

Order number	Total number of observations in the data	Conditional probability of observing purchase occasion $t+1$ in the data if occasion t is observed*	Average amount of purchase
1	81	NA	$49.51
2	55	55 ÷ 81 = 68%	$62.28
3	44	44 ÷ 55 = 80%	$57.01
4	34	77%	$62.03
5	31	91%	$63.06
6	28	90%	$72.90
7	23	82%	$60.30
8	21	91%	$63.68
9	20	95%	$72.04
10	19	95%	$67.89
11	17	89%	$70.07
12	17	100%	$82.48
13	16	94%	$82.17
14	15	94%	$61.12
15	14	93%	$65.79
16	13	93%	$82.29
17	13	100%	$65.32
18	13	100%	$99.20
19	13	100%	$73.74
20	12	92%	$92.91
21	10	83%	$59.57
22	10	100%	$75.69
23	9	90%	$60.33
24	9	100%	$84.83
25	8	89%	$87.55
26	7	88%	$60.99
27	7	100%	$87.95
28	7	100%	$99.33
29	6	86%	$77.30
30	6	100%	$99.70

Source: Data courtesy of Retail Relay.
* For example, in the pilot study, if a customer made two purchases, the probability of a third purchase is 80%.

TABLE 5.3. **Descriptive statistics of customer purchases conditioned on how many times an individual ordered from Retail Relay (full study)**

Order number	Total number of observations in the data	Conditional probability of observing purchase occasion $t+1$ in the data if occasion t is observed	Average amount of purchase
1	587	NA	$46.71
2	322	$322 \div 587 = 55\%$	$56.71
3	240	$240 \div 322 = 75\%$	$57.93
4	188	78%	$56.87
5	156	83%	$58.26
6	127	81%	$66.90
7	103	81%	$63.62
8	89	86%	$70.27
9	73	82%	$63.03
10	62	85%	$62.60
11	56	90%	$71.81
12	52	93%	$76.76
13	44	85%	$78.14
14	39	89%	$65.65
15	33	85%	$74.84
16	30	91%	$81.11
17	29	97%	$72.08
18	28	97%	$87.30
19	27	96%	$71.94
20	23	85%	$75.44
21	19	83%	$70.35
22	17	89%	$72.86
23	14	82%	$66.68
24	11	79%	$79.90
25	9	82%	$93.91
26	8	89%	$61.08
27	7	88%	$94.16
28	6	86%	$100.40
29	4	67%	$77.89
30	3	75%	$99.70

Source: Data courtesy of Retail Relay.

received a 5% discount coupon for a third purchase. The redemption rate of these coupons on qualified purchases was high, around 80%.

Relay tested the value of home-delivered flyers as well, distributing 2,000 of them to homes in a Charlottesville subdivision. The flyers contained a coupon for 10% off the total price of a Relay order. The cost of this door-to-door program, including printing, transportation, and labor, was approximately $1,200, and the program produced a total of seven uses, all by new customers.

Relay also tested coupons inserted in Valpak "blue envelopes," mailers that contained coupons and promotional offers from many companies, most of them local. Relay's coupon offered $5 off any purchase of $25 or more and $15 off a purchase of $100 or more. Purchasing insert coverage across three separate mailings at a cost of $1,100, Relay was able to reach approximately 60,000 homes in the greater Charlottesville area. Based on coupon redemptions, which required customers to input a promotional code when they submitted their online order, and previous purchase data, management determined these Valpak inserts were redeemed by 58 new customers and 10 existing customers.

Management wanted to determine the profitability of these promotions. A CLV analysis of its customer-level data would allow Relay to answer the question, "If I acquire a new customer, on average how much money is that customer really worth?"

New Customer Acquisition and Retention

Besides its limited foray into direct-to-consumer price promotions, Relay employed several tactics to recruit new customers and retain existing ones. It set up informational booths at various community functions around Charlottesville (e.g., the Discovery Museum Fair, the Vegetarian Festival, and the Virginia Festival of the Book), and management was available for local talk radio programs that catered to Relay's target audience. But by far its largest promotional investment, in terms of both time and money, was in its email and social media campaigns. Beginning each Sunday, promotional Relay emails were distributed to thousands of existing customers, as well as to others whose email addresses had been obtained during other promotional activities. Because repeat customers often developed a regular pattern in their orders, Relay was able to predict the most likely day of the week for their purchases, based on their previous ordering days. It staggered email delivery to these existing customers so they would receive messages one day prior to their regular order day, thereby using the email as a reminder as well as a way to offer special information in a timely manner. To further promote awareness through this medium, Relay established partnerships with large local employers who sent email blasts out to its employee base, offering exposure to an expanded group of potential customers. Individuals could also become fans of Relay on Facebook, where its page was regularly updated with new information on suppliers, recipe suggestions, and comments on what produce was starting to come in season.

CONCLUSION

Through all this activity, Zach Buckner and his recently hired new president—Arnon Katz, a 2009 graduate of the University of Virginia's Darden School of Business—wondered if the customer acquisition and retention activities were really worth what they cost the business in time, money, and aggravation. As the customer base grew, perhaps they should simply allow word-of-mouth advertising from existing customers to filter through the rest of their target audience. Relay's growth rate was robust, averaging 25% per month over the previous six months, and ramping up the home-delivered flyers or Valpak mailers did not seem to be a great use of time and money, particularly in the small market of Charlottesville.

Buckner and Katz needed more than their gut feeling to figure out which marketing activities to invest in, and how to quantify their customers in terms of lifetime value to the company.

Marketing Experiments

Regression models, as explored especially in chapters 4 and 9, make it possible for marketing managers to extrapolate and predict future customer behavior based on historical information. Their importance can't be overstated. However, without historical data—as in the case of a start-up or a new approach within an established company—regression models are impossible.

Marketing experiments offer an effective, data-driven alternative to regression models, and one that does not rely on historical data. Indeed, the recent explosion in digital marketing analytics is largely driven by marketing experiments. Given the rise in online business and especially online marketing, it is easier than ever to run real-time digital experiments. The results from these experiments, however, will be meaningless without effective experimental design. Before jumping into marketing experiments, it is crucial to take time to design your experiment thoughtfully and effectively.

HYPOTHETICAL CASE: BIGHONEY

In her quarterly budget presentation, Elena Flores, brand manager for BigHoney cereal, requests funds for an advertising campaign highlighting new packaging that retains freshness better and longer. In response, Malini Agrawal, BigHoney CFO, asks Flores, "Can you convince me that sales of BigHoney will be hurt if you do not advertise?" As a follow-up, she asks, "You have requested $500,000 for a national campaign. Is that the right amount? Can you get the same result for $250,000?" How can Flores convince Agrawal?

The challenge for Flores is typical for marketing managers who need to invest in the marketing mix in order to increase sales in the future. Attributing an increase in sales to a specific marketing action is a major challenge, because the effect on a brand of any single marketing activity is difficult to isolate. Each marketing action consists of several levers being pulled at the same time, including price promotion, new product introductions, competitive actions, television advertising, PR events, and seasonality. Also, sales resulting from such inputs take time; a television advertisement is unlikely to compel a viewer to immediately jump off the couch, run to the store, and buy a soda. Isolating the influence of a specific event on consumer behavior can be a daunting task.

One way to isolate such influences is through experiments. In our example, Flores could, on a smaller scale, measure the effect of her proposed campaign on the brand's sales. She could then estimate the return on marketing investment (ROMI)—and a prospective budget—by projecting any identified lift to a national scale. But how can she design an experiment that would provide accurate results?

ESTABLISHING CAUSALITY

Four key rules determine a causal relationship between two variables or factors. Let us consider the challenge. The marketing campaign may be considered effective if it satisfies the following **conditions of causality**:

- Launching the marketing campaign increases unit sales.
- Not launching the marketing campaign causes no change to the sales figures.
- Launching the marketing campaign today affects unit sales in subsequent time periods.
- There are no other established external factors (e.g., competitive action) affecting unit sales.

To ascertain clearly whether the targeted sales increase could be achieved without spending marketing dollars or whether any marketing spend is warranted, Flores needs to establish causality.

DESIGNING MARKETING EXPERIMENTS

Evidence-based practices, from medicine to marketing, rely on experiments to establish causality. An experiment provides a mechanism to manipulate one or more input factors (the independent variables, such as advertising investments), and observe changes in an output of interest (the dependent variable, such as sales or brand awareness), while controlling all other factors that may also affect the output (such as price).

Experiments involve at least two situations, often including a **control** group, where the independent variable is not changed, and a **treatment** or **test** group, where the independent variable is changed—for example, by introducing a new marketing activity. A statistically significant difference between the test and control groups suggests causality, meaning that the marketing activity likely has an effect on the dependent variable. These experiments are also called A/B testing, where A is the control group and B is the test group. An experimenter will be more confident in the results if the participants in the two groups are as similar as possible, to reduce the effects of other factors that differ between the two groups and may skew the results.

EXPERIMENT TYPES

After-Only Experiment

A very basic experiment that Flores can design is illustrated in **figure 6.1**. Flores recruits 1,000 participating customers, half of whom—the test group—are exposed to

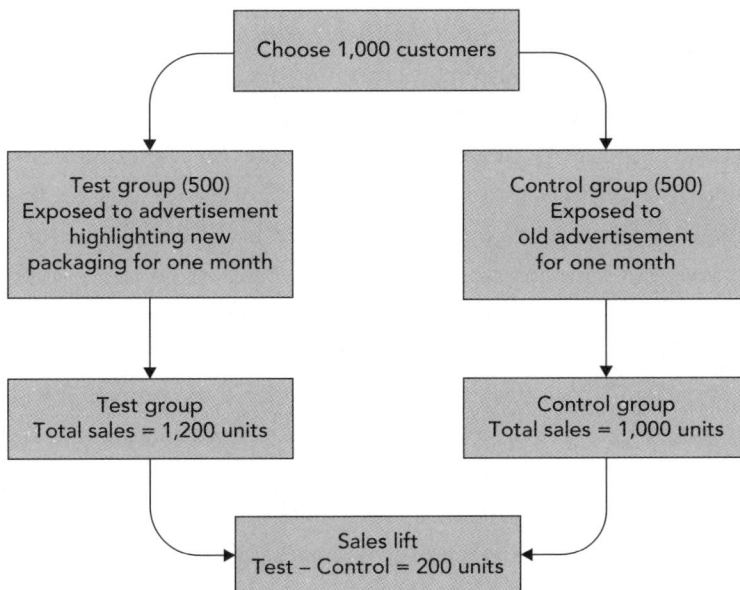

FIGURE 6.1. After-only experiment design

the *new* advertisement highlighting the new packaging technology; the other half—the control group—are exposed to the *old* advertisements. If cereal purchases by all 1,000 customers are tracked, the difference in sales between the test and control groups will indicate the magnitude of the potential sales lift provided by the new advertising campaign. Such an experimental design is called **after-only** because sales are measured only after exposure; in this experiment, Flores measures BigHoney sales among the participants of the experiment only after they are exposed to the advertisement (whether new or old).

The after-only design satisfies two of the four conditions for causality: sales increase in the short term and in subsequent periods. It cannot indicate whether the increase might have occurred without the new advertisement, nor whether preference differences existed prior to the experiment. These two conditions are more likely to be satisfied if the two groups are more similar in terms of relevant factors. The more the two pools of subjects are exposed to the same external environment—store promotions, competitive reactions, even the same weather—the more reliable are the causal inferences, because the only difference would be the advertisement campaign to which each was exposed.

Deciding how to distribute customers between the test group and the control group is critical. The key issue is the extent to which the participants in the test and control groups are similar *in terms of the factors relevant to the experiment*. There are two primary ways to select groups: randomization and attribute matching.

Randomization involves allocating participants randomly between the treatment group and control group. With a big enough sample size, randomization will help improve the similarity between the test and control groups. Consider that Flores is using an email advertisement campaign and has at her disposal a list of 1,000 BigHoney customers. In a random assignment, she would assign every other customer to the test group and the rest of the customers to the control group. Randomization creates fairly homogeneous test and control groups because it removes all sources of extraneous variation, which the experimenter is unable to control. The chance that the test and control groups end up being different even with random assignment decreases as the sample size increases. For most practical marketing applications, a sample size needs to exceed 100 participants for a reliable random assignment process.

Attribute matching is used when the available sample size is not large enough to permit random assignment. Participants are assigned based on certain known attributes such as demography, geography, or annual income. If Flores were testing the effect of a TV advertisement campaign, for example, she would be better off choosing cities that are similar to each other in key demographic or psychographic attributes critical to BigHoney's sales.

Before-After Experiment

A **before-after** design (**figure 6.2**) requires an experimenter to measure the output of interest both before and after the participants have been exposed to the inputs.

In this before-after design for an email advertising campaign, Flores would randomly divide the 1,000 participants into test and control groups, as with the after-only

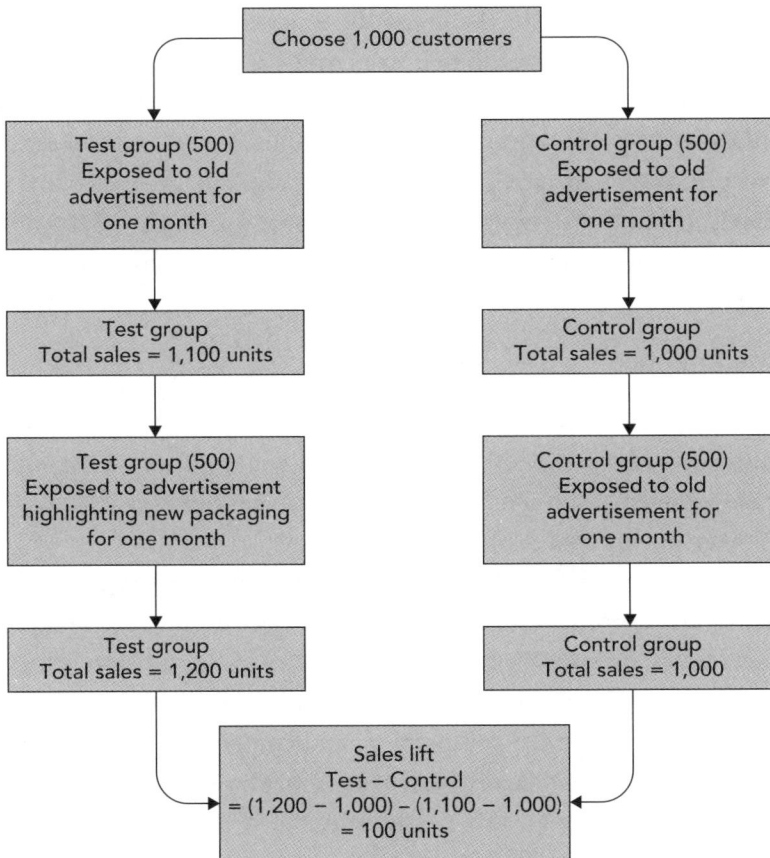

FIGURE 6.2. Before-after experiment design

design. Both groups would be exposed to the old advertising campaign and sales in the respective campaigns recorded. Let $\Delta Sales_{before}$ be the difference in unit sales between the test and control groups when they are exposed to the old campaign. The test group is then exposed to the new advertising campaign, whereas the control group is still exposed to the old campaign. Difference in sales between the test and control group now is termed $\Delta Sales_{after}$. The lift in sales due to the new advertising campaign is then calculated as $\Delta Sales = \Delta Sales_{after} - \Delta Sales_{before}$. Subtracting $\Delta Sales_{before}$ from $\Delta Sales_{after}$ allows the experimenter to control for preexisting differences between the test and control groups. This before-after design, along with random or matched assignment of participants, provides a belt-and-suspenders approach for controlling for all external differences between test and control groups.

If BigHoney cereal is sold to retailers for $1.59, and the cost of goods is $0.99, the unit contribution equals $0.60. The lift of 100 units in the experiment translates to $60.00. If the cost of a single email sent to a customer is $0.10, the cost of emails to 500 test-group customers is $50.00. The experiment suggests that the email campaign provides ROMI of 20%. Flores can use this ROMI estimate to plan national campaigns. Alternatively, if 500 emails provide $10.00 in contribution, the contribution from a single email is $0.02. If the target lift from a national campaign is $100,000.00, the experiment suggests that Flores would require 5 million emails to attain the target lift.

Field Experiments

Experiments conducted within a natural setting are termed **field experiments**. In some industries, field experiments are a part of everyday business. Retail outfits regularly use catalogs or emails to conduct massive field experiments that assess consumer price sensitivity and optimal catalog design.

A major advantage of field experiments is that people are seldom aware that they are subjects in an experiment, so the collected data are more likely to represent the realities prevalent in the marketplace. A related disadvantage is that it is very difficult to control extraneous variables or to manipulate inputs precisely. Field experiments are also very transparent to the competition, and competitive reaction could cloud the results. If, during Flores's experiment, her competition, BigSugar, launches a promotion, the results could be overly pessimistic. But field experiments are still preferred because they allow the marketer to test a campaign with customers in a natural setting, increasing the accuracy of any prediction. In general, in field experiments, it is

TABLE 6.1. BigHoney sales data

	Product price	Sales	Profit
City 1	$1.59	$1,000,000	$600,000
City 2	$1.89	$600,000	$540,000
City 3	$2.15	$500,000	$380,000

easier to experiment with pricing, product, or promotion decisions than with place or channel management decisions.

Flores also wants to determine the best price for her new packaging, so she creates test conditions that differ only in price: advertising, promotions, and coupons are all the same. As part of the experiment, Flores introduces BigHoney with its new packaging in three cities, which she selects because they are similar in factors that affect BigHoney's sales. The only difference is that the products are priced differently in each city: $1.59, $1.89, and $2.15. She then tracks the sales figures in the three cities over time. She expects the city where the product is priced at $1.59 to have higher sales volume—the question will be *how much* higher? The experiment results, based as before on the original cost of goods sold being $0.99, are given in **table 6.1**.

Given these data, Flores is better off introducing the product at the $1.59 price point, because it provides the highest profit.

Web Experiments

A subset of field experiments, **web experiments** can be executed quickly and cheaply, giving them a significant edge over traditional offline field experiments. Consider the difference between TV and email advertising campaigns. With TV advertising, Flores has to buy spots on different channels in the test markets with significant lead time. Once the copy is shot, it is difficult, time consuming, and very expensive to change it. Furthermore, the cost of the experiment increases rapidly with each new copy that she would like to test. The email advertisement, on the other hand, can be created much more quickly and at a much lower cost, making it easier and less expensive for Flores to test different copies.

The faster execution and lower cost of web experiments allow marketers to easily test the simultaneous influence of multiple inputs. Say Flores wants to test three different copies: "Longer Shelf Life," "Tastes Better," and the current campaign, "Good

TABLE 6.2. Full factorial design

Advertisement copy	Price		
	$1.59	$1.89*	$2.15
"Lasts Longer"	$1,315	$1,112	$1,206
"Tastes Better"	$957	$1,030	$1,500
"Good for You"*	$930	$820	$770

Note: The current price is $1.89, so it can be considered the control (*). The values within each shaded cell represent profits obtained from each combination of price and advertisement copy.

for You," each at three different price points, $1.59, $1.89, and $2.15. To do this, she can create a **full factorial design**—meaning one involving all possible combinations of campaign and price—as shown in **table 6.2**.

Since Flores is testing three types of copy and three price points, the total number of possible combinations that need to be tested is $3 \times 3 = 9$. The profit from each combination is provided within each shaded cell of **table 6.2**; for example, the profit for the combination of "Lasts Longer" ad copy and a $2.15 per-box price is $1,206.00.

The full factorial design allows Flores to test combinations of the advertisement message and price point. In **table 6.2**, we see that the "Tastes Better" message with a price point of $2.15 provides the highest profit, followed by the "Lasts Longer" campaign at the $1.59 price point. We also see that when the price is maintained at the current level of $1.89, the "Lasts Longer" campaign provides the highest profit. At least in this case, had Flores tested only the advertisement copies and not the different prices, she would have wrongly concluded that the "Lasts Longer" copy provided the highest profit.

If BigHoney is sold direct to consumers through a website, then Flores can randomize the emails sent to consumers to match one of the nine combination cells in **table 6.2**. Web experiments like this one would also allow her to track email open rates, click-throughs to the website, and the subsequent online purchases, for each consumer. This kind of data provides Flores with a much stronger sense of the effectiveness of the campaign, because the same consumer is tracked from exposure to purchase. By contrast, a TV advertisement campaign would have required Flores to recruit nine different cities for the experiment (one for each cell), as well as retailers in each city willing to manipulate the prices, a very expensive and time-consuming process.

Natural Experiments

In a **natural experiment**, a marketer observes the effect of certain naturally occurring incidents on customer behavior and other factors, such as sales volume. Recognizing such occurrences allows companies to learn about their customers at no or little additional expense. A classic example is Amazon collecting sales tax data from California residents. Analyzing the effect of a newly levied tax on sales volume will give Amazon an opportunity to discover how a sales tax affects online retailing. Amazon could compare sales before and after the sales tax introduction for customers living on either side of the state's border. The only change would be the new taxation of online purchases, which affects consumers only on one side of the border.

The key in identifying and analyzing natural experiments is to find treatment and control groups created by some external factor. Many marketers resort to geographic segmentation for natural experiments, but that is not always a distinguishing characteristic. For example, when the Ford Motor Company introduced an employee pricing promotion, there was no natural geographic separation; all customers were offered the same deal. Instead, marketers compared sales in the weeks immediately before and after the program was introduced.

Ford Motor Company discovered that the jump in sales levels was accompanied by a sharp increase in prices. Customers presumed that they were getting a good deal, but the prices on many models were actually lower before the promotion than at the time of the employee discount prices. Customers responded to the promotion *despite* the prices, not *because* of the prices. The program led to many happy customers, even though they were paying higher prices.

CHALLENGES

Experiment duration. The accuracy of data obtained from a marketing experiment increases with the experiment's duration. Experiments with shorter durations might not adequately account for the carryover effects of marketing interventions.

Time between experiment and campaign. Most marketing decisions are sensitive to time, highlighting the tension between quick and accurate decisions. The longer the gap between the field experiment and the full campaign, the less accurate the prediction from the field experiment. Yet the time required to obtain buy-in for the field experiment results could delay the timing of the full campaign and thereby the relevance of the field experiment.

Demand effect. If an experiment involves salespeople, the mere knowledge of being in an experiment could change their behavior, leading to biased conclusions; this is known as the **demand effect**.

Experiments provide a bridge between new ideas and management decisions. Digital marketing has popularized experimentation in the marketing community. Organizations can succeed if they develop a system to learn from experiments and strive toward continuous improvement.

CONCEPT APPLICATION

As business is increasingly—and often exclusively—conducted online, web experiments are becoming an integral part of marketing analytics. In the Compare.com (Compare) case, a price-comparison website for car insurance is experiencing a drop in completion rates: potential customers are not finishing the online questionnaire that results in a list of insurance quotes.

The first challenge is to choose the best solution for lifting Compare's completion rate, with the goal of running experiments on the best way to implement that option. As you work on this,

- Write down a list of pros and cons of each option, keeping in mind considerations like fixed costs and risk.
- Think about Compare's business model, and why people might visit its website.
- Since the option chosen will need to be tested to see if it is actually effective, a marketing experiment will need to be run. Therefore, an important practical consideration is how each option would be used in experiments: Are all the options as easily tested?

Looking forward to the experiment, consider

- Why would Compare want an experiment?
- What is the goal of the experiment?
- In terms of experimental design, what should be included? Think about how to assign groups and what the experimental treatment(s) should be.

- Design an experiment to test versions of your chosen strategy for lifting completion rates.

CASE: COMPARE.COM

In March 2016, Andrew Rose, CEO of Compare, was looking for a simple solution to a troublesome problem. Headquartered in Richmond, Virginia, Compare was an aggregator of insurance—primarily automotive—that allowed customers to acquire a list of real-time available quotes from affiliated insurance providers. The offering was totally unique in that customers were given actual monthly quotes, as opposed to estimates, after completing a questionnaire. Rose saw a huge opportunity for Compare to leverage its accurate price offering to compete with the larger companies in the auto insurance space.

Ever since the company's launch in 2013, there had been ample good news for Rose: Compare had partnerships with nearly 100 insurance companies, and the site was reaching peak levels of traffic (over a million visitors per month, in both February and March 2016), the bulk of which (just over 50%) was increasingly coming from mobile devices such as phones and tablets (up from 5% at the start of 2014). The problem, however, was that the completion rates for Compare's questionnaire were at a dramatic low, with just 12% of site visitors finishing the required form in March, a sudden and unprecedented drop from an all-time high of 18% for the metric that January.

Over the past year, Rose and his leadership team had enacted several changes to the site in attempts to lift the completion rate, with efforts ranging from altering the order of the questions to removing the need for customers to create an account, making this rapid drop in the key performance indicator all the more alarming. Rose knew that customers' unwillingness to complete Compare's questionnaire posed a serious threat to the growth of his business, and he wanted to act fast to remedy the situation. In contemplating the problem, he mused, "Car insurance is an interesting space. It's the one product I'm aware of where both the buyer and seller hope it's never used. Trying to change consumer behavior around it is doubly interesting and doubly tough."[1]

Compare.com Background

The Admiral Group (Admiral), one of Britain's largest insurance companies, headquartered in Cardiff, Wales, had grown a successful European insurance business since its launch in 1993. The company entered the US market in 2009 with its establishment of Richmond, Virginia–based Elephant Insurance (Elephant), which followed Admiral's successful direct-to-consumer business model by serving customers via the phone and internet. In addition to Admiral's low-cost online auto and home insurance offerings in Europe, it also owned several auto insurance price-comparison sites such as Confused.com in the United Kingdom and its equivalents in Spain and France. In 2011, following the success of these sites in Europe and Elephant's growing foothold in the United States, Admiral started to investigate whether the American market was ready for its own insurance price-comparison site. After much analysis, Admiral ultimately decided to push forward with a Confused.com equivalent for the United States, and preparations commenced to launch Compare (then comparenow .com) in early 2013. Rose was tapped from sister company Elephant to be Compare's first CEO.

Rose, a graduate of the University of Virginia's Darden School of Business, brought over seven years' experience in the car insurance industry to the helm of Compare when he joined in 2012. After earning his MBA, he had spent three years as a product manager at Progressive and two years as the senior vice president of Auto Product Management at Countrywide before becoming the founding CEO of Elephant.

Similar to Admiral's Confused.com offering in the United Kingdom, Admiral's mission with Compare was to try to build a site that could make finding the best insurance price "a much easier, much quicker process" for US drivers. Before Compare, the process American consumers faced when shopping for car insurance was inefficient and messy, despite the legal mandate for nearly all drivers to have it (depending on their state's policy). Drivers looking online for the best policy had to fill out multiple forms for multiple insurers and play the waiting game before receiving quotes and comparing prices.

This lack of clarity inherent to auto insurance purchasing in the United States stood in stark contrast to the ease of comparison shopping for other products, such as airline tickets and hotels (through sites like Kayak.com and Hotels.com, respectively). In fact, in 2014, 90% of US consumers were comparing prices for airline tickets before making a purchase, but only 20% were comparison shopping for auto insurance.[2] Rose thought the opportunity to fill this gap was huge, and he set his targets on the large national carriers as his direct competition. "We were attempting to have a customer utilize our platform instead of a traditional shopping mechanism," he explained.

Despite these lofty goals, Compare's first year was a challenging one. Rose spent his first few months as CEO attempting to sign carriers up to a platform and concept that were totally unproven. "Pitching the business in those days was a real challenge; this was a completely different way of doing business, and so it wasn't easy to convince carriers that online comparison shopping was going to be a part of the future." He likened the decision on when to launch the site to a "chicken-and-egg scenario"—carriers were hard to sign without large volumes of consumers, and consumers weren't drawn to a site with no rates to compare. Compare's soft launch ultimately took place in March 2013 without any advertising; it had only one carrier partnered in one state at the time. Over the course of the year, Rose and his sales team pushed to grow the number of carriers quoting on the site, and by 2014 the company offered policies for customers in 46 states, with "varying carrier panels in each of those states." On average, a consumer still got only one rate back at that time, dependent on their location. Compare's revenues came from charging the insurance companies a flat referral fee (negotiated with each insurance provider) after a policy was purchased.

Growing Compare's Test-and-Learn Culture

The first state in which Compare was able to offer a handful of carrier quotes to site visitors was California, and its relatively robust panel prompted Compare to roll out its first TV advertising campaign in the state in January 2014. Because Compare was new to advertising and didn't know what kind of messaging would result in the best response, this advertising effort provided the company with a real opportunity to embrace the "deep test-and-learn culture" that it had inherited from its parent company, Admiral. Compare decided to treat the campaign as an experiment, testing 12 "truly distinct" creative campaigns across six markets. The divergence in copy for the 12 ads was extreme: some were animated, while others were fully scripted live action or featured a spokesperson; some were light on the Compare brand, and others pushed the brand name heavily. "We tried all different combinations of these," Rose recalled.

In order to achieve maximum learnings from the experiment, Compare kept its ad buys constant across the six markets (using the same shows, on the same channels, at the same times) and simply used different ads in the time slots according to region. This methodology allowed Compare to analyze the response rates and changes in web traffic in any region as direct responses to the ads that were run. "We could literally monitor the website, assessing baseline traffic before and after certain ads ran,"

TABLE 6.3. Visitors to Compare.com after targeted ad buys, by region, 2014

Region (California)	Ad	Ad type	TV households	Unique visitors	TV households/ visitor
Bakersfield	Obvious vignettes	Direct response	492,000	280	1,757
Chico	Narrator explains site to confused audience	Direct response	384,000	216	1,780
Fresno	Low-rider car	Story line/ direct response	1,300,000	487	2,683
Monterey	Playing cards represent site	Direct response	489,000	307	1,592
Palm Springs	CEO explains	Direct response	296,000	587	505
Santa Barbara	Distinguished gentleman explains site to couple	Story line/ direct response	472,000	382	1,523

Source: Data from Compare.com company documents, used with permission.

Rose explained. Because Compare did not engage in any other promotional methods at the time, any change was attributable to the TV advertising. Tentatively identifying which ads were winners and losers based on initial results, Compare then took "the worst performing ad and put it in the best market, and the best performing ad and put it in the worst market" to confirm its hypotheses on effective campaigns. Ultimately these swaps revealed that the best-performing ad improved sales in the worst market and the worst-performing ad did not improve sales in the best market.

After running several rounds of these tests, Compare was able to "home in on the ads that worked the best," and it went from "12 ads quickly down to three or four that were the true winners," Rose recalled. In January 2014, Compare had targeted buys of 80 reach and 2 frequency in each market. **Reach** refers to the percentage of the target audience that is exposed to an ad, and **frequency** means the average number of times each individual is exposed to the ad. **Table 6.3** shows response rates (measured as visitors to the Compare site) for six of the tested ads.

Many of the insights the company learned around messaging and effective language served all subsequent advertising campaigns across all channels.

Following Compare's public investment in advertising, a wave of new carriers joined the site. By March 2015, Compare caught Google's attention, and the two established a partnership that would allow Google access to many of Compare's 41 different insurance partners for its own comparison platform, Google Compare. By 2016, Compare had grown to a team of 50 employees, offered policies to consumers in 48 states, and partnered with nearly 100 brands across the country.

Shopping for Auto Insurance

The US auto insurance industry had a $214.3 billion market value in 2015, having experienced a growth rate of 3.9%[3] over the past year. The industry was highly fragmented, with over 300 providers active in 2015, the vast majority of which (267) were active on a state or regional basis; only 35 providers operated in more than 40 states.[4] (For a representation of car insurance demand by state, see **table 6.4**.)

Of those national carriers, seven accounted for 56.2% of market share in 2012,[5] and the industry was seeing an explosion of marketing wars as the large name-brand carriers battled for new customers. Within the crowded market, consumers often behaved as passive loyalists, easily pried away from incumbent policies for meaningful savings; 66% of consumers who shopped for insurance in 2015 claimed they were motivated by price.[6] Customers also looked into changing carriers toward the end of a current policy, when a rate spiked, or if they had a bad experience with a provider. New car purchases and new drivers in the family also prompted the purchase of new policies. Despite these motivations, Rose explained the reality that "most everyone hates shopping for insurance." In fact, in 2015, only 13% of people switched auto insurers.[7]

In 2016, there were multiple distribution channels active in the auto insurance sector. Many consumers worked directly with insurance companies to select and purchase coverage, often through their exclusive agents' local offices or over the phone, while others used independent agents or brokers who worked with multiple carriers. ("Captive agents" described those who represented a single brand, utilized by companies such as Allstate and State Farm, whereas "independent agents" worked with multiple carriers.) Historically, there was a preference for exclusive agents working with single providers, and by 2013, these agents continued to dominate auto insurance sales, with over 70% of net premiums written coming directly from either the insurance company or their captive agents.[8]

TABLE 6.4. Total market premiums by state in 2014

State	Total market premiums	State	Total market premiums
California	$20.556 billion	Alabama	$2.511 billion
Texas	$15.729 billion	Kentucky	$2.469 billion
Florida	$14.353 billion	Oregon	$2.158 billion
New York	$11.294 billion	Nevada	$1.729 billion
Pennsylvania	$7.367 billion	Kansas	$1.534 billion
Michigan	$7.129 billion	Mississippi	$1.514 billion
New Jersey	$6.878 billion	Arkansas	$1.493 billion
Georgia	$6.064 billion	Iowa	$1.415 billion
Illinois	$5.898 billion	Utah	$1.311 billion
Ohio	$5.570 billion	West Virginia	$1.134 billion
North Carolina	$4.758 billion	New Mexico	$1.094 billion
Virginia	$4.595 billion	Nebraska	$998 million
Massachusetts	$4.376 billion	Rhode Island	$745 million
Maryland	$4.071 billion	Delaware	$718 million
Washington	$3.937 billion	New Hampshire	$687 million
Arizona	$3.590 billion	Hawaii	$650 million
Louisiana	$3.365 billion	Idaho	$599 million
Tennessee	$3.272 billion	Maine	$591 million
Colorado	$3.213 billion	Montana	$536 million
Minnesota	$2.987 billion	Alaska	$427 million
Missouri	$2.982 billion	South Dakota	$398 million
Indiana	$2.981 billion	North Dakota	$392 million
South Carolina	$2.920 billion	Vermont	$315 million
Connecticut	$2.558 billion	Wyoming	$296 million
Wisconsin	$2.536 billion	District of Columbia	$289 million

Source: Data from NAIC Autoinsurance Database Report 2013/2014.
Note: Premiums represent what customer paid for automotive insurance in aggregate; insurance insiders usually looked at premiums when evaluating a state's attractiveness.

At the same time, the industry was experiencing a macro shift in distribution away from human intermediaries, as consumers increasingly turned to carriers' websites and independent broker sites to buy policies online. In 2014, 71% of consumers who shopped for auto insurance reportedly did so online, up from 67% in 2013.[9] As insurance providers and brokers adapted to sell policies online, carriers such as Progressive began providing "comparison" price-shopping tools on their websites, although these prices were often very rough—even inaccurate—estimates. Not only was digital shopping for insurance convenient for consumers, it also provided better collection and analysis of customer information for the insurance companies, making it easier to upsell and cross-sell customers.[10]

As options for finding estimates and quotes over the internet grew, many shoppers were fooled by lead generators, or insurance lead services, when they were not sure from which company to buy. Once lured to these sites (which were especially active from the years of the dot-com boom until Compare's arrival in the United States), consumers entered various personal details in the hopes of receiving accurate pricing, only to be barraged with calls and emails from agents who had received their contact information. As a result, many customers were leery of online insurance marketplaces and overly protective of their personal information when shopping for car insurance. In fact, 74% of consumers who had never purchased a policy online by 2015 cited the desire to meet or speak with an agent as the top barrier to future online policy purchases.[11]

It was against this backdrop that aggregators, or price-comparison sites, entered the market and attempted to give customers an unprecedented ease of price comparison and policy purchasing online. Similar to Compare, quote-comparison sites like the Zebra and CoverHound emerged in 2012 and 2010, respectively; the Zebra provided loose estimates and a team of licensed insurance agents to call, while CoverHound's offering was so similar to Compare's that it had its own partnership with Google Compare.

How It Really Worked—Compare.com's Process

Since its founding, Compare worked with three main channels to market its brand and attract consumers to its site. The first channel of acquisition was advertising through TV. Although this channel was highly effective and actually drove real-time spikes of site hits during airtime, as the company learned during its 2014 California testing, its high costs kept Compare's use of it moderate. The second channel of acquisition was marketing through Google AdWords (pay-per-click), which more easily targeted consumers actively investigating car insurance. The final channel was advertising on broker websites. Broker website visitors typically searched for phrases like "compare auto insurance quotes" or "save money on car insurance" through a search engine, and once they clicked on a broker's link, they were asked to answer some basic questions such as age, marital status, zip code, and current insurance carrier. These brokers then "sold" these customers to insurance carriers such as Geico or to comparison sites like Compare. The benefit of broker traffic to the insurance companies was that they were able to purchase traffic based on demographic variables, enabling Compare to purchase traffic with the same characteristics of its highest-converting groups.

Using the broker channel became increasingly popular for Compare over time, largely due to its low costs, but consumers coming to Compare from this channel presented the lowest completion percentage. A likely explanation for this was that consumers had just answered basic questions through the broker sites, and another questionnaire through Compare immediately disengaged them. Many brokers also actively encouraged customers to engage with multiple providers, amplifying the competition for their business. Finally, some members of the team hypothesized that many of these visitors were mostly interested in seeing if they could find a cheaper plan than their current insurance. While Compare allowed them to do this, these visitors were not "motivated" shoppers and were therefore more likely to drop off due to the length of the questionnaire.

Managing the Purchase Funnel

Regardless of the channel of acquisition, upon arrival to Compare's site, all consumers were met with an identical questionnaire. Compare described the process of a customer completing the questionnaire and ultimately moving to the selected partner's page as the customer journey, or CJ. In 2016, the first step in Compare's questionnaire, and thus also the first CJ step, asked site visitors to give the year, make, and model of the vehicle they were interested in insuring; the top of the page included a banner giving the visitor a sense of overall progress, with the four CJ steps in order: Vehicle, Driver, History, Quote. (A screenshot of this page is on the online supplement at http://store.darden.virginia.edu/marketing-analytics-supplements.) The minimum basic information required for partner insurance companies to calculate their costs included the driver's zip code, name, date of birth, vehicle make and model, and recent driving record. Upon completion, the drivers were presented with a list of quotes tailored to their situation that they could click to buy immediately from the insurer's site. (See **figure 6.3** and the online supplement for a screenshot of an example of quotes presented at the end of the process.) Consumers were also given the option to call the insurance company with a specific quote number to complete the purchase process over the phone; the rate did not vary by method of purchase.

Pay monthly | Pay in full | All results

Sorted by **Monthly Equivalent**

MERCURY INSURANCE
6 MONTH POLICY
Pay monthly **$49** due today
+5 payments of $43 ($262 total)
Pay in full **$231** due today
(equates to $38 a month)
Talk to an advisor

metromile
6 MONTH POLICY
Pay monthly **$101** due today
+5 payments of $39 ($232 total)
Pay in full **$232** due today
(equates to $39 a month)
Checkout online
Soft quote includes base rate plus per-mile rate times reported mileage.
How does this work?

Safeco Insurance A Liberty Mutual Company
12 MONTH POLICY
Pay monthly **$57** due today
+11 payments of $47 (572 total)
Pay in full **$500** due today
(equates to $42 a month)
Talk to an advisor
If your windshield is damaged and can be repaired, we'll repair it for free with no deductible

Elephant
12 MONTH POLICY
Pay monthly **$53** due today
+11 payments of $53 ($638 total)
Pay in full **$524** due today
(equates to $44 a month)
Checkout online
Talk to an advisor
Rated A+ by the Better Business Bureau. We provide "More Care & Less Cost".

Nationwide
6 MONTH POLICY
Pay monthly **$44** due today
+5 payments of $44 ($264 total)
Pay in full **$264** due today
(equates to $44 a month)
Checkout online
Talk to an advisor
Get The Support & Protection You Deserve. Nationwide is On Your Side.

esurance
6 MONTH POLICY
Pay monthly **$97** due today
+4 payments of $49 ($292 total)
Pay in full **$275** due today
(equates to $46 a month)
Checkout online
Talk to an advisor

FIGURE 6.3. Compare.com quote page

Customers could also create price alerts if they didn't see anything cheaper than their current policy. Compare maintained a detailed database of all historical quotes provided to each customer at the end of the questionnaire, in addition to the quote that was ultimately purchased and the customer input that resulted in each customer's quote range.

By summer 2016, Compare's questionnaire consisted of at least 31 total questions split across the four sections: vehicle information, driver information, driving history, and information related to current insurance policy in the "quote" section. (The total number of questions could increase if a customer entered multiple drivers or vehicles.) Other comparison sites required visitors to answer fewer questions before displaying quotes. The Zebra, for example, asked visitors only four questions prior to displaying estimate quote information.[12] Compare's questionnaire was more detailed than other similar sites and required more time for the customers to complete in order to receive accurate, bindable quotes. On average, it took customers approximately 4.5 minutes to complete the Compare survey and see their rate options, as opposed to 45 seconds on the Zebra.

Compare's detailed purchase funnel was the source of constant testing and learning for Rose's team. The purchase funnel, depicted in **figure 6.4**, led a consumer from a state of awareness, in which they visited the website; to interest, in which they began the quote process; to desire, in which they completed the quote; and finally to action, in which they clicked on a partner site.

In describing Compare's approach to the purchase funnel, Rose explained:

> As we went through the purchase funnel, through the history of the organization, we optimized at a step then moved on, optimized at another step and moved on. Early on we said, "First things first—we've got to get people to the site. What is the lowest we can get our cost per unique visitor?" And we would hammer away, testing and learning all these different pieces and parts, and we would discover what each opportunity cost per unique visitor was.

In accordance with this culture of testing and learning (and similar to the experiments testing the California ad campaigns in 2014), Compare's marketing team frequently employed web experiments, using both before-after and A/B (after-only) testing to optimize the language, subject lines, and cadence of its marketing emails in order to draw people to the site. Compare's A/B testing was an after-only experiment,

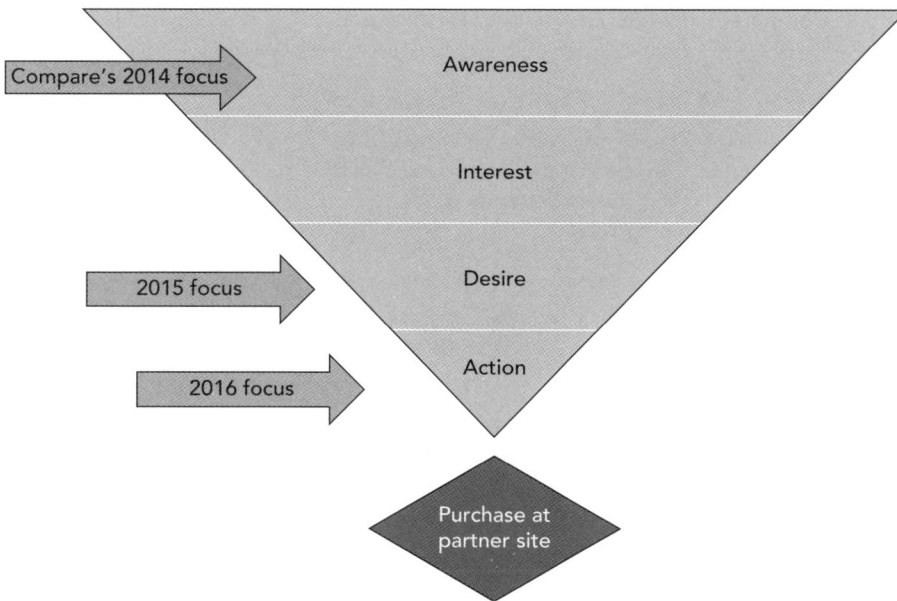

FIGURE 6.4. Visual representation of Compare.com's purchase funnel. (Adapted from conversations with company representatives)

in which the control group saw the current (prior to testing) marketing email, and one or more test groups were sent experimental emails. The response of the control group was then compared to that of the test group(s) to determine which version was preferred by consumers. The firm had data on completion and conversion rates for both the test and control groups before conducting the experiment. For data on the outcome of three example marketing tests (two before-after tests, and one after-only test), see **table 6.5**.

Once consumers had arrived to the site, the next challenge was to engage them and ensure they filled in the form. Describing this step, Rose explained, "This is where you get into the long part of the funnel, which is the website, and there's an enormous amount of work that goes there, but you optimize on getting people to the bottom of the quote," at which point they actually receive rates. The final part of the process, which Rose described as "last but not least," was to get the visitor to "ultimately buy."

Rose and his team "constantly challenged the assumptions" that their method was the best and, emboldened by a willingness to fail, were always running new experiments in order to gather data and learn from them. Rose explained:

TABLE 6.5. **Compare.com email campaign testing examples**

1. Before-after test results

	Test 1	Test 2
Customer journey step	Email inviting customer who quoted last year to get a new quote.	Email inviting customer who quoted only on site to review top three prices and buy one.
Process before	Customer clicks on link in email and is taken to beginning of quote process; details are prefilled but process must be redone.	Customer clicks on a price in email and is taken to Compare's price page that shows all their prices.
Process after	Customer clicks on email and is asked to update two pieces of out-of-date data (existing policy end date and desired new policy start date) on existing policy before reaching end of process.	Customer clicks on a price in email and is taken to the company's page offering the price they selected.
Timeline	Before June 2016; after September 2016	Before June 2016; after November 2016
Success criteria	Email click to buy click*	Email send to buy click
Before-after	0.42%/4.62%	0.62%/4.28%
Sample size	96,177 before; 80,383 after	172,868 before; 82,222 after

2. A/B (after-only) test results

Customer journey	Email inviting customer who quoted last year to get a new quote.
Subject line A	2016 Ford Focus Insurance as Low as $89
Subject line B	Your Renewal Reminder: *2016 Ford Focus* Insurance as Low as *$89*
Timeline	January 2017
Success criteria	Email open rate
A/B	4.0%/5.4%
Sample size[†]	62,500

Source: Data from Compare.com company documents, used with permission.
* Figure refers to a customer who has already clicked on the link within the email and ultimately chose to click to transfer to partner's website with desired quote.
† Different subject lines assigned to recipients randomly using Salesforce Marketing Cloud.

Our DNA is test and learn. We have a test ongoing right now with a contact center. So if you get deep enough into our quote process in a couple of states, you'll see phone numbers there so that you can call and talk to somebody. It's not because we necessarily want to do that. The thinking is, "This is a test. Let's see what happens."

Compare's ability to adapt and optimize at so many stages of its purchase funnel was in large part due to its agile development process, in which it conducted regular test "sprints" as it tweaked its site. The company was divided into three teams: customer journey, carrier (also called partner integration), and data. Each group carried out its own test sprints for periods of two to four weeks. The three main business owners of each team met briefly every day to be sure they were aware of other groups' sprints; this allowed them to identify tests that affected more than one business team during the planning phase. For such cross-group tests, the sprints were conducted in tandem; priority was decided by an executive team that met every two weeks and included Rose, but it was very much a consensus process. For sprints that affected only one group, the business owner of that area set the sprint priority based on expected business impact.

Compare, like its parent company Admiral, employed a very transparent company culture. Failure was acceptable; colleagues worked alongside each other without walls; and numerous storyboards showing work in progress and goals associated with each sprint were on display in the office. Ideas around ways to optimize the customer journey were frequently posted to the CJ group's backlog, for example, and these ideas originated from all levels of employees within that team "whenever they had an idea that they thought was good enough to write down." The backlog was reviewed regularly so that high-value ideas could be given priority, and some ideas might sit in the backlog for almost a year before the business owner of that team decided to prioritize the corresponding test.

The Problem

In early 2016, Compare's drop-off problem became acute, with the completion rate sinking from 18% in January to 13% in February and dropping further to 12% in March. To adapt, Rose and his team developed the ability to measure page-by-page drop-off on a granular level, and several changes to the site quickly followed.

One of the first changes to hit the website was the removal of the account language. During Compare's first few years of business, consumers were required to provide their email addresses in order to set up a free account to get quotes at the end of the questionnaire process, a point at which the site experienced high drop-off. The account phrasing was ultimately removed, and the updated process just asked customers for their email address at the final stage of the questionnaire, allowing Compare to send them a unique link to see their quotes again if they were more inclined to purchase later.

Once the unpopular account requirement had been remedied, Rose and his team noticed that the first page of the questionnaire, which initially requested driver information, suffered from the highest drop-off rates; once consumers completed the first page, they were far more likely to complete the process. Armed with this information, the team altered the order of question categories on the questionnaire, moving high drop-off questions seeking name and phone number from the beginning to the end of the process and placing vehicle information at the start. The resulting questionnaire was a four-page sequence: (1) vehicle information, headed "Tell us about your vehicle . . ."; (2) driver information, headed "Tell us about yourself . . ."; (3) information about the driver's current or recent insurance, headed "We need just a few more details . . ."; and (4) contact information, headed "One last thing . . ."; the final page was the list of quotes from partner insurance carriers (for screenshots of these pages in June 2016, see the online supplement).

The irony of this change was that if consumers had been willing to give their personal information at the beginning, the questionnaire process would have been shortened, as Compare would have been able to look up the drivers' car information automatically and prefill the vehicle page of the site. As a result, in the spring of 2016, the development team at Compare decided to test giving customers the option of having their vehicle information located if they were willing to start the form with personal information.

Other changes Compare tested included adapting its questionnaire from multiple pages to a single (albeit lengthy) page that didn't require reloading, and buttonizing the "easier" questions; it soon found that the single-page conversion had no impact on completion rates (and thus was not implemented), whereas buttonized answers did (and were thus made permanent in the process; see the online supplement for an example). In early 2016, following a collaboration with online brokers that advertised Compare on their platforms, Compare was able to prefill data for consumers arriving from those brokers' sites, removing the need to enter personal information twice. These changes created some lift in the completion rates, but not for long.

Solution Options

As Rose and his team searched for more effective solutions to permanently lift the lingering problem of the low completion rates, they considered several promising options proposed by the leadership team.

Mobile App

Some team members felt that the rising number of visitors on mobile devices signaled that the development of a mobile app would encourage those consumers to complete the form from their devices at a time convenient for them. Mobile apps were, after all, relatively easy to develop, although Rose knew the marketing efforts to convince users to download an app for a single use represented a more significant investment. However, Rose and his management team acknowledged that having the app preinstalled on consumer devices would bolster customer loyalty to future product lines should Compare expand into property, renters', or other forms of insurance in the future.

Midprocess, Saved Quote

The second potential remedy on the table entailed building an entry box into several points in the questionnaire that would allow customers to provide their email addresses, receive a link to their saved questionnaire, and complete it at a more convenient time—in essence, a "save my quote" option. Many of Rose's colleagues felt this was distinct from the previous "create an account" language and it would encourage site visitors to eventually complete their forms, while others felt past problems obtaining consumers' email addresses midprocess heralded a larger aversion to email address sharing.

Estimates

The final potential solution Rose was asked to consider seemed incompatible with Compare's value proposition, and that was to provide site visitors with quote estimates early in their questionnaire process in order to encourage them to stay and complete the form. Those supporting this solution believed that many customers would be happy with a broad estimate if it was easily attainable sooner, while others feared that such estimates, especially if inaccurate, could severely weaken Compare's value proposition of real, accurate prices. This ensuing internal debate begged further questions—how did customers define "accurate" quotes, and how broad could estimate ranges be to satisfy a customer? Should all customers be given an estimate option, or just a select few? If a few, who? Finally, what amount of information would be sufficient to provide a satisfactory estimate?

CONCLUSION

Stuck between his site's lingering poor completion rates and an array of potential solutions to explore, Rose faced a critical question—how should he invest Compare's resources to combat the problem? He knew the company needed to run more marketing experiments to help clarify the way forward. He also understood that to obtain the most informative and relevant results, he needed to think carefully about experimental design.

7

Paid Search Advertising

I magine you're in the market for a baseball cap, an espresso maker, and a Ferrari F430 (lucky you). You decide you'd like to purchase each of the items in an online auction. You'd like to pay $10 for the hat, $1,000 for the coffee maker, and $150,000 for the Ferrari, so you set aside $151,010 to make sure you land your items. Without understanding the nuances of the bidding structure, you decide to take an average of your total budget and allocate that as your bid amount on each item—$50,336.67 for the hat, $50,336.67 for the espresso maker, and $50,336.67 for the Ferrari.

Much to your dismay, you later learn you've won the auctions for the hat and espresso machine but missed out on the Ferrari. As ridiculous as the strategy sounds, this is what can happen when businesses run paid search advertising campaigns without targeting their efforts to the business context and nuances of the system at hand.

Now imagine that instead of a customer wanting to buy different products such as hats and Ferraris, you are a business targeting customers with different levels of worth. Paid search advertising campaigns are based on the technology of online auctions: search engines allow businesses to bid on the opportunity to put their ads in front of certain types of customers. Fortunately, there are better strategies available to you than the one you followed to get your hat and coffee maker; you do not need to divide your company budget equally among all your customers. Instead, the campaigns themselves generate enough data about your potential customers to ensure that your company will know what customers' expected values are before deciding whether it is worth it to place your ad in front of them.

WHAT IS PAID SEARCH?

Traditional advertising pushes a firm's message to consumers regardless of whether they are interested in the product—think of TV commercials or highway billboards.

Direct mail and store signage are more targeted: they are meant to create demand by putting a company's message in front of people who have been identified as likely customers but who don't yet realize they want its products.

Unlike these kinds of marketing, **paid search advertising** targets *intent*. Paid search advertisements appear in response to online keyword searches, so they are designed to capture prospective customers right at the moment they are expressing an interest in a particular product. Paid search is also, of course, distinct from traditional advertising in that it is wholly online. Part of a broader view of search engine optimization (SEO), paid search advertising is a way to improve a company's performance in keyword searches on popular search engines (most notably Google). As such, it is an important strategy for companies to increase their digital visibility.

When a user types keywords into a search engine (e.g., "car insurance"), two types of results are listed: websites the engine's algorithm has organically determined to be valuable, and websites advertisers have paid to promote based on the keyword searched (**figure 7.1**). To see these two kinds of results for yourself, type your own keywords into Google. You'll see a clutter that includes both paid ads (identified as such, often in more than one location on the page) and organic results. Which of the paid ads you see depend on a set of factors we'll explore in this chapter.

Because of the large amounts of data produced in paid search advertising campaigns, the returns from paid search advertising can be improved through marketing analytics, whereas organic search results are influenced more by website architecture.

Although paid search is only one of the platforms companies can use to increase their digital visibility, it is the dominant online marketing vehicle and is still growing (**figure 7.2**). Display advertising and social media have been growing faster than search in recent years, but search remains a key part of digital media.

Paid search advertising empowers a company to deliver offers that resonate with customers. It is an effective tool that can deliver a robust return on marketing investment (ROMI), when optimized through appropriate data analytics techniques. Which customers to target, how to reach them effectively, and how much to pay to advertise to them: all these crucial questions can be answered by appropriate data analytics and implemented as paid search campaigns.

In this chapter, you will learn about paid search advertising and its strategic objective. Specifically, we'll go through the auction-like structure of advertising spending, the principal metrics used to track the success of campaigns, the relationship between customer lifetime value (CLV) and search ads, how to overcome sparse data problems

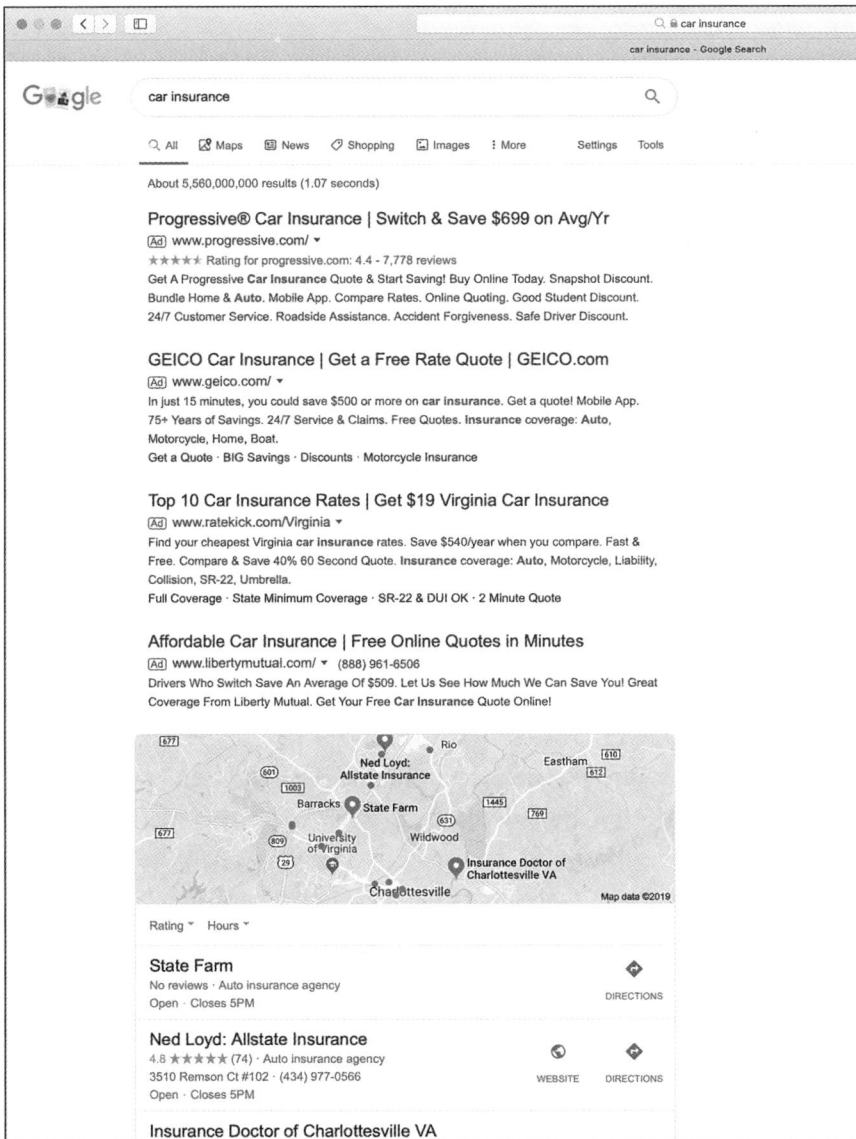

FIGURE 7.1. Search results. (Google and the Google logo are registered trademarks of Google LLC, used with permission)

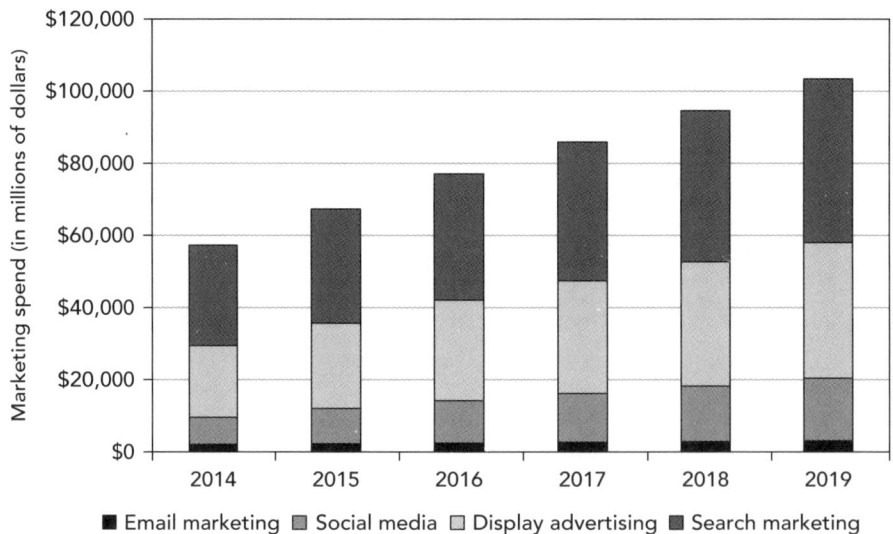

FIGURE 7.2. Interactive marketing spending in the United States, 2014–19. (Data from Lindsay Blankenship, "4 Takeaways to Forrester's US Digital Marketing Forecast," Search Discovery, November 18, 2014, https://www.searchdiscovery .com/blog/forrester-report-us-digital-marketing-forecast-2014-2019/ [accessed Nov. 19, 2019])

using keyword clouds, and the nature of Google AdWords' enhanced campaigns. Finally, the case follows an online clothing start-up whose primary marketing is through Google AdWords. Given access to its paid search data, you have the opportunity to practice the kind of analytics that optimize paid search advertising.

Using linear and logistic regressions (see chapters 4 and 9), cluster analyses (see chapter 2), and CLV calculations (see chapter 5), modern marketing managers can optimize their paid search advertising campaigns to ensure that they don't spend $50,000 on a customer who only wants to buy a hat.

STRATEGIC OBJECTIVE

The goal of paid search advertising is to marry the ad a company is serving and the price it is willing to pay for it to the intent of the consumer at the moment they see the ad.

Modern paid search systems allow their advertisers to stipulate exactly what they are willing to pay to advertise to a given customer based on everything they know

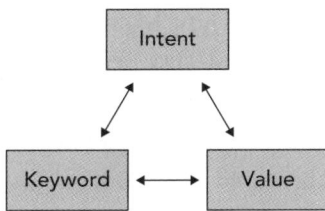

FIGURE 7.3. **Strategic objective**

about that customer. This information includes the specific search terms entered into a system ("car insurance" versus "cheap car insurance"), the type of device on which the search is being conducted, the time of day of the search, and the location of the person searching, allowing a company to estimate how valuable they think the searcher might be. For example, data generated by companies using paid search advertising has shown that people are more likely to buy at some times of the day than at others. Individuals searching at 1:00 a.m. might just be making a wish list, but those searching at 9:00 a.m. while at work typically are trying to be more efficient.

Using all this information about customers, the company can estimate their value, which then relates to their intent to buy and to the keywords they use, as depicted in **figure 7.3**. This value estimate will inform the company's bidding decisions, as explained in the next section.

The two most common types of ads are text ads, which contain roughly a dozen words, and product listings, which are more pictographic and are growing in importance for e-commerce. If you look back at the results you got from the keyword search you did at the beginning of this chapter, you'll see both text ads and more pictographic product listings (their format and look change quickly, but see if you can identify each type in your search window). Both types of advertisement must have messages that are appropriate and attractive to a user based on the user's search terms.

In paid search advertising, the goal of targeting ad copy to customers becomes even more difficult to achieve. For a retailer such as Walmart that sells hundreds of thousands of products, targeting means creating appropriate ad copy (the words displayed in the paid search link) for millions of possible search-term combinations. For example, the company might want to promote high-definition televisions with one group of advertisements and women's clothing with another. That means creating a campaign that hits the top search terms for televisions (high definition, hi-def, HD, flat screen, LCD, digital television, and so on) and a completely separate campaign for clothing (blouse, skirt, dress, and so on).

Management's challenge is not only understanding how to create copy that is relevant for those different potential search queries, but also performing controlled marketing experiments to ensure the copy resonates with the types of users who are encountering it. This improves the advertisement's click-through rate, which also increases the visibility of the ad since the search engine algorithm responds to more activity by displaying the ad to more customers.

In addition to the ad copy, the landing page to which the customer is directed must be appropriate. Although it is simple to send every potential customer to a company's homepage, most consumers expect to be taken directly to the product or service they are seeking.

The most critical piece of the paid advertising system is paying for the ads, which means bidding on ad space. Determining exactly how much a company is willing to pay for which customers, and setting the system up to enter the appropriate bid, are complex processes. Because all customers are not of equal value to a company, the bid a company is willing to make on any piece of web traffic should be commensurate with the anticipated value of the traffic to the business. A good management system should measure the value extracted from each user and use that information to anticipate the value of similar customers in the future. This is where marketing analytics enter into the process, since regression analysis, field testing, CLV, and cluster analysis all play critical roles in optimizing bids.

PAID SEARCH BIDDING

Not only does paid search target consumers looking for specific products, it targets them in specific ways based on a range of variables including customer characteristics, product characteristics, types of keyword, and even location, device, and time of day of search. All of these factor into how much a company will pay a search engine to display its ad—or rather, how much a company is *willing to pay* to a search engine to display its ad, since paid search advertising campaigns are structured like auctions.

Cost-per-Click

The structure of paid search advertising has become increasingly complex and granular. Still, it is based on the maximum **cost-per-click** (**CPC**) bid, which is the highest amount an advertiser would be willing to pay for an individual click. The search engine will typically sell the link placement to the highest bidder at a rate just above the next-highest bid. This means the maximum CPC a company is willing to pay can be considerably higher than the average cost they actually pay. In order to control spending, search engines allow marketers to specify maximum daily spends.

The search engine provider allows the advertiser to bid how much it would be willing to pay for the user to click on its link (a pay-per-click pricing structure). If the company's bid is high enough, its ad will be placed at the top of the page. Although payment is made only when someone clicks on the ad, the advertiser can be pushed farther down the page if competitors' ads are more effective at producing clicks.

Google's Paid Search Bidding Engine

Google is the largest and most important player in the paid search advertising arena. The search engine has captured about 80% of the market for these types of ads and essentially makes the rules of the game. Bing is also a player, holding about 7.2% of the market share. Comparison engines such as Yelp and Amazon also deserve attention from companies whose products are sold in those arenas.[1] Other pay-per-click advertising media, such as the one offered by Facebook, are focused on display ads pushed toward people who have expressed an interest in categories of products and lifestyles.

Even with these other players, the digital marketer with the most cachet to reach potential customers is still Google AdWords. Potential advertisers can sign up for Google AdWords for free, but have to agree to the type and amount of bid they are willing to spend on certain keywords for their ads to appear. The keywords a company chooses to trigger its ads are highly important—the more words that match a user's search, the greater the chance an ad will be shown. Bids can be placed automatically or manually and are determined by the Google AdWords customer's budget. Advertisers can restrict their budget on a daily schedule if desired.

Google decides which ads appear on a Google user's search results based on an auction. Based on the keywords Google users search, an AdWords algorithm engine looks at its customers' ads for the best match to the search words and assigns quality scores to the matching ads. If a Google user looks for "car insurance," for example, the Google engine examines all ads that closely match those words. Eligible ads are then ranked based on "bid amount, quality of ad and website, and expected impact"[2] and appear with the user's search results.

Advertisers choose from numerous AdWords pricing structures. For a company interested in driving traffic to its website, it is charged a fee (CPC) when a Google user clicks on its website ad or phones the vendor. If a company prefers to focus on impressions, it would pay depending on the number of times its ad is viewed (cost per thousand viewable impressions). If the Google AdWords customer wants to focus on conversions (a sale, an email sign-up, or whatever action the company wants the customer to take), the system would try for as many conversions as possible at a given cost per acquisition. And for a company using TrueView video ads, each time its video is watched—even if the viewer stops watching it—the company is charged using cost-per-view bidding.

Example: "Cheap Car Insurance"

Consider three firms—Progressive, Geico, and Liberty Mutual (similar to the top results, marked "Ad" in **figure 7.1**)—bidding for the keywords "car insurance" on Google. As shown in **table 7.1** (hypothetical data), Progressive has stated that the maximum amount it is willing to pay for a single click is $0.40. Geico and Liberty Mutual have set their maximum bids as $0.65 and $0.25, respectively.

Based on its proprietary algorithm, Google has assigned a quality score of 1.8 to Progressive for the keywords "cheap car insurance." For the same keywords, Google assigns Geico and Liberty Mutual quality scores of 1.0 and 1.5, respectively. In general, a higher quality score indicates that the firm's advertisement (and the firm's products) has a higher match with, or is more relevant to, the search keyword. This implies that Google has determined that a consumer who searches for the keywords "cheap car insurance" is more likely to click on Progressive's ad than on Geico's or Liberty Mutual's ads.

TABLE 7.1. Cost-per-click calculations

Advertising firm	Cost-per-click (CPC) bid	Quality score	Rank number	Position	Actual CPC
Progressive	$0.40	1.8	0.40 × 1.8 = 0.72	1	$0.37
Geico	$0.65	1.0	0.65 × 1 = 0.65	2	$0.39
Liberty Mutual	$0.25	1.5	0.25 × 1.5 = 0.38	3	$0.01

Note: Hypothetical data used.

Google AdWords uses the product of the maximum CPC bid and the quality score to compute a company's rank number. The firm with the highest rank number is provided the top spot in the paid search advertising listing. The belief is that consumers are more likely to click on a paid search advertisement that is at the top of the list than on the ads lower down. In this example, Progressive has the highest rank number (0.72) and therefore occupies the top listing in the paid search advertisement section for the keywords "cheap car insurance," followed by Geico and then Liberty Mutual. Although Liberty Mutual had a better quality score than Geico, it was given the third spot, because Liberty Mutual's maximum CPC bid was much lower than Geico's.

The final piece of information to consider is the actual CPC paid by the advertising firms. Although Progressive was willing to pay $0.40, Google charges only $0.37. The formula for calculating the actual CPC paid is

$$\$0.37 = \frac{0.65}{1.8} + \$0.01.$$

The minimum Progressive would have to pay to obtain the number-one position is $0.37, since Geico has a rank number of 0.65 and Progressive has a quality score of 1.8. At the actual CPC of $0.37, and a quality score of 1.8, Progressive's rank number—(actual CPC × quality score)—is 0.667, and for a CPC of $0.36 and a quality score of 1.8, Progressive's rank number would be 0.648. So, given Geico's quality score and maximum CPC bid, Progressive would need to bid $0.37 to have the highest rank number.

Similarly, even though Geico's maximum CPC bid is $0.65, its actual CPC is $0.39. At a CPC bid of $0.39 and a quality score of 1, Geico's rank number would be 0.39 × 1 = 0.39, sufficient for Geico to have a higher rank number than Liberty Mutual.

This auction process is similar to the second-price sealed-bid system that is common in government contract jobs. In the **second-price sealed-bid** system, the winner of the contract is paid the price quoted by the second-lowest bidder, not the price the winning contractor itself quoted. In contrast, in a first-price sealed-bid system, the winner would be paid the amount they themselves quoted. (The difference in paid search advertising, as opposed to the second-price sealed-bid system, is the quality score.) Academic research has shown that a second-price sealed-bid auction system increases the number of people willing to participate in the auction system and motivates people to bid at their true willingness to pay.[3] The second-price sealed-bid system has been found empirically to have a higher average clearing price than a first-price sealed-bid system.

METRICS OF SEARCH ADVERTISING

Before examining the efficacy of a paid search advertising campaign, marketers should be familiar with several metrics used to understand web traffic in general. The **visits** metric measures the number of sessions on a website, whereas the **visitors** metric measures the number of people making those visits. ("Visitors" and "unique visitors" are the same metric.) When a user creates a shopping cart on a website that does not result in a purchase, this is known as **abandonment**, and the **abandonment rate** is the ratio of the number of abandoned shopping carts to the total number of carts created by users. **Table 7.2** offers a list of additional terms useful for understanding paid search advertising metrics.

Remember that the success of a company's paid search advertising campaign depends on its ability to put the right message in front of the right consumer and influence them to perform an action. **Impressions** represents the number of opportunities consumers are given to see an advertisement. Many recorded impressions are not actually perceived by the intended viewer, however, so some marketers refer to this metric as **opportunities to see**.

Less-refined metrics for understanding how often an ad is viewed are page views and hits. **Page views** represents the number of times a website is accessed, and **hits**

TABLE 7.2. Paid search advertising metrics

Keyword	Term identified as one a customer might use to search for a given product.
CPC bid	The amount an advertiser is willing to spend to place its ad in front of a potential customer given the keywords entered, device used, geographic location, and other factors.
Quality score	An estimate of how relevant a company's ads, keywords, and landing page (website to which the ad points the customer) are to a person seeing an ad.
Realized CPC	The actual amount a company spends to place its ad in front of a potential customer. This cost is determined as a function of bid amount, amount of the next-highest bid, and quality score.

Source: Adapted from Paul W. Farris, Neil T. Bendle, Phillip E. Pfeifer, and David J. Reibstein, *Marketing Metrics, The Definitive Guide to Measuring Marketing Performance* (Upper Saddle River, NJ: FT Press, 2010).

measures the number of file requests by a website. The notion of page views was intended to more accurately measure the number of times a site has been displayed to a user. But for marketing purposes, a further distinction must be made as to how many times an advertisement has been viewed by unique visitors. For example, the advertisement may be a banner ad that changes depending on the visitor. So, for a single advertisement served to all visitors on a site, impressions are equal to the number of page views. If a page carries multiple advertisements, the total number of all ad impressions will exceed the number of page views.

Cost per impression, **cost per click**, **cost per order**, and **cost per customer acquired** are the most critical marketing metrics for paid search advertisers. All four are calculated in the same way: by dividing advertising cost by, respectively, number of impressions, number of clicks, number of orders, and number of customers acquired. As explained earlier, a company advertising through Google AdWords can choose the marketing metric most appropriate for its particular goals.

Click-through rate is the percentage of impressions that lead a user to click on an ad. It describes the fraction of impressions that motivate users to visit the web location intended by the advertiser. Most internet-based businesses use click-through metrics, and the growth of paid search advertising has made them more common. Advertisers should remember, however, that click-throughs are only a step on the road to a final sale, and other metrics must be observed to understand the true value of a paid search ad.

CLV-BASED OPTIMIZATION: STICKS KEBOB SHOP

One way to get the most out of paid search advertising is to set customer lifetime value (CLV) as the objective function. In other words, the goal of the campaign should be to maximize CLV. In the earliest days of paid search advertising, firms typically focused on optimizing conversion rate. But all orders are not equally valuable, so measuring sales dollars rather than conversions (or number of orders) makes more sense.

Consider the example of Sticks Kebob Shop in **table 7.3**. Recall from chapter 2 that Sticks's management performed cluster analyses on its potential customers in order to make an informed decision about where to locate its new store. It has also calculated the CLV of each of the customer segments it identified (see chapter 5). Using the results of both of these analyses, as well as historical data on web searches,

TABLE 7.3. Optimizing paid search bids to maximize CLV

	Health conscious		Convenience	
Keywords	Click-through rate	Conversion rate	Click-through rate	Conversion rate
"Kids healthy fast food"	35%	40%	5%	15%
"Convenient fast food"	10%	5%	40%	30%
CLV		$1,200		$700

Sticks can now determine which keywords are more likely to appeal to customers with higher CLV, and therefore how to allocate its advertising dollars.

Management has realized that customers who first visit the Sticks website based on the keywords "kids healthy fast food" are more likely to belong to the Health Conscious segment of the Sticks customer base. Customers who first visit the Sticks website through the search keywords "convenient fast food," however, are more likely to belong to the Convenience segment. Sticks also knows from its customer database that customers in the Health Conscious segment have a CLV of $1,200, and customers in the Convenience segment have a CLV of $700. Management decides to bid higher for the keywords "kids healthy fast food" than for "convenient fast food," even though the click-through and conversion rates for these keywords are similar.

But there is still more to the picture: profit margin rates are also different depending on the product, and return rates can vary significantly. For example, people who buy paint rarely return it, but shoe buyers return their purchases regularly.

Different orders have different values to a business in the long term, so the goal of a company engaged in a paid search advertising campaign should be to use the data it has about its existing customers' behavior to optimize CLV. For companies looking to generate only sales leads through their online ads, the process is similar, as all leads are not equally valuable. Furthermore, what happens online isn't the whole story, as some consumers browse on a mobile device before making an in-store purchase. Others shop on a laptop and then contact a call center. Companies must make an effort to capture some of these data in order to gain an accurate sense of CLV.

While some of the elements of CLV might seem obvious to a marketing manager (a customer searching for "Lexus insurance" is more valuable than a customer searching for "cheap car insurance"), the ability to track the performance of a paid search ad granularly allows managers to confirm their intuition.

KEYWORD CLOUDS

A challenge does arise for companies that use a large volume of keywords, such as big-box retailers. This leads to a number of keywords with relatively sparse performance (**figure 7.4**), meaning not enough is known about the people who click on the ads after entering those words to make any significant claims about who they are relative to groups of people who click on other terms.

To account for sparse data concerns, companies must attempt to aggregate data. For example, on the keyword level, the company might group certain words with their "cousins." The firm might have sparse data on "blue steel widgets," but it might recognize that the phrase "blue wood widgets" behaves in a similar fashion. By grouping these words into **keyword clouds**, or families of search terms, the business can build a statistically significant data set and make viable claims about the people who are attracted to the keywords, including for example where they are from, how they surf the internet, and whether they are likely to be repeat customers.

On the location level, although a firm might have little data on how a keyword performs in, for instance, Charlottesville, Virginia, it might be able to create a statistically significant amount of data on small cities in the southeastern United States with above-average income levels. That data can then be used to make assumptions about what type of keyword will be effective in those types of geographic location.

Because there is no downside to using a very large number of keywords (the cost increases per click, not keyword), even smaller companies may discover that some of their words do not produce a large number of clicks, meaning little is known about

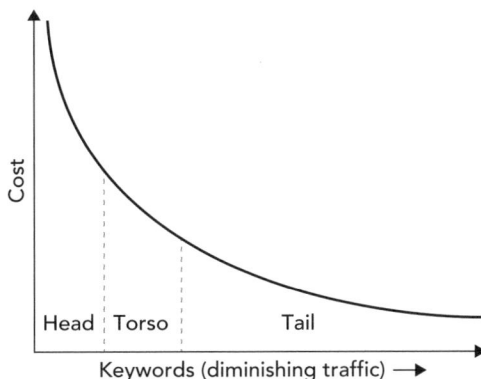

FIGURE 7.4. The long tail of keywords

the customers who are drawn to those words. Cluster analysis comes into play again here: because keywords are tied to the intent of consumers who are part of the same market segment, marketers can group keywords just as they would customers in a given marketplace segment.

ENHANCED CAMPAIGNS

Google recognized early on that a keyword on a smartphone would be worth a different amount to a company than the same keyword on a home computer, and a keyword entered within a mile of a brick-and-mortar store would be worth more than the same keyword entered 100 miles away. So Google initially set up its AdWords system to allow businesses wanting to advertise on Google to create different campaigns for each modifier to a keyword. In other words, if a company had a base campaign of 10,000 keywords, it would create a separate 10,000-word campaign for those keywords searched on a smartphone; another 10,000-word campaign for those keywords searched on a tablet computer; and a third 10,000-word campaign for the same keywords searched on a desktop computer. If the company wanted to further modify the campaign for geography, it would have to create another three campaigns for searches within a mile of a brick-and-mortar store, and another three campaigns for searches more than 100 miles from a brick-and-mortar store. This led to a replication model that was not scalable for large customers.

To correct this problem, in July 2013, Google rolled out an enhanced campaign that allows companies to modify their base campaigns. This meant firms had to condense back to a single version of every keyword and create a system where they could bid up for certain conditions or bid down for others. But one problem remains—the modifiers in the 2013 iteration are stacked on top of one another. For example, if a firm determined that smartphone traffic is worth 20% of desktop traffic because of the difficulty of shopping on a smartphone, it might set its bid for keywords on smartphones to one-fifth of its bid on desktops. But if the smartphone search is conducted within a mile of a brick-and-mortar store, the company might consider it to be worth the same as desktop traffic and therefore want to increase the bid by a factor of five. In Google's current system, this would also increase the cost of desktop traffic for that keyword by a factor of five if the desktop is located within a mile of a brick-and-mortar store. If the company wanted to further customize the campaign to double its bid for

TABLE 7.4. Enhanced campaigns

Device	Bid amount for "television"	Bid amount for "television" within one mile of store	Bid amount for "television" within one mile of store in high-value geographic location
Laptop	$5 (base bid)	$25	$50
Smartphone	$1 (20% of base)	$5	$10

smartphone users within a mile of a brick-and-mortar store who also reside in a high-value geographic location, the desktop bid would again be doubled based on the larger bid, even if that were not the company's intention (**table 7.4**).

Search engines deliver reports that marry each click to the geography from which it came, and the goal of the manager is to synthesize that information to determine the value of each type of click. For smaller businesses, Google's optimize-conversion option delivers advertisements with some success. The rules are applied across the board, however, and don't take into account CLV or conditions unique to a company, such as promotions.

DIAGNOSING OMITTED FACTORS

As with any marketing measure, paid search advertising campaigns must be refined through numerous iterations. Marketing managers must gather the data available, revisit their campaigns, and hone and focus them over time based on historical data as well as through experiments.

So how does the ability to target customers based on the different factors analyzed by search engines actually work? Imagine Suck-It-Up Vacuums determines that the average search for "vacuum cleaner" is worth $0.45 (**table 7.5**). The company then determines that factors including search location, day of the week, search device, kind of internet connection, time of day, and whether the customer has bought from Suck-It-Up previously can all modify the value of the search, and therefore its bid. Specifically, it decides to reduce the bid by 5% when the search is performed at least 10 miles away from a store and by 2.5% on Mondays, but to increase it by 10% when the search is on a tablet, 3% when over a wireless internet connection, 7% for morning

TABLE 7.5. Matching bids to value

Modifier	Bid
Desktop—search engine	$0.45
More than 10 miles from store	−5%
Smartphone or tablet	+10%
Free Wi-Fi hotspot	+3%
Early morning	+7%
Repeat purchase	+13%
Monday	−2.5%

TABLE 7.6. Regional variance in value per click

Location	Bid adjustment
Indiana	+25%
Kentucky	+25%
Michigan	+25%
Missouri	+25%
Tennessee	+25%
Virginia	+25%
Florida	−10%

searches, and 13% when the person searching is a repeat buyer. With all these factors, the value of the search term at that moment is $0.56.

As with any model, there is a risk of making faulty assumptions based on incomplete data and omitted variables. Consider a furniture retailer's campaign, shown in **table 7.6**. The company wanted to determine which regions were performing best nationally, and it found statistically significant differences in a variety of locations. Further inquiry, however, determined that proximity to shipping locations was an omitted variable in the model. Shipping costs within 100 miles of the company's discrete distribution centers were reasonable, but they skyrocketed outside those locations. Understanding that the conversion rate was higher within those regions, the company was able to use enhanced campaigns to change bids for specific locations without creating duplicate campaigns.

LOOKING FORWARD

Paid search advertising is a powerful tool for marketers hoping to match their offers with consumers who are looking for their products. Because it is an auction-like system, wherein marketers bid an amount to put their ad in front of a customer, the data available from existing customers' behavior can ensure an optimal marriage between customer value and the price of the ad.

What's more, paid search advertising systems are only growing more powerful. Our discussion of consumer data here was limited to location, device, and search time, but there are far-reaching possibilities for search advertising. If data are available, search engines might also be able to feed marketers data about consumers including such granular information as whether they have put something in their carts but never made a purchase; the speed of their internet connections; whether they are at home or work; whether they are traveling at 5 miles per hour or 60; whether they tend to buy online or offline; and whether they are existing customers of a competitor.

The basics of marketing analytics still hold true when analyzing the effectiveness of paid search advertising campaigns. The advertisements can be customized to the needs of the advertiser through varying bid amounts. Keywords represent customer intent, so they can be grouped in terms of their value, just as customers can be grouped into segments. And finally, the whole process can be improved over time through feedback loops, just like marketing measures in traditional channels.

CONCEPT APPLICATION

The company in the following case—Historical Emporium Inc. (HEI), an online period-clothing store—uses Google AdWords and analytics as its primary marketing efforts. As you read the case, have open the related data sets, available in the online supplement at http://store.darden.virginia.edu/marketing-analytics-supplements. These include real Google Analytics and AdWords data about the company.

- What conclusions can you draw from the Google Analytics site data and the AdWords ad data (use the Google definitions table for reference)? How would this help HEI?
- To drive new customers, what should HEI do, in terms of paid search advertising and/or other marketing options?

- What resources would HEI require to carry out your recommendation(s)?
- Based on case information and the accompanying data set, can you make recommendations about metrics HEI might focus on? Should it pay for cost per click, per impression, per order, or per customer acquired? For which keywords should it bid more? What characteristics (of the potential customer, customer context or geography, and keyword, for example) should it place most value on?
- Should HEI use, or test the use of, a new social media component in its marketing strategy?
- Does the company have the ability to employ a recommendation system (turn to chapter 10) or to usefully employ its user reviews (turn to chapter 8)?
- What challenges does HEI face? Identify some in the case itself, and also consider what some others might be that aren't explicitly mentioned. Can paid search advertising help with any of these, and if so, how?

CASE: MARKETING A PURE PLAY E-TAILER: HISTORICAL EMPORIUM INC.

Chris Allen, HEI's CFO, had always wanted to become an entrepreneur, though he had never envisioned himself in the historical clothing retail business. He was a financial professional who had worked for Hewlett-Packard and several start-ups and consultancies in Silicon Valley. His father, Terry, had become a Civil War reenactor and operated a small traveling store that offered Civil War–style clothing for men throughout the US Midwest.[4]

Chris's wife, Alicia, a techie with a business degree, worked as a product development consultant and helped develop business websites. By the time Chris and Alicia had two children, they were ready to pursue a business that would offer more flexibility than the average start-up in Silicon Valley. So in 2003, they decided to take a crack at selling historical costumes and took over Chris's father's business, but with a twist—instead of a traveling store, they would be an online retailer.

From their garage to a 16,000-square-foot warehouse and office in San José, California, the Allens built a business that generated nearly $8 million in sales in 2015. And in true techie fashion, the pair continually thought about other ways they could use digital tools to increase sales and enhance customer experience. The number of available online marketing campaigns was vast, but each one cost money, and the Allens were looking for the best bang for their click.

Online Retailers

Not that long ago, customers headed to a real store, poked around, and maybe even tried something on. Some simply enjoyed the experience but didn't buy anything. For others, shopping was a necessity and they entered stores only to purchase—they were less likely to leave empty-handed. As shopping moved from physical stores to online, online customers exhibited many of the same habits leading to a purchase or decision not to buy, and companies wanting to sell to these customers developed frameworks to understand shoppers in the digital market. Online vendors used the data from these models to craft marketing tools to attract customers. Digital marketers, such as Google AdWords, Yahoo! Gemini, and Bing Ads, provided analytics to those using their services to track visitor behavior.

As the Allens delved more deeply into the world of online shopping, they realized they needed to take advantage of these digital marketing tools to reach customers and grow their business.

E-Commerce and HEI

Initially, the HEI website mimicked the product offerings of the traveling store. At the end of the first year, the Allens were disappointed to learn that the target market, Civil War enthusiasts, did not shop online for items that they could easily purchase at the next reenactment that they visited. But they also realized that a new market niche—Victorian clothing for men—seemed to be in demand and underserved. They revamped the website, removed all references to the Civil War, and focused instead on men's Victorian clothing and accessories. Alicia stopped tech consulting and worked full time on the historical clothing business. Sales began to take off, and the Allens decided to branch out. By 2006, Chris had quit his job and joined Alicia in working full time from their garage. A year later, they moved the business from their home to a warehouse, hired their first employee, and offered 764 products.

The site's success was based on its unique products: high-quality, authentically styled clothing, not costumes. It also focused on customer service: unlike most of its competitors, HEI offered items off the rack, shipped them quickly, and had a generous return policy. The website included a broad assortment of items and sizes. To assist customers in their decision-making, complete outfits were available and could be purchased with one click (see **figure 7.5** for an example).

FIGURE 7.5. "Solomon Brewer, Bank Officer." (Provided by HEI, used with permission)

While price and selection were prominent determiners for online demand, the Allens tried to mimic the in-store values of lifestyle, experience, and superior service. They offered a full-service shop and had five customer service representatives available to answer questions and resolve issues. Chris explained their approach:

> We have a high-touch business model with an easy-to-reach customer service team—unlike some of our competition who don't answer their phones, return emails, or deliver the product that was ordered. Our return policy is very open and for good reason. For example, some of our customers are theater companies. They want to order costumes in plenty of time but if they have an actor change and need a different size, we want to make sure they get it easily. This high-touch customer service has earned us high ratings from our customers but comes at a cost in both time and money.

Revenues grew to $981,012 in 2007, $1.8 million in 2008, and $2.4 million in 2009.[5] Men's clothing represented roughly 85% of sales, and 60% of HEI's customers were male. Focusing on growth, HEI expanded into the adjacent businesses of ladies' Victorian wear, western historical clothing, and steampunk (a mixture of Victorian, Goth, and burlesque styles made popular by movies such as *Sherlock Holmes* and *The Raven*). Each of these businesses had its own domain name—Gentleman's Emporium, Ladies' Emporium, Western Emporium, and Steampunk Emporium—that directed back to HEI. HEI also sold products through other engines that directed people to its website for purchases. Along the way, the Allens added a blog (http://www.civilizedfashion.com/) and hired 13 salaried employees.

HEI's customers were a rather eclectic group of shoppers. Purchasers included repeat visitors such as role-play enthusiasts, entertainment professionals, reenactors, theater companies, movie studios, museums, opera companies, and historical societies (see **table 7.7** for customer segment information). One-time purchasers tended to be those attending theme weddings, school proms, or historical celebrations.

HEI Marketing Initiatives

From the beginning, the Allens used Google AdWords. Indeed, they were the first advertiser to use the keyword phrase "Victorian clothing," and at the time, each click cost a mere nickel. "In 2006, Google actually sent us a branded mini fridge as a thank-you

TABLE 7.7. HEI market segments

Market segment	Sample customer	Primary needs
Production companies: Theater, TV, and movie	*Hell on Wheels*	Immediate delivery
	The Big Bang Theory	Availability (sizing and style)
	Unbreakable Kimmie Schmidt	Available in volume
	In a Valley of Violence	Lenient return policy
Performance: Group and individual	Band	Style
	Magician	Quality
		Durability
		Sizing availability
Dress events	Weddings	Complete outfits
	Proms	Timing critical
	Formal dances	Sizing availability
Historical locations and events	Historical sites	Authentic appearance
	Old-fashioned store	Availability (sizing and style)
Steampunk enthusiasts	College-age enthusiasts	Historically inspired
	Burning Man	Full line of basics to allow
	Edwardian Ball	individual modes to suit style
	SteamCon	Brassy bling and accessories
Individual enthusiasts	Dickens Fair	Complete outfits
	Halloween	Reduced risk
	Christmas party	Quality
	Edwardian Ball	Build outfit over time

Source: Provided by HEI, used with permission.

for our business," said Alicia. The program was very successful for the store and was the company's sole form of marketing for five or six years. This allowed the Allens to focus on business operations and the difficult task of sourcing new products. But competition in the historical wear category and the increased cost of advertising required them to reevaluate how their advertising dollars were spent.

As costs increased, the company began a variety of new marketing initiatives (see **table 7.8** for a timeline).

The efforts took many forms, from sponsorship to e-communication to offline advertising. To communicate with customers and encourage visitors to their websites,

TABLE 7.8. HEI's marketing timeline

2003	Google AdWords
2005	Froogle (early Google Shopping) Bing advertising
2007	Yahoo! advertising
2009	Facebook
2011	Hired ad agency to manage Google AdWords Facebook ad test Offline postcard mailing
2012	Google Shopping (formerly Froogle, Google Product Search, Google Products) Offline advertising: *Make* magazine
2013	Shopzilla/Connexity eBay Commerce Network Pinterest boards
2014	Free shipping offer Product videos Email program (newsletters, shopping cart abandonment, remarketing) First store sale (not clearance items)
2015	Amazon store

Source: Data provided by HEI, used with permission.

the Allens turned to social media and created Facebook pages for each of the websites in 2009. Through this channel, they announced new products and initiatives, provided advice on the best times to shop, and collected information on how customers used HEI's products and what new products they desired. Facebook changed its business model in 2013 and required payment for posts to reach new followers, which made it costly to collect the marketing insights the business had previously enjoyed for free. Still, Facebook marketing was highly effective, and the couple paid Facebook to build up their audience to over 28,000 followers on Gentleman's Emporium and over 46,000 on Steampunk Emporium (see **table 7.9**).

Although HEI began using Pinterest on its websites in 2013, it had not fully developed its presence or refined posts to increase sales. Most Pinterest users were women, and the bulk of what HEI sold was men's clothing.

Other tools HEI used to reach out and attract shoppers were Google Shopping—on which HEI had relied since 2005—Shopzilla, eBay Commerce Network, and Bing

TABLE 7.9. HEI Facebook followers, December 1, 2015

Website	Number of followers
Steampunk Emporium	46,750
Gentleman's Emporium	28,545
Ladies' Emporium	4,671
Western Emporium	3,494

Source: Provided by HEI, used with permission.

product ads. On these comparison shopping sites, the Allens focused on mainstream products like vests and shirts. High costs and low conversion prompted HEI to remove its listings from Shopzilla, but the company remained on the other selling platforms.

In the spring and summer of 2014, HEI also ran a free-shipping campaign for orders over $150. "We heard from other retailers that offering free shipping resulted in a 10%-to-20% increase in sales," Alicia said. The offer ran for five months but was unsuccessful. Although it pushed up average order size slightly, the uptick was insufficient to make up for the increased shipping costs, and the promotion was discontinued in August 2014. Alicia described other initiatives:

> We tried adding product videos to our website in the fall of 2014—others had seen a 15%-to-20% increase in sales conversion rate; we did not. We performed an A/B test [see chapter 6] to see the specific effect of the product videos and found that just showing the link to a product video caused a decline in product conversion. We ultimately removed the links from all of our product categories.

In 2014, the Allens also began an email marketing campaign. They added multiple ways for visitors to join their email list from the website. Within less than a year of launching email tools, HEI's reachable list had grown from 10,000 to 67,000. "We don't send as many emails as we could," Alicia said. "But when we do, we have high click and conversion rates."

In 2015, the Allens opened a storefront on the Amazon marketplace; Google Adwords continued to do ad placement on Amazon. To maintain control of products and pricing, the Allens put only a small section of custom-made products on the Amazon storefront (see **table 7.8**).

Despite all of these initiatives, Google AdWords remained the largest source of traffic to the store. With the use of a monthly sales funnel report that showed them customer behavior from arrival to purchasing (see online supplement), the Allens would sift through impressions and steps to conversions and revenue to determine where there might be issues and highlight areas where they could or should adjust resources. "We can have a long sale cycle, months long, when shoppers leave things in the cart, often for six months, and then come back and buy it," Chris said. "Who gets credit for that sale, Google ads that brought the shopper in or the reminder that they had something in their cart that we sent?"

Part of the analytics involved running numbers on first touch and last touch—which initiative was the last one customers touched before they bought? But even that ignored the lifetime value of that customer. For example, consider a gateway product—say, a monocle. According to the numbers, this product didn't do much for HEI because it was a single-sale, $16 product. But it was something that only people who were interested in old-fashioned, uncommon clothes would buy, and it brought them in the door. Chris explained how the Allens used data from their own websites:

> We have an ad agency that manages our AdWords program. They have campaigns with groups of keywords and groups of ad copy that pertain to looking for theater, for regency, whatever we are trying to track. It's a 30-to-35-word grouping campaign, and then we look at how engaged that visitor was—did they click out to our ad page on our site? How long did they spend on the site? How many pages did they visit? Did it convert to a sale? How big is it?

After five years of relatively fast growth, things began to level off at HEI. There was a decline in steampunk queries as well as an overall decrease in Google search volume. Research showed that users were starting at larger gateway websites such as Amazon or eBay, which offered large marketplaces for a wide variety of products.

Popping Up Everywhere

One of the main drivers of HEI's rapid growth had been the steampunk trend that started back in 2006. Steampunk enthusiasts had actually contacted the Allens about offering the fashion. Initially there were few competitors in the space, but as the size of the market grew, so did the competition. Although many trend watchers suggested the market would continue to grow, it seemed to peak in 2012.

Noticing the dip in their sales, the Allens wanted to pursue avenues to backfill the loss of that business. They returned to the analytics (see online supplement)—what should they concentrate on to draw new customers and keep existing customers engaged?

CONCLUSION

Given what you've learned about the bidding structure of paid search advertising, and having worked through the challenges for HEI and suggesting solutions, think back to the absurdity of bidding equal amounts for a hat, an espresso maker, and a Ferrari. What have you learned about bidding structure? How would you apply those learnings, perhaps to marketing strategies for these three very different (and differently priced!) commodities?

8

Text Analytics

The searchable internet contains, as of this writing, almost 2 billion websites. And new, text-rich sites are being added at a rapid pace: more than 700 million popped up from 2016 to 2017, according to the International Real Time Statistics Project.[1]

Just how text-rich is the internet? Estimates in 2016 suggested that it would take 305.5 billion letter-size pages to print out all the words on the web.[2]

A lot of the web-based text published every day is relevant to marketers. This includes online product reviews, information about purchasing behavior, customer-to-customer interactions, and transcribed sales calls. Such text constitutes a plentiful source of information about customer emotions, which firms can analyze to find valuable insights.

Marketers now have more information from consumers in the form of written words than ever before, and it is only increasing. The problem, as with any extremely large data set, is determining how best to use the information. The relatively new fields of text analytics and sentiment analysis offer solutions that enable marketers to turn vast amounts of emotion-rich, word-based data into actionable information about consumers.

And companies are indeed using these tools, to great advantage. The Yankee Candle Company, for example, used text mining to determine the scents its customers most desired, for a highly successful seasonal lineup.[3] Consulting firm Sentifi uses text analytics, along with traditional financial metrics, to give customers investment insights.[4]

WHAT IS SENTIMENT ANALYSIS?

Sentiment analysis is a tool commonly used by companies to mine text for usable consumer insights. The approach involves converting a chunk of text into a score that represents either a positive or negative overall emotion. **Sentiment scores** higher than zero imply positive emotions, while those below zero imply negative emotions.

The target of sentiment analysis can be text in the form of a few words, clauses, sentences, paragraphs, or even a traditional book chapter. Think of Charles Dickens's seminal opening paragraph in *A Tale of Two Cities*:[5]

> It was the best of times, it was the worst of times, it was the age of wisdom, it was the age of foolishness, it was the epoch of belief, it was the epoch of incredulity, it was the season of Light, it was the season of Darkness, it was the spring of hope, it was the winter of despair, we had everything before us, we had nothing before us . . .

The paragraph begins in an unequivocally positive way: "It was the best of times." It then reverses course, and the second clause is negative: "it was the worst of times." From the perspective of sentiment analysis, the two clauses cancel one another out, yielding a neutral sentiment.

Consumer-focused websites like Netflix and Airbnb offer more marketing-relevant examples of text analysis. Netflix, which derives significant value from its ability to recommend new titles to viewers and keep them engaged with the streaming service, might use text analytics to better identify the kind of content descriptions its customers like most. Airbnb could analyze its online reviews (**figure 8.1**) to determine how its star ratings match up with text-based user comments.

A human reader can quickly determine the sentiment, positive or negative, implied by an Airbnb review, comments on a Netflix movie, or a Dickens novel. The challenge for quantitative sentiment analysis is to take the countless collections of text across the internet and quickly make the same determination for them.

The two principal methods of conducting sentiment analyses are dictionary-based and empirical. The dictionary-based approach is the fastest and most commonly used method of sentiment analysis. The empirical approach involves data regressions or neural network–based analyses.

THE DICTIONARY-BASED APPROACH

The **dictionary** in a dictionary-based approach is a predefined list of words classified in terms of sentiment: the simplest version classifies each word in a set as either posi-

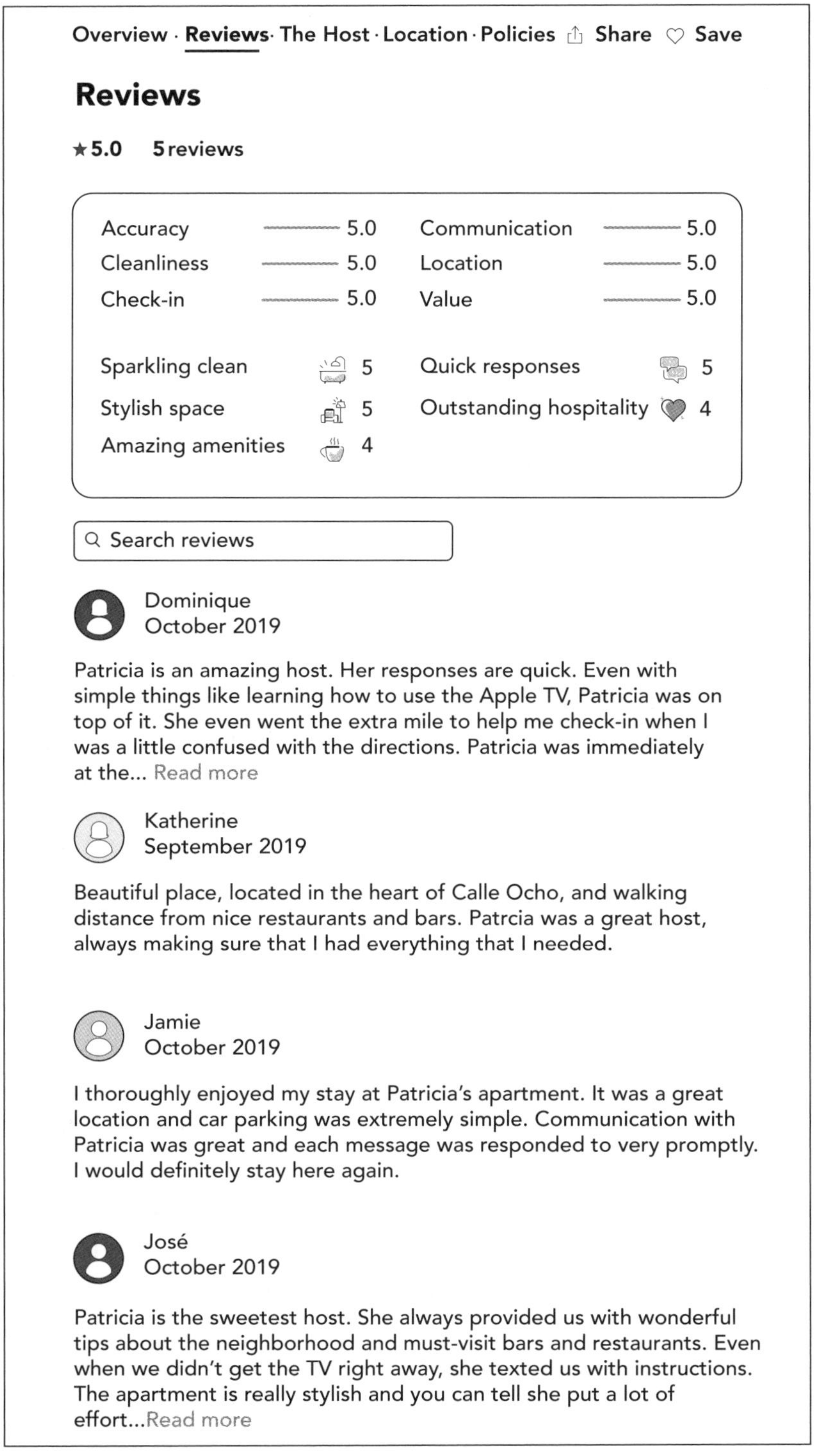
Overview · Reviews · The Host · Location · Policies
Share
Save
Reviews
★5.0 5 reviews
Accuracy 5.0
Cleanliness 5.0
Check-in 5.0
Communication 5.0
Location 5.0
Value 5.0
Sparkling clean 5
Stylish space 5
Amazing amenities 4
Quick responses 5
Outstanding hospitality 4
Search reviews
Dominique
October 2019
Patricia is an amazing host. Her responses are quick. Even with simple things like learning how to use the Apple TV, Patricia was on top of it. She even went the extra mile to help me check-in when I was a little confused with the directions. Patricia was immediately at the... Read more
Katherine
September 2019
Beautiful place, located in the heart of Calle Ocho, and walking distance from nice restaurants and bars. Patrcia was a great host, always making sure that I had everything that I needed.
Jamie
October 2019
I thoroughly enjoyed my stay at Patricia's apartment. It was a great location and car parking was extremely simple. Communication with Patricia was great and each message was responded to very promptly. I would definitely stay here again.
José
October 2019
Patricia is the sweetest host. She always provided us with wonderful tips about the neighborhood and must-visit bars and restaurants. Even when we didn't get the TV right away, she texted us with instructions. The apartment is really stylish and you can tell she put a lot of effort...Read more

FIGURE 8.1. Airbnb review page

tive or negative, which can then be converted into numbers, or scores. To prepare for **dictionary-based sentiment analysis**, the analyst must first process the given text data. Text is inherently messy and must be "cleaned" prior to being entered into an analytics algorithm. The text-processing steps are generally defined as follows:

1. Load text data as a flat file (e.g., comma-separated).
2. Remove punctuation.
3. Remove numbers.
4. Change text to lower case.
5. Remove special characters.
6. Feed the data into text analytics software.

Consider the following text of a review for a specific Airbnb property:

We had so much fun in South Beach! Merce's apartment is conveniently located close to the beach. Merce was very helpful in recommending us to a great restaurant nearby and another place within walking distance.

Removing punctuation and numbers, toggling to lower case, and removing special characters, the text becomes:

we had so much fun in south beach merces apartment is conveniently located close to the beach merce was very helpful in recommending us to a great restaurant nearby and another place within walking distance

An analyst can then load this cleaned text into **R**, a statistical computing and graphics language and environment (an integrated suite of software facilities for data manipulation). R is used for a variety of statistical techniques, including linear and nonlinear modeling, classical statistical tests, time-series analysis, classification, clustering—and sentiment analysis. A basic sentiment analysis might treat each word or combination of words in text as data. In one of the most common sentiment analysis algorithms in R, the conversion of text into data results in what is known as a **tidy data** structure.[6] Tidy data sets can be used to count the frequency of words in a document, find the polarity or sentiment of those words, and develop models predicting text sentiment.

Let's consider another Airbnb review example and manipulate it as we might in R:

> text <- c("Nicolas is a great host everything was perfect and the flat is amazing
And the location is great in a quiet area the subway I definitely come back here")

Using the tidy data set framework,[7] the review can be broken down into constituent parts, as shown in **table 8.1**.

Using a simple, single-column examination of the text, we can easily count the frequency of each word in the document. The results can then be used to create a word cloud or other marketing-relevant tool.

The same tidy data set can be used to determine the positive or negative score of each word and append it as an additional column in the table (**table 8.2**). The positive/negative score, or **lexicon score**, is obtained from many available dictionaries, such as AFINN, Bing, and NRC.[8] The dictionaries are built through crowdsourcing on Amazon Mechanical Turk or through manual labor by authors.

The review's sentiment score is determined through a simple sum of the positive/negative score column. Here, Nicolas and his property earn a positive sentiment score of 6.

Grouping Words in the Dictionary-Based Approach

Single-word analyses of text create inherent problems. Imagine a slightly different review of Nicolas's flat. Consider the following sentence and its tidy data set based on single-word lexicon lookup (**table 8.3**): "Nicolas is not a great host everything was not perfect and the flat is not amazing And the location is bad I definitely come back here."

The sum of the sentiments for each word in **table 8.3** would provide a neutral outcome of 0. However, the sentiment of the review is clearly negative. The error results from the algorithm treating each word independently, even when a connection exists between the words. The algorithm treats context-shifting words as stand-alone items, for example by leaving positive words to contribute a sentiment score of one, even when they have been shifted negative.

To overcome this issue, we can use two or more words at a time in the analysis. The resulting word sets are known as **bigrams** (if we use two words at a time) and **n-grams** (if we use some variable *n* words at a time). Consider once again our negative example, but regroup the words as bigrams: "Nicolas is not a great host everything was not perfect and the flat is not amazing And the location is bad I definitely come back here" (**table 8.4**).

TABLE 8.1. Tidy data set for Airbnb review

Word
Nicolas
is
a
great
host
everything
was
perfect
and
the
flat
is
amazing
And
the
location
is
great
in
a
quiet
area
the
subway
I
definitely
come
back
here

TABLE 8.2. Tidy data set for Airbnb review with sentiment scores

Word	Sentiment
Nicolas	0
is	0
a	0
great	1
host	0
everything	0
was	0
perfect	1
and	0
the	0
flat	0
is	0
amazing	1
And	0
the	0
location	0
is	0
great	1
in	0
a	0
quiet	1
area	0
the	0
subway	0
I	0
definitely	1
come	0
back	0
here	0

Using the bigram approach, we can neutralize or even reverse the score of a word. The pairs "not perfect" and "not amazing" both receive scores of −1. The resulting overall sentiment analysis also settles on −1, a better representation of the text data than had been achieved using single-word analyses.

Sentiment analysis algorithms also can move beyond n-grams to identify specific phrases that warrant consideration. Using fixed syntactic word structures often used to express opinions, we can find a more nuanced measure for sentiment in three steps:[9]

TABLE 8.3. Tidy data set for negative Airbnb review with sentiment scores

Word	Sentiment
Nicolas	0
is	0
not	−1
a	0
great	1
host	0
everything	0
was	0
not	−1
perfect	1
and	0
the	0
flat	0
is	0
not	−1
amazing	1
And	0
the	0
location	0
is	0
bad	−1
I	0
definitely	1
come	0
back	0
here	0

TABLE 8.4. Tidy data set with bigrams for negative Airbnb review with sentiment scores

Bigram 1	Bigram 2	Sentiment
Nicolas	is	0
not	a	0
great	host	1
everything	was	0
not	perfect	−1
and	the	0
flat	is	0
not	amazing	−1
and	the	0
location	is	0
bad	I	−1
definitely	come	1
back	here	0

Step 1. Extract phrases containing adjectives or adverbs. These two parts of speech often indicate subjectivity; however, they frequently lack context. An algorithm therefore extracts several combinations of words around each adjective and adverb. In our example, "Nicolas is not a great host everything was not perfect and the flat is not amazing and the location is bad I definitely come back here," "great host" would be extracted, among other combinations.

Step 2. Estimate the extracted phrases' sentiment orientation using **pointwise mutual information** (PMI), expressed as:

$$\text{PMI}(\text{term}_1, \text{term}_2) = \log_2 \frac{p(\text{term}_1 \wedge \text{term}_2)}{p(\text{term}_1)\, p(\text{term}_2)},$$

where $p(\text{term}_1 \wedge \text{term}_2)$ is the probability that the two terms will occur together on a web page. The denominator indicates the probability that the terms will appear together if they are statistically independent. The pre-log ratio ($p[\text{term}_1 \wedge \text{term}_2]$ / $p[\text{term}_1]\, p[\text{term}_2]$) therefore expresses the statistical dependence between the terms, and PMI, or the log of that ratio, tells us what we learn about one of the words appearing when the other is present.

We then determine the **opinion orientation (oo)** of the given phrase using the positive word "excellent" and negative word "poor" as reference points. Opinion orientation can be expressed as:

$$\text{oo}(\text{phrase}) = \text{PMI}(\text{phrase}, \text{``excellent''}) - \text{PMI}(\text{phrase}, \text{``poor''}).$$

To complete step 2, we calculate the probabilities of the terms appearing together using internet searches. Using search engine returns, we can calculate:

$$\text{oo}(\text{phrase}) = \log_2 \frac{\text{hits}(\text{phrase AROUND}(10)\text{``excellent''})\,\text{hits}(\text{``poor''})}{\text{hits}(\text{phrase AROUND}(10)\text{``poor''})\,\text{hits}(\text{``excellent''})},$$

where hits(query) is the number of search engine returns for the keywords entered. Google's AROUND(X) operator can find web pages with two words or phrases within a certain number of words of each other; other search engines have similar operators, like AltaVista's NEAR operator.

Step 3. The algorithm finds the average opinion orientation of all phrases in the text being examined. If average opinion orientation is positive, the text is considered positive in sentiment. For example, review text would be considered a recommendation if its average opinion orientation were above zero.

Using the Sentiment Algorithm in R

The dictionary-based sentiment package in R is capable of examining phrases and context shifters, and it allows two levels of analysis: granular (one review at a time) and high level (multiple reviews at the same time).

Before testing the sentiment algorithm in R with several examples, remember that **R:**

- uses a prespecified dictionary of positive and negative words
- uses context-shifting words around the positive and negative words; these **context shifters** can be negators, amplifiers, deamplifiers, or adversative conjunctions:
  - **negators** flip the sign of polarized words (e.g., "everything was not perfect")
  - **amplifiers** increase the impact of polarized words (e.g., "absolutely perfect")
  - **deamplifiers** reduce the impact of polarized words (e.g., "almost perfect")
  - **adversative conjunctions** overrule the previous clause containing a polarized word (e.g., "not perfect but pretty good")
- is not affected by neutral words
- uses four words before and two words after a positive or negative word to identify context shifters
- considers words to be positive or negative net of the number of amplifiers and deamplifiers present
- makes double negatives positives
- computes the weighted average of positive and negative words in a sentence, with weights dependent on the valence of the words and context shifters

Let's consider how R analyzes the positive review of Nicolas's Airbnb flat, which reads, "Nicolas is a great host everything was perfect and the flat is amazing And the location is great in a quiet area the subway I definitely come back here." First, we break the example into clusters of four words before and two words after a positive or negative word. The word "great" first determines sentiment:

```
> text = c("Nicolas is a great host everything")

> sentiment(text)$sentiment

[1] 0.2041241
```

Next, we create another cluster using the words "great" and "perfect":

```
> text=c("great host everything was perfect and the flat")

> sentiment(text)$sentiment

[1] 0.4419417
```

When we add a context shifter, "absolutely," to the positive word, the sentiment improves:

```
> text=c("great host everything was absolutely perfect and the flat")

> sentiment(text)$sentiment

[1] 0.6166667
```

When we add a negative and positive context shifter, the negative takes precedence because it is closest to the positive word, and sentiment decreases:

```
> text=c("great host everything was absolutely not perfect and the flat")

> sentiment(text)$sentiment

[1] 0.1106797
```

In all, the review of Nicolas's flat (not including the context shifters added to the two final examples) contains the positive words "great," "perfect," "amazing," "great," and "quiet." It contains no negative words. Its overall polarity score according to R is 1.22.

Now let's consider a different negative review: "Nicolas is a bad host everything was horrible and the flat is dirty And the location is great in a quiet area the subway I will not come back here." Here, the positive words are "great" and "quiet," while the negative words are "bad," "horrible," and "dirty." The review's overall polarity score is −0.036.

Adding amplifiers to the negative words in the review, we might arrive at "Nicolas is an extremely bad host absolutely everything was horrible and the flat is very dirty And the location is bad in a noisy area the subway I will not come back here." Here, we have no positive words, and the negative words are "bad," "horrible," "dirty," "bad," and "noisy." R gives us a polarity score of −1.01.

To understand coding in R, let's consider the review of Merce's South Beach–based Airbnb property: "We had so much fun in South Beach! Merce's apartment is conveniently located close to the beach. Merce was very helpful in recommending us to a great restaurant nearby and another place within walking distance." The R code would appear as follows:

```
setwd("~/Dropbox/text mining case study/Airbnb Case/text analysis/textdata")

install.packages("sentimentr")

install.packages("tm")

library(tm)

library(sentimentr)

##########Read Text Data###################################

text<-c("We had so much fun in South Beach! Merce's apartment is conveniently
located close to the beach. Merce was very helpful in recommending us to a
great restaurant nearby and another place within walking distance.")

require(tm)

arev<-Corpus(VectorSource(text))

###########preprocess Text Data###################

revc1<-tm_map(arev,removePunctuation)

revc1<-tm_map(revc1,removeNumbers)

revc1<-tm_map(revc1,tolower)

revc2<-tm_map(revc1,PlainTextDocument)

###############collect polarity scores for each property###############
####

sentiment(revc2[[1]]$content)$sentiment
```

The dictionary method of determining text sentiment can be effective in many applications important to marketers. However, it has its drawbacks. First, the resulting sentiment scores depend largely on the quality of the dictionary used, and dictionary definitions can change with context. Prior to going forward with the method, analysts must determine the appropriateness of the available dictionaries or supply one themselves.

EMPIRICAL SENTIMENT ANALYSIS METHODS

Empirical methods of sentiment analysis use regressions or neural network–type models, in which words, n-grams, or phrases are independent variables, and known text sentiment is the dependent variable. For example, an Airbnb text review might be paired with a star rating, which could be used to score corresponding text sentiment.

Google offers an empirical sentiment analysis product known as Natural Language Application Programming Interface (API; see **figure 8.2**).[10] While its operational details are proprietary, Google describes the tool as using machine learning to explore internet-based text in order to extract relevant marketing information and consumer sentiment (machine learning and its similarities with analytics are also discussed in chapter 11).

Alternatively, human coders (e.g., as sourced through Mechanical Turk) can manually provide sentiment scores for reviews. The sentiment score then becomes the dependent variable in a regression, neural network, or random-forest tree model, and the words, n-grams, or phrases appearing in the reviews can be used to predict sentiment in other reviews. Lasso regressions, or other data reduction techniques, can reduce the dimensionality of the independent variables to a smaller number that are really effective at predicting sentiment. (For more on neural networks, random forest, and lasso regressions, see chapter 11.)

CONCEPT APPLICATION

With its text-rich online platform connecting homeowners with renters, Airbnb overturned the hospitality industry. The unstructured text of customer reviews on its site offers a wealth of information about consumer preferences and behaviors, if marketers can find ways to manipulate and analyze that text. As you turn to the Airbnb, Inc., case, consider the following questions:

- What value proposition does Airbnb offer its customers?
- How does Airbnb make money?
- How could you calculate the potential revenue of a property on Airbnb using the available data?
- How does review sentiment affect a property's potential to be rented on Airbnb?

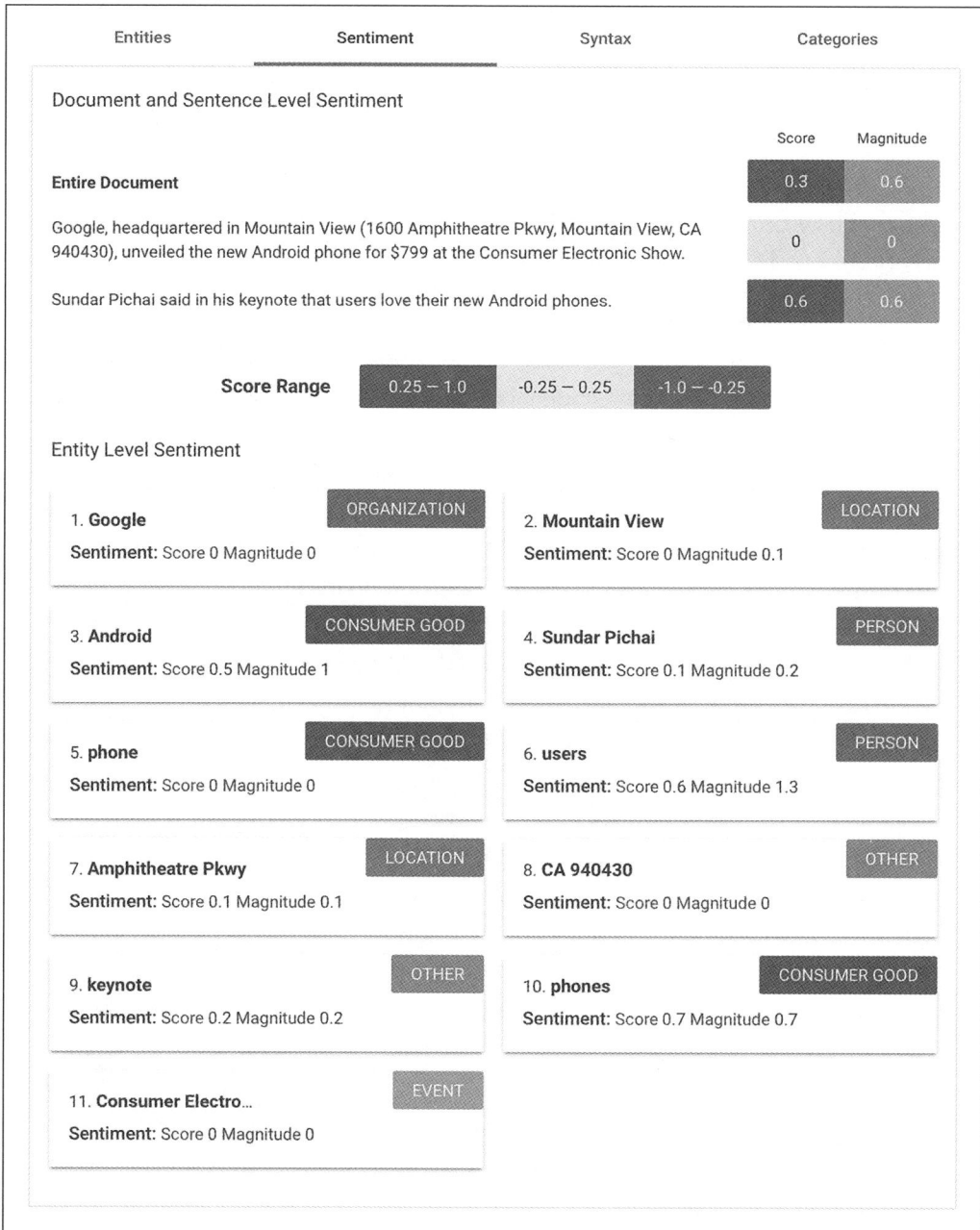

FIGURE 8.2. Google Natural Language API. (Google and the Google logo are registered trademarks of Google LLC, used with permission)

- What are the drivers of Airbnb property revenues in Miami, Florida, and Paris, France?
- How would you optimize Airbnb property revenues in Miami and Paris? Are your strategies different or the same in these cities?

CASE: HAVE TEXT, WILL TRAVEL: CAN AIRBNB USE REVIEW TEXT DATA TO OPTIMIZE PROFITS?

Hundreds of thousands of would-be hoteliers have been popping up all around you. One might be your unassuming 60-year-old neighbor, looking to pad her pension—others might include the young couple down the hall from your Chicago high-rise apartment.

The one thing all these individuals have in common is that they list their properties online in order to invite complete strangers into their homes and charge them a premium to treat the space as their own. More often than not, these entrepreneurs have zero experience in the hospitality industry and no idea how to run a successful guesthouse. Welcome to the Airbnb era.

The goal of Airbnb's aspiring hosts is to use the Airbnb website (www.airbnb.com) to attract guests willing to pay the highest rates for brief stays in their homes. Airbnb's goal is to increase profits by improving customer review performance. How can the company achieve this? Enter text mining, a technique that allows businesses to scour websites, decipher the meaning of groups of words, and assign the words a sentiment proxy through the use of a software package.

In order for Airbnb to use text mining to its advantage, its marketing professionals needed access to customer review data on the vacation rental firm's own website. The team then had to analyze the data to find ways to improve property performance. Were the text data in the reviews adequate to the company's purposes? Would the team be able to leverage this large amount of data to determine a strategy (e.g., a location-specific approach) going forward?

If the marketing team was successful, hosts would be more likely to continue to list their properties on the Airbnb site, rather than choosing one of the growing number of competitors in the market.

Taking Flight: The Rise of Airbnb

Founded in 2008 and based in San Francisco, California, Airbnb was an online platform that connected owners of homes, condos, apartments, villas—even castles—to prospective renters. This platform overturned the hospitality industry in the half decade after its founding and continued to gain traction in the market. Indeed, Airbnb's rise came at a time when **shared economies**—wherein the creation, production, distribution, trade, and consumption of goods and services were performed by a disparate group of individuals—were increasingly popular. The strategy had become entrenched in retail settings (e.g., eBay and Craigslist) and was gaining a foothold in other areas such as transportation (e.g., Zipcar and Uber).

Airbnb's specific model involved charging both its hosts and guests a fee for using its online connection service. Anywhere from 6% to 12% of the reservation subtotal went to Airbnb, and this reservation fee decreased as the price of the accommodation increased. Hosts paid a 3% service fee. To grow revenues, Airbnb looked for ways to help its hosts market their homes. For example, it encouraged homeowners to use professional photographers,[11] and in winter 2014, it launched *Pineapple*, a magazine in which users in several key markets told their personal stories.[12]

This strategy made Airbnb the world's leading peer-driven home-rental website. As of 2019, the company offered properties in more than 65,000 cities in 190 countries. Over six million homes were listed on the site worldwide. And up to 2019, there had been over half a billion Airbnb stays.[13]

A 2012 study by real estate consulting firm HR&A Advisors indicated that Airbnb provided a significant economic boost to both its users and the locations they visited. In an examination of San Francisco, the firm found that people who rented their homes on Airbnb used the income they earned to stay afloat in difficult economic times, and that travelers who used Airbnb spent more money in the cities they visited and brought more income to less-visited neighborhoods than did travelers who used traditional accommodations. From April 2011 to May 2012, guests and hosts utilizing Airbnb contributed $56 million in total spending to San Francisco's economy. "Airbnb represents a new form of travel," said Brian Chesky, Airbnb's CEO and cofounder, at the time of the study. "This study shows that Airbnb is having a huge positive impact—not just on the lives of our guests and hosts, but also on the local neighborhoods they visit and live in."[14]

Further investigations of Airbnb's economic impact found that the service had generated $61 million from February 2013 to January 2014 in Portland, Oregon;[15] $175 million from August 2012 to July 2013 in Barcelona, Spain;[16] $240 million from May 2012 to April 2013 in Paris, France;[17] and $632 million from August 2012 to July 2013 in New York, New York.[18]

Airbnb was not alone in its dominion over the user-generated vacation-rentals market. HomeAway, which operated a number of rental platforms such as VRBO and VacationRentals.com, was a large and growing competitor that had shifted its business model to more closely match that of Airbnb. HomeAway had previously charged its hosts on a per-listing basis, but it changed a portion of its services to charge users only when they successfully rented their properties.[19]

Airbnb was unique, however, in that all its listings were located in one place: its website. This made it easier to collect large amounts of text data using a web-scraping tool, and these data represented a way for the company's marketing team to gain an advantage over its fast-growing competition.

Gathering Text Data

The idea of gathering and using text data from internet-based sources was not new. It had been used with some success to examine other large online marketplaces such as Yelp, and it proved useful in automotive market segmentation.[20]

At the same time as Airbnb was growing, several commercially available tools were developed that made text mining far more practical. Anywhere in the world, businesses large and small could profitably use these tools to turn their web text into actionable information. Import.io was a fully web-based tool that was simple to use and could be customized to individual data-mining projects.[21] By deploying the tool on a set number of sample pages, the software could learn the type of information available and then use that model to extract data from a large number of pages in a short amount of time. The data output was in a simple **CSV** (comma separated values, a kind of plain text) export that could be used in the subsequent analysis.

Although text-mining tools still have their limitations, they are becoming smarter every day, and the latest packages are capable of sophisticated sentiment analysis that can turn written words into quantifiable consumer preferences.

Analyzing Sentiment and Developing a Revenue Model

Imagine that Airbnb marketing professionals have received text data from the company's IT department and asked that the data be cleaned and whittled down to only two sample cities: Paris, France, and Miami, Florida. (A sample of the raw data is shown in **table 8.5**.)

Text is not usable in a regression model, so in order to analyze consumer reviews in a model designed to optimize property performance, Airbnb's marketing team needed to apply numerical values to the sentiments implied in a group of related words. The team chose to use dictionary-based sentiment analysis, and at the time, several forms of sentiment-analysis tools were available. The software that Airbnb chose for this particular analysis was called qdap in R. Once the raw data were imported into this sentiment-analysis tool, all the data could be mapped to the variables shown in **table 8.6**.

TABLE 8.5. Airbnb sample data

	Price	Reviews	Rating	Accommodates	Extpeop	Savwish	Min_stay	Sentiment
1	$70	45	4.5	2	0	934	3	3.704471
2	$100	13	5	3	0	171	5	3.355278
3	$90	0	NA	4	1	0	1	2.962161
4	$125	20	4	4	0	460	7	2.139501
5	$99	10	5	6	0	589	1	3.628548
6	$129	22	5	4	1	560	7	3.334242
7	$99	72	4.5	4	0	1464	1	0.772571
8	$1,300	0	NA	4	0	0	5	NA

	Secdep	Cleanfee	Weekfee	Monthfee	Bedroom	Bathroom	Beds
1	1	0	0	0	1	1	1
2	1	0	1	1	1	1	1
3	0	0	0	0	0	1	1
4	0	1	0	0	1	1	2
5	1	1	1	1	2	2	3
6	1	1	1	1	1	1	1
7	1	1	0	0	1	1	1
8	1	1	0	0	2	2	2

Source: Data from Airbnb public website (accessed Apr. 2014).

TABLE 8.6. **Descriptions of variables in data**

Variable	Description
rating	Average user rating on a scale of 1 to 5, with 5 being the top rating
reviews	Number of user reviews
price	Daily rental price of the property
savwish	Number of times property was saved to the wish list
review_text	Raw dump of all the user reviews
sentiment	Numeric value assigned to review text describing its positivity or negativity
accommodates	Number of people the property can accommodate
bedroom	Number of bedrooms
bathroom	Number of bathrooms
beds	Number of beds
min_stay	Minimum number of days required for rental
secdep	Security deposit necessary?
cleanfee	Fees for cleaning services
weekfee	Discount for weekly stay
monthfee	Discount for monthly stay
extpeop	Fees for extra people

Source: Variables from Airbnb public website (accessed Apr. 2014).

Using qdap in R, the Airbnb marketing team had two options when determining how to represent sentiment in its model: granular, meaning at the level of each review, or high level, using multiple reviews. The team in this case selected the high-level analysis and created a polarity metric to represent sentiment.

The qdap in R polarity algorithm used a prespecified dictionary of positive and negative words, as well as context shifters. The polarity score computed the weighted average of positive and negative words in a sentence, and the weights were dependent on the combination of the words and the context shifters.

Once a numerical value was assigned to the sentiment present in each review, Airbnb's marketing managers could use it as a variable in a regression analysis designed to optimize revenues just as it would any other variable. The Airbnb marketing team might consider *price, reviews, savwish,* and *min_stay,* for example. The team might then consider drivers of these metrics, which might include price; whether people rent out entire homes, private rooms, or shared rooms; and number of bedrooms.

Optimizing Price and Beyond

The goal of Airbnb's marketing team in this exercise was to improve its users' performance so it could reap the benefits of ongoing host and renter fees. If the hosts were not happy, they were less likely to continue listing their properties through Airbnb; in a competitive and burgeoning marketplace, such attrition could be devastating.

With an almost completely online marketing presence, and an ever-increasing stash of customer information, especially in the form of text reviews, Airbnb was a perfect test case for the practicability and value of text analytics. While it had the data, and the tools were increasingly available and useful, it also needed to make decisions about how to use its findings in order to increase use of its site and therefore profits.

CONCLUSION

Internet-based text is rapidly becoming one of the largest data sets in the world. Traditionally, though, marketers have not been able to quantify word-based data in a meaningful way.

Through sentiment analysis, marketers can place a value on the way consumers feel about products when they write reviews, discuss products in online forums, publish blogs, and post to social media. The number of tools that marketers can use to access such information also continues to grow, from dictionary-based sentiment analyses like R to empirical models to off-the-shelf products like Google Natural Language API. These tools convert big text into big data, which can then be analyzed—using many of the other tools in this book—to optimize marketing efforts.

Logistic Regression

We all have some familiarity with odds. How likely is rain this weekend? What are the chances you will get the job you applied for? What's the probability that your favorite game-show contestant will win today? What you might be less familiar with is how odds can be applied to marketing analytics. What are the chances a customer will buy your product? How likely are you to retain a customer versus lose them?

When you are using odds, you are examining two opposing outcomes, meaning the outcome can be only one thing or another. Odds involve either/or chances, not a range of possibilities. Any such either/or unknown is called a **dummy variable**. If you know how to examine dummy variables properly, the results are anything but dumb.

WHEN LOGISTIC REGRESSION TRUMPS LINEAR REGRESSION

Logistic regression (also known as **logit**) is similar to linear regression—both are powerful tools for analyzing and interpreting historical data—but with one important distinction that has critical consequences.

Think about an important metric in marketing: customer retention. If Keepmoney Bank wants to use a regression analysis to examine whether it will retain a customer, it will set customer retention as its dependent variable, and see how retention changes as a result of variations in independent variables (like bank promotions or kinds of accounts held). Unlike continuous variables, which are distributed in a normal, or bell, curve (**figure 9.1**), however, customer retention is a dummy variable whose only two possible outcomes are customer retention and customer loss. For its analysis, Keepmoney Bank assigns a 1 to represent customer retention and a 0 to customer loss.

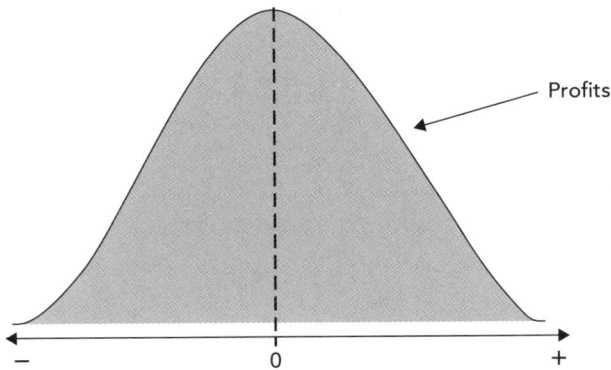

FIGURE 9.1. A normal distribution

Studies have shown that **binomial logistic regression** is the best model for examining dummy variables such as customer retention.[1] Why can't Keepmoney use its trusty linear regression to determine the likelihood of customer retention given its set of independent variables? Remember that linear regressions assume a **normal distribution** of outcomes that reaches from negative infinity to infinity. Many things in life follow this sort of distribution. Think of human height or school grades—a few people typically earn Cs, a few more earn a B−, the majority will earn Bs, and a very few will earn an A+. But when examining a dummy variable such as customer retention, there is no curve across a range of outcomes. The outcome can only be 1 or 0.

If Keepmoney attempts to use a linear regression to examine customer retention, nonsensical predictions may result. The bank may find its chances of customer retention are greater than 1—meaning the likelihood that it will retain a customer is over 100%—or less than 0. One can round up for those predictions that are less than 0 or round down for those greater than 1, but the results of the regression will not be precise.

CHOICE BEHAVIOR: HYPOTHETICAL CASE OF A FLIGHT TO MIAMI

The objective of logistic regression in this example is to represent consumers' choice behavior as accurately as possible.

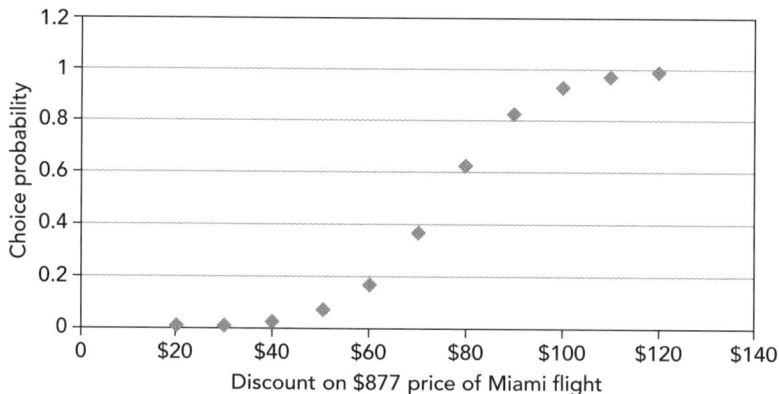

FIGURE 9.2. Choice behavior with flight discounts

Of course, the factors that go into a customer's choice are not always either/or propositions, but can include features that range, for example, from a low to a high price. When an individual consumer chooses a product, the value they place on it does not typically increase linearly with increases in its preferred features. Instead, research indicates that consumer valuation of a product typically follows an S-shaped curve with increases in the levels of a preferred attribute.

We can test whether the S-shaped curve represents consumers' choice behavior with a simple exercise. Imagine that on the x axis we have the level of discount on an $877 plane ticket from your town to Miami, Florida (see **figure 9.2**). Ask your friends if they would purchase this flight. Then offer a discount of $20. How many additional people say they would buy the ticket? Probably not many. Increase the discount to $40. Maybe one person half-heartedly jumps in. At $60, you are likely to see a spike in purchasers. And from $60 to $100, the number of purchasers should increase at every level; however, at a discount of about $100, the number of additional purchasers will taper off, as you have reached the upper threshold.

In most real-life situations, this S-shaped curve represents how people make decisions. As a discount (or in marketing terms, a promotion) increases, the odds that people will choose to buy will increase. In this example, at a $60 discount, 2 in 10 people are likely to purchase the flight to Miami; 8 in 10 are unlikely to purchase the flight.

But what does this S curve have to do with linear and logistic regression?

THE LOGISTIC TRANSFORMATION

We now see that a linear regression would not accurately represent individual consumers' choices, since reducing an S curve to a straight line would lose information and result in a misleading representation. A predictive and prescriptive model should reflect as much as possible the distribution of the data, which in this case is an S-shaped curve.

Consumer choices depend on how they value a particular product or service. Recall from the discussion in chapter 3 of conjoint analysis that **utility** represents the value to a consumer of a product or service, in terms of satisfaction rather than, say, a monetary amount. Utility is thus a key element in finding how people make purchasing choices.

The **utility function** (u_p), otherwise known as a **value function**, is used to describe the value a person places on a certain good or service. To return to the example of a flight to Miami, its utility—or value—must include all the variables that go into the decision to buy the flight: the airline, the flight's duration (is it nonstop?), the time of day, the day of the week, the cost, and tangential factors like availability of lodging in New York. Perhaps a simpler example is coffee. To find the utility of a cup of coffee, again you must consider the variables that factor into your decision to buy that particular cup: its taste, price, logo, store location, your personal habits, and the caffeine jolt it gives you in the morning. Based on behavioral studies[2] indicating how people process variables in an additive way, the utility function (u_p) is assumed to be linear.

Utilities capture the value consumers place on products, and a logistic function mathematically connects utilities to a consumer choice. The logistic function (p) takes the form of the exponent of the utility over the sum of 1 and the exponent of the utility. If we consider a consumer's decision whether to renew a monthly subscription service such as Netflix, the outcome of (p) is consumer retention. Consumer choice is whether to renew the subscription; the product is the streaming service; and the outcome is whether the customer decides to renew the subscription or not.

Mathematically, the logistic function that describes consumer choice, or probability of retention, is:

$$p(\text{customer retention}=1)=\frac{\exp(u_p)}{1+\exp(u_p)},$$

where u_p is the utility the consumer obtains from product $a + b_1 X$ (a linear function), and $p(\text{customer retention} = 1)$ means the probability that a customer is retained. The

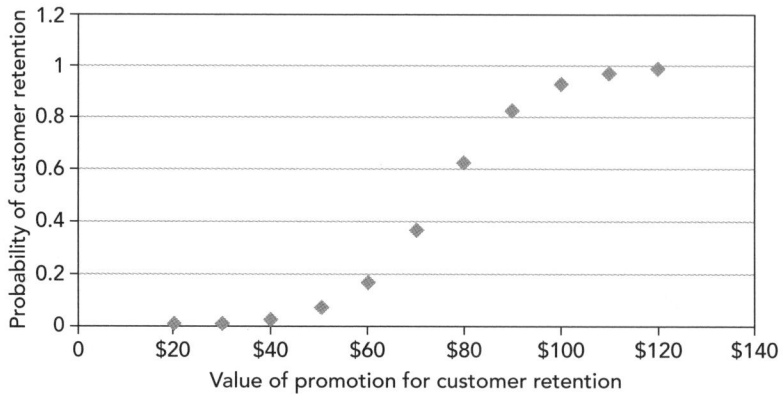

FIGURE 9.3. Logistic distribution of probabilities

retention variable (a dummy variable) is 1 when the customer is retained, and 0 otherwise; this retention variable can then be used to calibrate coefficients that would predict the probability of retention, based on the independent variables in u_p. Typically, the customer can be predicted to stay with the company if the retention probability is found to be greater than 0.5.

The resulting distribution looks like an S-shaped curve, as shown in **figure 9.3**—this is the same curve as in **figure 9.2**, you'll recognize, because it represents the same probabilistic distribution of choice behavior. The predictions from this function are bound between 0 and 1, meaning they add to 1; thus if one outcome is 0.1, the opposite outcome is 0.9.

If we continue with the example of a subscription service like Netflix, the x axis, value of promotion, could for example be a limited-time cash-back offer that Netflix provides in an effort to boost retention.

The opposite of consumer retention is **churn**, or failure to retain a consumer because the customer decides not to purchase the good or service in question. In our example of the plane ticket to Miami, churn would happen when your friend decides not to buy, or decides to buy a ticket with a different airline. The probability of success (retention) versus failure (churn) is

$$\frac{p}{1-p},$$

where p is the probability of retention.

This is known as the **odds ratio**. For example, if there are 10 outcomes with 1 success and 9 failures, the odds ratio is 1/9. In other words, if we do 10 random draws from this distribution that is estimated from the logit model, an odds ratio of 1/9 would imply that we would observe customer retention once out of the 10 draws and customer churn 9 times out of 10.

Substituting for p (probability of retention) using the logistic function describing probability of retention, the odds ratio is equal to $e^{(a+b_1X)}$: an exponential function. For a marketing manager interested in trends over time, a linear view—a straight line—is likely more useful than a logistic distribution, which is a curved line. Fortunately, there is a mathematical way to transform a logistic function to a linear function, using an exponential function and its counterpart, a logarithmic function.

UNDERSTANDING EXPONENTIAL FUNCTIONS

In order to understand logistic regressions, it is helpful to first examine exponential functions. Recall the S curve of the logistic function: an exponential curve covers the numerator of the logistic function, and when two exponential functions are involved, the curve becomes an S shape. **Figure 9.4** shows a classic example of an **exponential distribution**. When considering the cumulative sales of a product that has gained market acceptance over time (such as ultrasound machines), we see that sales are slow at first but begin to increase at a greater and greater rate once they have reached critical mass. In the graph, the dotted line is the actual data, or number of sales per year since introduction. What stands out is that the curve is not a straight line, like those in linear regressions. This is an exponential distribution.

In **figure 9.4**, the solid black line (the regression line) represents a function, created using a computer program, that best accounts for the data shown in the graph (for more information on how to perform a logistic regression using computer software, see the online supplement at http://store.darden.virginia.edu/marketing-analytics-supplements). The regression analysis of the available data has produced a line defined by the form $y = 4.0858e^{0.3225x}$, where 4.0858 is the intercept of the line, the slope is 0.3225, and x is time. (The **constant e** is an irrational number approximately equal to 2.71828, which is related to the rate of change in an exponential function and is the base of the natural logarithm.) This function is found in a similar way as a straight-line function when performing a linear regression analysis: by finding a line of best fit for the data points.

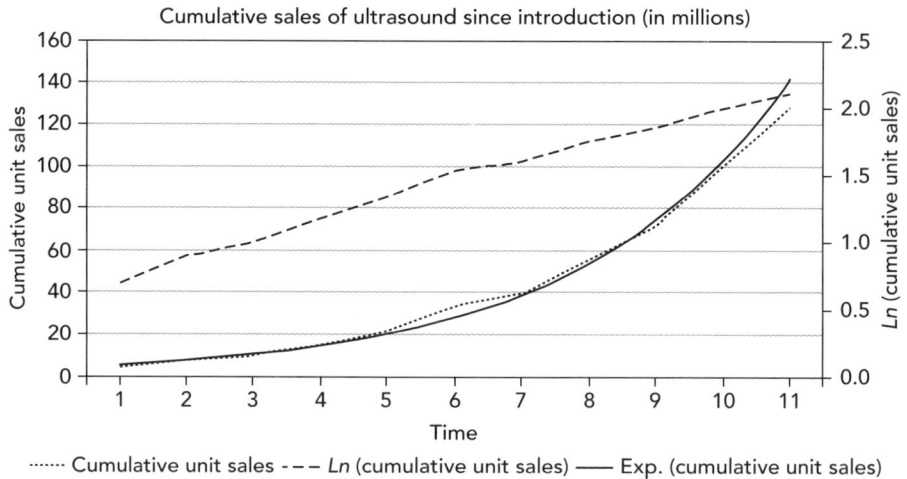

FIGURE 9.4. An example of an exponential function

One thing to note about this analysis is that the regression line fits almost perfectly. Because of the volume of data used, r squareds of up to 99% are possible, as compared with the r squareds of 20% to 30% one finds when developing a true predictive model. This is because we are looking at the adoption of a new product several years after its launch. If a true predictive model were constructed, wherein the same analysis of cumulative ultrasound sales was conducted in year two, it would be difficult to predict what would happen in years three, four, or five, because r squared breaks down at that point.

What does this have to do with logistic regressions? Consider the dashed line in **figure 9.4**, which represents the natural log of cumulative sales at each time period x. The line is nearly straight, meaning a linear regression analysis could produce an accurate function describing the data. In other words, a **logistic transformation** of exponentially distributed data allows you to view the outputs of the regression in the same way you would a linear regression. In algebraic terms, if $y = 4.0858e^{0.3225x}$, the natural log of y will equal $4.0858 + 3.225x$, a linear function where the intercept is 4.0858 and the slope is 3.225.

To return to our example of your friend deciding whether to fly to Miami, the airline would like to see a linear value function in order to get a sense of the relationship between aspects of the flight's utility and customer choice; as in linear regressions, this will help the airline figure out which aspects to manipulate to increase unit

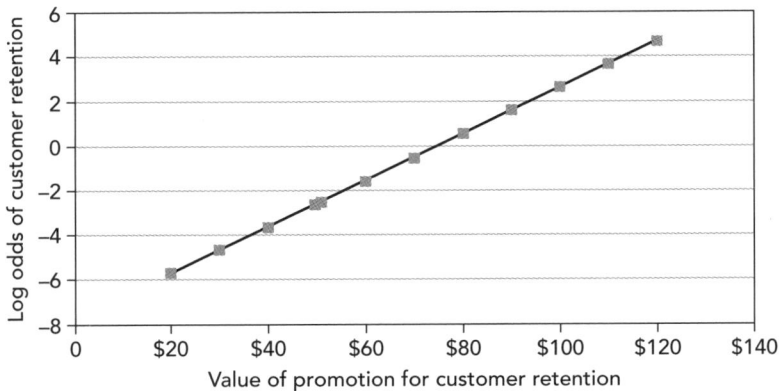

FIGURE 9.5. Log odds function

sales. If we are to transform the S-shaped logistic function in **figure 9.3** to a linear function via the natural log, we will find the **log odds function**, which is

$$Ln\left(\frac{p}{1-p}\right) = a + b_1 X.$$

(See **figure 9.5**.) This is equivalent to the value function.

Essentially, we have assumed there is a linear value function—or utility function—underlying your friend's decision to buy a plane ticket. We have then transformed that value function into something useful about the chances they will decide to buy or not, by mapping the utilities to consumer choices about buying at each utility value. Therefore, the critical output of a logistic regression is the probability, or percentage chance, a customer will stay with a company or leave the company, and that probability is defined in terms of the value the customer places on the company's product.

HYPOTHETICAL CASE: ASSESSING VIDEO GAME PURCHASERS

Let's consider another example to see how a marketing manager can use logistic regression techniques to find useful information about customer behavior. Consider the data in **table 9.1**, which tally the number of Xbox game sales through Best Buy's

TABLE 9.1. Sales of Xbox games through Best Buy's mobile app

SKU	Game	Num sales	AB median	Browsetime	New	Regular price	Customer review count	Customer review average
1004622	Sniper: Ghost Warrior—Xbox 360	53	1	(0.00017)	0	$19.99	7	3.4
1010544	Monopoly Streets—Xbox 360	12	1	(0.00285)	0	$29.99	3	4
1011067	MySims SkyHeroes—Xbox 360	3	1	(0.00157)	0	$19.99	1	2
1011491	FIFA Soccer 11—Xbox 360	85	1	(479.80822)	0	$12.99	18	4.6
1011831	Hasbro Family Game Night 3—Xbox 360	6	1	0.00094	0	$9.99	2	3.5
1012721	The Sims 3—Xbox 360	140	1	(0.00031)	0	$19.99	13	3.8
1012876	Two Worlds II—Xbox 360	5	1	0.00047	0	$39.99	8	3.4
1013666	Call of Duty: The War Collection—Xbox 360	41	1	0.00115	0	$68.18	2	4.5
1014064	Castlevania: Lords of Shadow—Xbox 360	15	1	(0.00235)	0	$7.99	4	4.8
1032361	Need for Speed: Hot Pursuit—Xbox 360	168	1	(0.00039)	0	$19.99	45	4.2
1052221	Marvel vs. Capcom 3: Fate of Two Worlds—Xbox 360	28	1	(0.00092)	0	$19.99	11	4

Source: Data from Kaggle, "Data Mining Hackathon on BIG DATA (7GB) Best Buy Mobile Web Site," http://www.kaggle.com/c/acm-sf-chapter-hackathon-big (accessed Nov. 5, 2013).

mobile app, as reported by Kaggle, a user-generated business analytics community (see https://www.kaggle.com).

Each of the games shown in this data set boasts above-median sales compared with the other games available. In other words, a dummy variable has been set: "above-median sales" is represented by 1, and "below-median sales" is represented by 0. Now, which independent variables shown in the chart (time browsed, whether the game is new, price, number of reviews, and review average) are good predictors of 1—that is, above-median sales?

The output of a logistic regression of these data (**tables 9.2** and **9.3**) looks similar to the output of a linear regression, and the most important data points, in addition to the coefficients, are r squared and p-value; other predictors of accuracy and significance go by a variety of names. The abbreviations that appear in these outputs are easily available in any basic statistics book; for convenience and review, they are as follows: Nrx_ind is popularity of video games, equal to 1 if the game sales are above median, and 0 otherwise; DF is degrees of freedom; AIC is Akaike Information Criteria; SBC is Schwartz Bayesian Information Criteria; SE is standard error; and $p > \text{Chi}^2$ means probability greater than Wald Chi Square or p-value.

The key difference in the logistic regression output, as opposed to a linear regression output, is that the coefficients are not interpreted as such. In order for the coefficients to add value to your analysis, you must calculate the odds ratio.

To do this, let us consider the logistic regression output in **table 9.2** and the log odds ratios presented in **table 9.4**. The **log odds ratio** is defined as the probability of observing an event (p) versus the probability of not observing an event $(1 - p)$. In the context of the choice of games on the mobile app, we are considering the factor by which the log odds of purchasing a game increases when the review for the product increases from 3 to 4. A simple way to calculate this would be to take the exponent of the coefficient of reviews from the logistic regression output. In our case, the coefficient of reviews equals 0.399. So the log odds will increase by a factor of 1.49, or 149% ($\exp[0.399]$), when the review average for a product increases by one unit.

Therefore, if a logistic regression yields a coefficient b of 2.303, the odds ratio says that for every one-unit increase in the independent variable (e.g., number of promotions), the odds that the dependent variable will be equal to 1 (e.g., the product is purchased) will increase by a factor determined by taking the exponent of the coefficient: $e^b = e^{2.303} = 10$. This is not the same as a direct linear transformation.

TABLE 9.2. Output of logistic regression

Summary statistics

Variable	Categories	Frequencies	Percentage
nrx_ind	0	1128	44.183%
	1	1425	55.817%

Variable	Observations	Observations with missing data	Observations without missing data
Sales calls	2553	0	2553

Minimum	Maximum	Mean	Standard deviation
0.000	12.000	2.396	2.128

Goodness-of-fit statistics (variable nrx_ind)

Statistic	Independent	Full
Observations	2553	2553
Sum of weights	2553.000	2553.000
DF	2552	2551
−2 Log(likelihood)	3504.580	3216.666
R^2(Cox and Snell)	0.000	0.107
AIC	3508.580	3220.666
SBC	3520.270	3232.356
Iterations	0	6

TABLE 9.3. Model estimates

Model parameters (variable abmedian)

Source	Value	SE	Wald Chi Square	$p > \text{Chi}^2$
Intercept	(1.097)	0.502	4.769	0.029
New	(1.595)	1.467	1.182	0.277
Regular price	0.006	0.011	0.279	0.597
Customer review count	0.066	0.030	4.943	0.026
Customer review average	0.399	0.116	11.878	0.001

TABLE 9.4. Log odds ratio and logistic probabilities

		Customer review average = 3	Customer review average = 4
Coefficient of customer review average (b_{review})	0.399		
$\exp(b_{review})$	1.490		
Utility(u) = $a + bx$		0.76	1.159
p(popular game) $= \dfrac{\exp(u_p)}{1+\exp(u_p)}$		0.68	0.76
Difference in probability		0.079	

Note: u is the utility function, which is the sum product of the coefficients and independent variables as provided in table 9.3. We fix all independent variables except customer review average at their sample mean.

So, examining the p-values shown in the far-right column of **table 9.3**, which variables appear to predict whether a game will be a top seller?

Customer review average is the most significant variable, followed by the number of customer reviews. Price is relatively insignificant, in this case most likely due to the fact that the price range of the games is small.

Using the coefficients determined in the regression analysis, the marketing manager can then determine how much the odds of a game being a top seller increase if review average increases by one point (**table 9.4**). In other words, if a customer review average of 3 yields a certain probability of success, what happens if the average increases to 4? On average, the coefficient of customer review (coefficient b, the slope of the line) is 0.399, and the exponent of b is 1.49, which means that a single-point increase in reviews increases the odds of a game being a top seller by a factor of about 1.5.

CONCEPT APPLICATION

Marketing managers often want to predict customer behaviors that are either/or, not distributed across a range of outcomes: buy or don't buy, customer retention versus customer loss, and so on. When only one of two outcomes is possible, if the manager attempts to use a traditional linear regression to examine them, nonsensical predictions can result. A better way to represent consumers' choice behavior is logistic regression. By transforming the value function into a logistic function, the manager can model how the value a consumer places on a product increases with a preferred feature of the product. The critical output of the logistic regression is therefore the increase (or decrease) in the percentage chance a customer will perform a behavior based on a unit increase in a variable correlated with that behavior.

In the following case, you will be reintroduced to a familiar start-up: Retail Relay (Relay), the grocery-delivery company that back in chapter 5 was calculating customer lifetime value (CLV) to help determine how to optimize its promotions to acquire more customers. As you'll recall, CLV is the value to a company of a customer relationship, taking into account estimated future cash flows from a current or a newly acquired customer. Of course, the customer has a choice: whether to stay with Relay or not.

Now, rather than figuring out how to acquire new customers, Relay is interested in predicting and improving its customer retention (a key component in CLV). The case is short, but the opportunities for analysis are rich, given the wealth of customer data the company has collected (available to you via http://store.darden.virginia.edu /marketing-analytics-supplements).

As is explained in the case, Relay has split its customer-level data into two sets, "train" and "test."

- First, use the Relay train data to develop a model to predict customer retention. Use logistic regression to predict the dependent variable *retained*, along with any combination of the independent variables available in the data to obtain a model with the best predictive ability and usability. Feel free to use different transformations and combinations of the independent variables.
- As you develop your model, consider the cross-sectional and summary nature of the data. You have only one observation per customer that summarizes their entire relationship with Relay. What are the consequences of this for predicting retention using variables such as *Total # of emails*?
- Once you have the best model that you can find, turn to the company's test data. Using the coefficients you obtained from the model you made using the train data, predict retention now in the test data. Name this predicted retention value *pretain*.
- Finally, calculate the hit rate, or the percentage of matches between the value of *pretain* and *retained* in the test data.
- Based on your analyses, what are your recommendations to Relay for improving customer retention?

CASE: RELAY, REVISITED

Because Relay was operating like a start-up, with all employees scrambling around to get everything done in a time of rapid growth, some important business processes had been left unattended. One of the processes that had received little attention was how to use the customer-level purchase information in its database to improve customer retention.

Relay understood that many of its existing customers were not only spending money with Relay, but also purchasing some of their grocery products from other vendors. This kind of customer behavior was evident from even a casual examination of Relay's customer-level purchase data. Some customers purchased from the company infrequently and sporadically. Clearly, these customers must be shopping somewhere else during the interludes between their Relay purchases. Since customers did not sign up for a subscription plan, Relay could never be certain if a customer stopped purchasing from Relay (that is, churned), or if they were merely dormant for a while. To overcome this challenge, Relay used a rule of thumb that classified customers as churned if their dormancy duration was more than two standard deviations above their mean interpurchase time. For example, for a customer whose mean interpurchase time was two months and standard deviation in interpurchase time was three months, Relay would classify this customer as churned if their dormancy duration was more than eight months.

Churned customers represented a loss of potential profit, and management believed that this loss was substantial. Yet Relay had not taken the time and energy to fully leverage its customer-level transaction data—an important customer-relationship asset—to improve customer retention. Because customers submitted their orders through Relay's website, Relay had a large and detailed database of customer orders. Among other information, when a customer placed an order, Relay knew which customer made the order, what items that customer ordered, and the customer's entire order history, including the dates and times of these orders. Relay decided to use the customer-level purchase data to better understand the factors that influenced customer retention. Were there any distinct characteristics of the retained customers that could instruct Relay about how to increase the retention of its not-so-regular customers?

Relay management knew that somewhere in these data lay the key to unlocking more of its current customers' grocery dollars. Now, it needed to dig until it found

TABLE 9.5. **Description of customer summary file**

Variable	Description
custid	Computer-generated ID to identify customers throughout the database
retained	1 if customer is assumed to be retained; 0 otherwise
created	Date when the contact was created in the database—when the customer joined
firstorder	Date when the customer placed first order
lastorder	Date when the customer placed last order
esent	Number of emails sent
eopenrate	Number of emails opened divided by number of emails sent
eclickrate	Number of emails clicked divided by number of emails sent
avgorder	Average order size for the customer
ordfreq	Number of orders divided by customer tenure
paperless	1 if customer subscribed for paperless communication (only online)
refill	1 if customer subscribed for automatic refill
doorstep	1 if customer subscribed for doorstep delivery
train	1 if customer is in the training database
favday	Customer's favorite delivery day
city	City where the customer resides

Source: Data from Retail Relay, used with permission.

that key. Would a logistic regression analysis reveal the keys to improving customer retention? To begin this process, Relay decided to explore the customer summary file described in **table 9.5**. To test the performance of its predictive model, Relay randomly split its customers into a "train" data set and a "test" data set (see http://store .darden.virginia.edu/marketing-analytics-supplements). The train data set was used to identify the best-fitting model to predict retention. The test data set was used to evaluate the accuracy of the predictions of the model identified in the train data set.

CONCLUSION

Marketing managers analyze historical data in order to find the factors that affect a desired outcome (like sales). Regression analyses are some of the most useful ways to represent data in a way that reveals those important relationships between aspects of a product or promotion and a desired outcome. And when data are either/or information, like customer choice, the best way to find these all-important relationships is to use logistic regression.

10

Recommendation Systems

You're ready to Netflix and chill. You pull up your browser and scroll through the new releases on Netflix.com. Nothing looks interesting. You turn your attention to the recommended titles, the "Top Picks" selected just for you. And there it is—the classic film you'd forgotten you wanted to see but has always been at the top of your to-watch list.

Netflix Top Picks, Amazon recommendations, the iTunes Genius button. They all have one thing in common: they are driven by clever algorithms that use a technique known as collaborative filtering.

Collaborative filtering is the process by which a firm like Netflix, Inc. (Netflix) generates predictions about a single user's preferences, using data taken from a large number of users. Just how much does Netflix depend on collaborative filtering? In January 2000, Netflix introduced its recommendation system, Cinematch, and just three years later, Cinematch was generating more than half of the firm's traffic.

DEFINING COLLABORATIVE FILTERING

Collaborative filtering is a term often encountered in machine learning operations. It is used by a variety of digital companies that recommend additional products to existing customers. Typically, the companies use one of two basic methods of collaborative filtering: slope one or ordinal logit.

The objective of collaborative filtering can be explained using a simple example. Imagine you have two doctors, each of whom has eaten an apple (**figure 10.1**). Doctor 1 has gone on to eat a strawberry. Doctor 2 is also considering eating an additional item. At its core, collaborative filtering attempts to guess what doctor 2 is going to eat next.

Because doctor 1 ate an apple and then a strawberry, and doctor 2, who shares a number of traits with doctor 1 (e.g., profession, age), also had an apple, we might

FIGURE 10.1. What doctors eat

guess he will eat a strawberry next. Or maybe he will eat another type of fruit, such as a banana. Companies like Netflix take the same intuition and apply it on a large scale to predict their customers' next moves.

A single prediction based on two doctors and two products represents a simple collaborative filtering calculation, but companies like Netflix must look at data from more than 100 million customers over almost 20,000 products. They require a collaborative filtering algorithm capable of running a real-time automated system in little computational time.

A firm uses preferences data—the fact that its customers enjoy eating apples and strawberries, for example—in one of two ways to arrive at predictions about what individual consumers will enjoy. One method, the **slope one strategy**, is nonparametric and does not assume a model or distribution. The algorithm simply performs calculations and makes predictions. Slope one users are not sure why their customers prefer what they prefer—slope one is a purely predictive nonparametric model that does not consider any characteristics of the customer or the product when making recommendations.

The second method, which is based on a parametric model, is known as an **ordinal logistic regression**, or **ordinal logit** model. If a binomial logit model predicts whether a customer will purchase a product or not, and a multinomial logit regression determines which of several brands a customer might buy, an ordinal logit model predicts the rating a customer would give to each of the brands under examination.

Slope One

The slope one strategy of collaborative filtering takes a nonparametric approach, meaning it treats all the available data in the same way. Imagine you are going to make a calculation to predict a consumer's rating for a movie they have not seen. Just as in the example of the two doctors, user 1 has watched two movies, then has assigned those movies ratings of 2 and 2.5 on a scale of 1 to 5, with 1 being the lowest rating and 5 being the highest (**table 10.1**).

User 2 has watched only one movie—the same movie as one of the films watched by user 1. If we assume user 2 is like user 1, we expect user 2 to like movie B more than movie A. This is the nonparametric intuition used in the slope one method. We take the difference between user 1's ratings of the two movies (we'll call this difference b) and add it to user 2's rating of movie A (we'll call this rating x) to arrive at user 2's likely rating of movie B:

$$f(x) = x + b, \text{ so}$$

User 2 rating for movie B $= 3 + (2.5 - 2) = 3.5$.

User 2's likely rating for movie B is 3.5, equal to user 2's rating of 3 for movie A, plus the difference between user 1's ratings for movie A and for movie B $(2.5 - 2 = 0.5)$. This is a simple example of a slope one calculation. The problem quickly becomes complex as we consider a third user and third movie (**table 10.2**).

Scott, Harry, and Mary have watched and rated some combination of movies A, B, and C. Scott is an avid movie watcher, having seen all three films. Harry has watched movies A and B; Mary has watched movies B and C. We would like to predict Mary's

TABLE 10.1. Two customers rating two movies

User	Movie A	Movie B
1	2	2.5
2	3	?

TABLE 10.2. Three customers rating three movies

User	Movie A	Movie B	Movie C
Scott	4	2	1
Harry	2	3	?
Mary	?	1	4

rating for movie A based on these data. One way to make this prediction is to look at the average difference between ratings for movies A and B. Scott rates movie A 2 points more than movie B. Harry rates movie A 1 point less than movie B. The average difference between ratings of the two films is therefore 0.5.

To predict Mary's score for movie A, we take her rating for movie B and add the average difference of ratings for movies A and B based on Scott and Harry's ratings. We therefore predict Mary will rate movie A as 1.5:

$$f(x) = x + b.$$

Average difference between movies A and B $= (2 + (-1)) / 2 = 0.5$, so

Predicted score of movie A for Mary $= 1 + 0.5 = 1.5$.

We might also predict Mary's rating for movie A by comparing ratings for movies C and A, both of which Scott has already rated. Scott likes movie A 3 points more than movie C. Using this comparison, Mary's predicted score for movie A would be 3 points greater than her rating for movie C:

Difference between Scott's ratings of movies A and C $= 4 - 1 = 3$, so

Predicted score of movie A for Mary $= 4 + 3 = 7$.

Which of the predictions is more accurate? Can we combine them to generate a prediction even more accurate than the two alone?

Yes: we can use **weighted averages** to combine the ratings. Using the slope one collaborative filtering strategy, we have two sources from which to predict Mary's score for movie A when we use movies A and B: Scott and Harry. We have only one

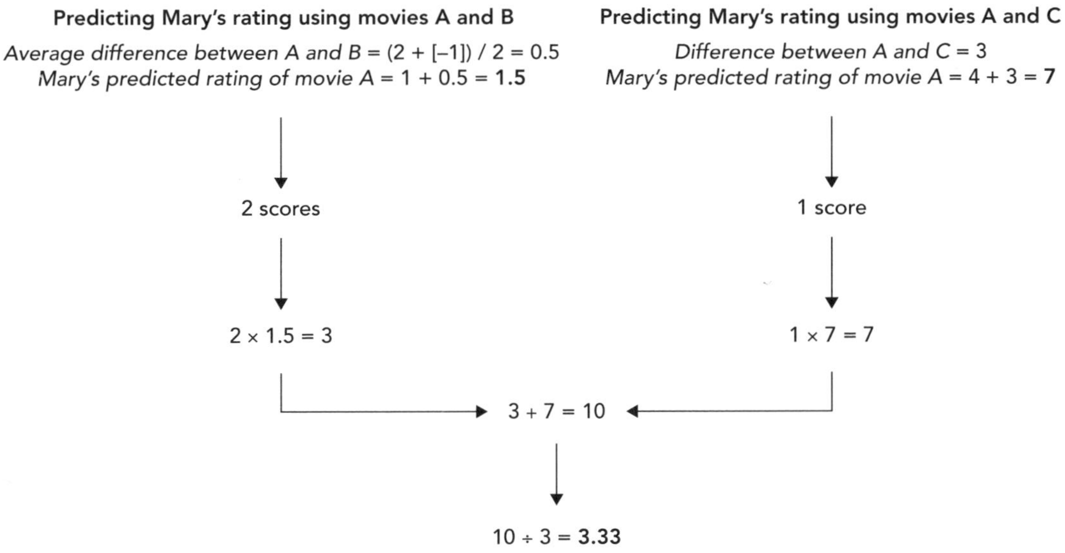

Predicting Mary's rating using movies A and B

Average difference between A and B = (2 + [–1]) / 2 = 0.5
Mary's predicted rating of movie A = 1 + 0.5 = 1.5

Predicting Mary's rating using movies A and C

Difference between A and C = 3
Mary's predicted rating of movie A = 4 + 3 = 7

2 scores

1 score

2 × 1.5 = 3

1 × 7 = 7

3 + 7 = 10

10 ÷ 3 = **3.33**

FIGURE 10.2. Predicting Mary's rating using combined scores

source when predicting Mary's rating for movie A using movies A and C: Scott. To combine the two predictions, we give the first prediction a weight of 2 and the second prediction a weight of 1, arriving at a combined rating of 3.33 (**figure 10.2**).

The weighted-average approach relies on the intuition that we are more confident in our comparisons when we have multiple sources. The first rating is weighted more heavily than the second because we can draw on ratings from both Scott and Harry, rather than only on Scott's.

The weighted-average approach significantly improves slope one collaborative filtering algorithms, particularly as the number of reference points increases. One way to further improve the algorithm would be to look at the correlation coefficients between the users to determine how predictive one is for another. For example, given a large number of ratings from Scott, Harry, and Mary, we might determine that Mary's predictions are more closely correlated with Scott's than with Harry's. We would then weight Scott's existing ratings more highly than Harry's when using them to predict ratings for Mary.

In each of these examples, we treat each customer as if they are the same, meaning we do not recognize that they have certain traits that are more closely aligned with some fellow customers than with others. Thus we might also improve our slope one collaborative filtering algorithm by performing a K-means cluster analysis (see chapter 2) and making predictions using only customers belonging to the same cluster.

Ordinal Logit

Whereas the slope one strategy represents a nonparametric way to drive a recommendation engine, ordinal logit is a parametric model–based strategy. The model considers the attributes of each item in the data set to understand what fuels consumer ratings, then makes predictions based on similarities.

Consider the movie rating data set known as MovieLens, developed by a group at the University of Minnesota. The group has made the data available to people all over the world to develop recommendation algorithms. **Table 10.3** provides the top-10 movies from the MovieLens database in 2016.

How can we use the ordinal logit strategy to make predictions using the Movie-Lens data?

First, it is important to keep in mind that the ordinal logit strategy is effective when the data set represents a rating scale satisfying the proportional odds assumption. In other words, if we have a rating scale from 1 to 5, we know 5 is greater than 4, 3 is greater than 2, and so on. In a standard numeric series, the difference between each rating is 1. But for a ratings scale like the one used by Netflix, this is not always the case. Individuals deciding whether a movie should receive a 4 or a 5 might set the

TABLE 10.3. **MovieLens top 10 (2016)**

Item	Average rating	Number of ratings	Item info
50	4.36	484	*Star Wars (1977)*
181	4.01	422	*Return of the Jedi (1983)*
258	3.82	402	*Contact (1997)*
100	4.11	395	*Fargo (1996)*
294	3.16	394	*Liar Liar (1997)*
288	3.45	391	*Scream (1996)*
286	3.64	388	*English Patient, The (1996)*
1	3.89	383	*Toy Story (1995)*
121	3.39	353	*Independence Day (1996)*
300	3.66	352	*Air Force One (1997)*

Source: Data from "MovieLens 100K Dataset," MovieLens Datasets, https://grouplens.org/datasets/movielens/ (accessed Aug. 8, 2019).

difference at closer to 2 points, as 5 is a premium rating. The difference between 3 and 4 might be 1.5, and the consumer might see little difference among scores below 3. The **proportional odds assumption** applies to both of these situations: even if the intercepts are different between levels, the coefficients and drivers of ratings are the same for all levels, so in the second case—the Netflix ratings—the different jumps from 1 to 2 and from 2 to 3 are determined by the intercepts.

The objective of any logistic regression in marketing analytics is to represent consumers' choice behavior. Recall from chapter 9 that the value consumers place on products typically does not increase linearly with increases in preferred features, but instead follows an S-shaped curve. The S curve shows how consumers make decisions in real-life situations. When an airline offers a small discount on a flight to Miami, a few new consumers might decide to buy a ticket. As the discount increases, many more consumers are likely to purchase the flight; however, the discount will eventually reach an upper threshold where the number of new consumers tapers off.

The proportional odds assumption can also be explained through an S curve (**figure 10.3**). The assumption dictates that for a rating scale of 1 to 5, the log of the odds of giving a particular rating is equal to the log of that rating's probability over the sum of all the probabilities for all ratings. For a rating scale of 1 to 5, the log of the odds of rating at each level are therefore:

$$1 = log \{p1 \ / \ [p1 + p2 + p3 + p4 + p5]\}.$$

$$2 = log \{p1 + p2] \ / \ [p1 + p2 + p3 + p4 + p5]\}.$$

$$3 = log \{p1 + p2 + p3] \ / \ [p1 + p2 + p3 + p4 + p5]\}.$$

$$4 = log \{p1 + p2 + p3 + p4] \ / \ [p1 + p2 + p3 + p4 + p5]\}.$$

$$5 = log \{p1 + p2 + p3 + p4 + p5] \ / \ [p1 + p2 + p3 + p4 + p5]\}.$$

Each probability is obtained from a logit function. The logit function provides the S-shaped curve that better represents people's choices in the context of movie ratings. The logit function for $p1$ is provided as:

$$p1 = logit \ (Xb) = exp(intercept \ 1 - Xb) \ / \ [1 + exp(intercept \ 1 - Xb)].$$

logit (x) = exp(x) / [1 + exp(x)]

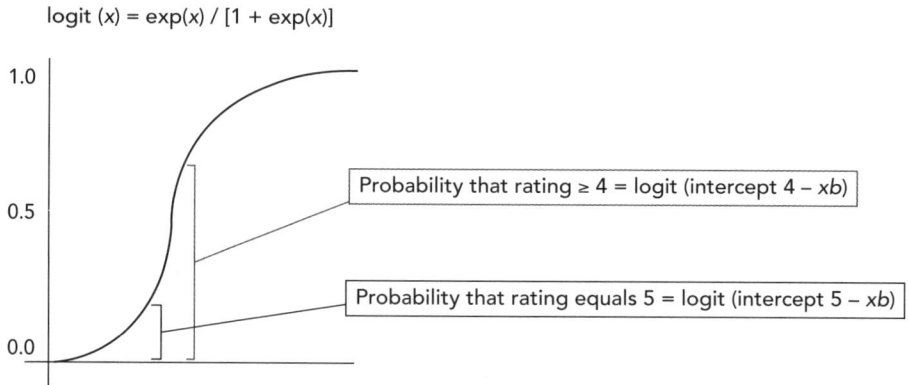

FIGURE 10.3. Proportional odds assumption ratings predictions

Xb here refers to the set of coefficients and predictor variables used in the ordinal logit. **Intercepts** in the ordinal logit model represent cutoffs between rating levels.

Ordinal data is the most frequently seen data type in the social sciences.[1] Examples include yes-maybe-no scales, Likert scales, always-frequently-rarely-sometimes-never series, educational achievement (no high school diploma, high school diploma, some college, bachelor's degree, master's degree, doctoral degree), free and reduced school lunch, income levels, and low-medium-high questions.

Using the data from MovieLens, we can run an ordinal logistic regression using consumer age and type of movie (action, adventure, animation, children's, comedy, drama) as the independent variables. *Xb* represents the utility of a movie rating, which includes the independent variables of consumer characteristics and movie type. As such, *Xb* forms the basis for the probability of a particular consumer giving a particular rating. The dependent variable, then, is the rating a customer gives a movie.

$$Xb = 0.004 \times \text{Age} - 0.15 \times \text{Action} + 0.13 \times \text{Adventure} + 0.58 \times$$
$$\text{Animation} - 0.36 \times \text{Children's} - 0.11 \times \text{Comedy} +$$
$$0.16 \times \text{Crime} + 0.46 \times \text{Documentary} + 0.39 \times \text{Drama}.$$

Table 10.4 shows the coefficients for each of our independent variables. Consumers in the data set show the least affinity for children's movies and the highest affinity for animated movies.

Below the coefficients for each of the independent variables, **table 10.4** includes values for four intercepts. The intercepts represent the four cutoffs between each level

TABLE 10.4. Ordinal logistic regression results

Source	Coefficient value	t-value
Action	−0.15	−8.68
Adventure	0.13	6.35
Animation	0.58	14.55
Children's	−0.36	−12.27
Comedy	−0.11	−6.72
Crime	0.16	7.31
Documentary	0.46	6.74
Drama	0.39	24.11
1/2	−2.55	−121.07
2/3	−1.35	−73.52
3/4	0.01	0.47
4/5	1.57	84.98

of the 5-point rating scale. The baseline, when all the intercepts are zero, is the cutoff for rating 1. Intercepts for ratings of 2, 3, 4, and 5 are also included. Thus the perceived difference between ratings 1 and 2 is a function of −2.55. The results show that all the independent variables and intercepts other than the intercept 3/4 are significant at $p < 0.10$.

How do we make predictions using the data and ordinal logit regression? The probability of each rating is the log of the appropriate intercept minus Xb, where Xb is the utility described by the sum of our independent variables and coefficients. Remember that Logit $(x) = \exp(x) / (1 + \exp(x))$.

Next, we find the probability that the rating equals 5, 4, 3, 2, and 1, and determine which is most likely to occur:

Probability of 5 = logit (intercept 5 − Xb).

Probability of 4 = logit (intercept 4 − Xb) − logit (intercept 5 − Xb).

Probability of 3 = logit (intercept 3 − Xb) − logit (intercept 4 − Xb).

Probability of 2 = logit (intercept 3 − Xb) − logit (intercept 2 − Xb).

Probability of 1 = logit (intercept 2 − Xb).

Alternative Least Squares

The alternative least squares technique is a robust collaborative filtering method that provides accurate, personalized predictions. It is particularly useful in overcoming two challenges that recommendation systems face, both related to sparse data.

The first of these is the **cold start problem**: this occurs when a recommendation system lacks data to make predictions. For recommendation systems like the one used by Netflix, the cold start problem is an issue for products newly added to the database and, more critically, for new users for whom no data are available.[2] The second is **popularity bias**, which arises when popular movies are recommended frequently while less popular, niche films are recommended rarely or not at all.

For new items like movies, we can use product characteristics (genre, actors, directors, and so on) to align them with similar films and make appropriate recommendations.[3] If a new *Star Wars* film joins the database, for example, we can base users' preferences on how they have reacted to previous *Star Wars* installments or other science fiction movies. However, this solution does not apply to niche films that are rarely recommended and are not obviously similar to other movies that are recommended more frequently.

For unknown users, the simplest strategy to overcome the cold start problem is to apply some baseline using popular titles or any available demographic data. We might also be able to use social network data, if available, for new users.[4] Shortly after a user joins a site like Netflix, the recommendation system can use click history to begin building preference data.[5]

Suppose we are attempting to provide recommendations for Mary in the slope one problem, but she has not yet watched any movies. If we assume Mary's preferences are aligned with those of Scott and Harry, we can take the average of their ratings to make predictions. If we can apply relevant demographic or social media data to Mary, we might be able to align her more closely with either Scott or Harry, thereby making more accurate predictions.

The **alternative least squares** method of building a recommendation system uses matrix factorization, which is a way to find hidden features of users or movies that might then predict future ratings. Finding these features allows the system to overcome a number of deficiencies in previous algorithms, including popularity bias and the cold start problem.[6] The Netflix data set, while robust, is both extremely large and relatively sparse, with only about 1% of the potential user-movie data points avail-

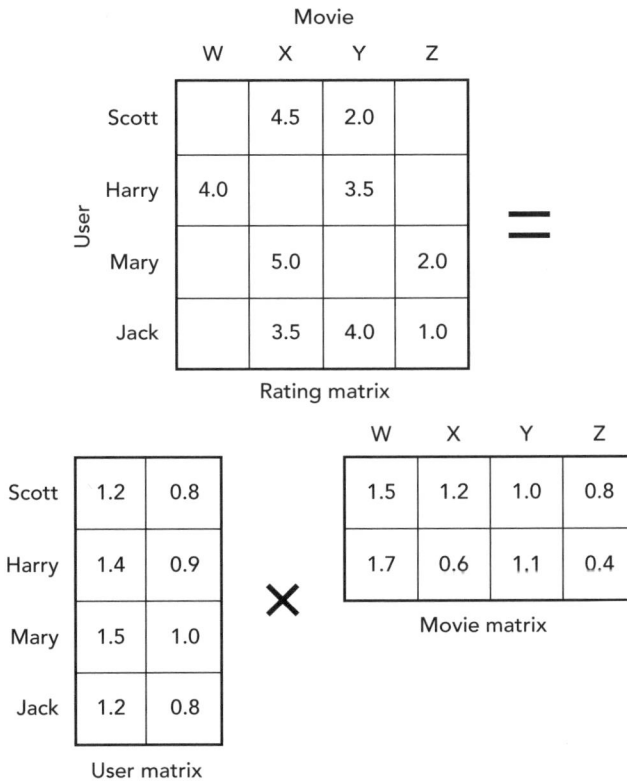

FIGURE 10.4. Matrix factorization

able. Furthermore, the ratings provided by users are inherently noisy,[7] because the ratings people report often don't reflect their actual behavior. Matrix factorization in the alternative least squares method is a way to fill in the missing data in order to generate likely ratings (and therefore accurate recommendations).

Matrix factorization means finding factors of the original matrix, or in other words, two or more matrices that, when multiplied, result in the original matrix. A matrix—like the one describing Scott's, Harry's, and Mary's ratings for movies (see **table 10.2**)—can be broken down, or factorized, into matrices of the users and films. See **figure 10.4** for an example of matrix factorization.

The goal is to predict the values of the missing ratings: Scott's rating for movies W and Z, and so on. To do that, we factorize the Rating matrix into a User matrix and a Movie matrix. These matrices yield latent factors of the users and films. **Latent factors** are lower-level characteristics that are not at first obvious but become clear through the factorization process, and which can then help fill in the missing data in the original matrix. The latent factors for the User matrix, for example, might be user age or preference for a particular actor. Similarly, Movie matrix breaks down each film by its latent factors, which might turn out to be features like genre, Oscar winner, or presence of a particular actor.

The alternative least squares method has four steps:

1. Initialize Movie matrix by placing the movie's average rating in the first row and random numbers in the remaining rows.
2. Fix Movie matrix, solving User matrix by minimizing the objective function, or in other words, by minimizing the difference between the Rating matrix and the product of User matrix and Movie matrix. (Remember that factorization means finding two matrices that are factors of the original matrix.)
3. Fix User matrix, solving Movie matrix by minimizing the objective function.
4. Repeat steps 2 and 3 until a stopping criterion set by the data scientist is reached. For example, a stopping criterion might be when the change in objective function is less than 0.01% in the last 100 iterations.

Once the stopping criterion is reached, the latent factors will have been identified, allowing Netflix to recommend movies to users based on those previously hidden features.

COLLABORATIVE FILTERING'S OUTSIZE VALUE

Netflix has pioneered collaborative filtering in two ways, each with distinct advantages for the company. The first of these uses may be familiar: collaborative filtering enables Netflix to make the recommendations that drive customers to consume more existing products similar to those they already like. The other way Netflix uses collaborative filtering may be a little more surprising: through insights derived from collaborative filtering, the company sources and develops new content that is tailored to its customers' tastes, enabling it to expand its portfolio of products. With all the data it has amassed about viewers' preferences, Netflix no longer has to guess what kind of original content will be successful. Collaborative filtering tells the company what its customers will like before they know themselves.

When a production team pitched a show called *House of Cards* in 2011,[8] Netflix saw value where others did not. Several networks and online video outlets had declined to buy the show, but through collaborative filtering, Netflix determined that *House of Cards* had many of the elements prized by its customers—the right actors, favored directors, the perfect genre. Netflix also knew its customers rated the BBC version of the show relatively highly. The online streaming service therefore jumped on the opportunity to buy *House of Cards*, acquiring one of its biggest hits at well below market value.

Amazon has also shown high regard for collaborative filtering engines, using them to inform customers what other individuals have purchased after buying certain items. Amazon's collaborative filtering–based recommendation system allows consumers to search efficiently for products and add more to their purchase lists.

But how exactly can we determine the value of collaborative filtering, beyond making purchase recommendations and understanding consumers' likelihood of buying goods? Imagine Disney announces *Star Wars* is up for sale. How could a service like Netflix determine what to pay for the property? Collaborative filtering strikes again.

Netflix might begin by determining its customers' expected viewing time of *Star Wars* as a portion of their total viewing time: that is, *Star Wars'* expected share of viewing time. Netflix could then look at movies similar to *Star Wars* and impute their viewership share, adjusting it based on *Star Wars'* relative consumer ratings strength. At the core of this strategy is knowing which movies are similar to *Star Wars*. A collaborative filtering recommendation engine enables Netflix to identify which films are most similar, and therefore which to use to price the franchise. The value of *Star Wars* for a streaming service like Netflix might therefore be determined by multiplying viewers' content budget by the ratio of expected *Star Wars* viewing time to total viewing time.

One of the challenges for companies developing recommendation engines based on collaborative filtering is gathering data—urging customers to rate the products they buy or movies they watch. Firms like Netflix can partially overcome this problem by also using various consumer habits to help develop their algorithms. Do customers watch certain movies in a single viewing session, or do they go back two or three times to complete a film? On what devices are they viewing movies? Such habits can be used as proxies for ratings and improve collaborative filtering algorithms.

Collaborative filtering, whether based on a nonparametric slope one algorithm or a model-based algorithm like ordinal logit, is an essential tool for companies like Netflix, iTunes, Amazon, and Spotify. The slope one strategy is fast but less accurate than an ordinal logit model, which takes time to build but provides context for why consumers make decisions. To improve collaborative filtering algorithms even further, companies can use even more consumer data about viewing habits as proxies for ratings, and they can cluster consumers within segments.

CONCEPT APPLICATION

As a marketing manager, you likely won't be running regressions or factorizing matrices yourself: you can ask your favorite data scientist to perform these feats. However, to be an effective manager, it is essential that you understand the bigger picture. You need to know what tools are available to you: as businesses are increasingly online, recommendation systems are becoming smarter, more efficient, and more expected by consumers. If you understand the potential of collaborative filtering to create value for your customers, you can suggest, invest in, and implement the right approach for your business and marketing goals. Likewise, after your data scientist friend has built a slope one or ordinal logit model and generated predictions, your understanding of those strategies will enable you to interpret the data and place your analysis in a larger context, in order to offer concrete product design recommendations.

Keep this in mind as you consider the case that follows. Netflix relies on a digital business model that combines content and technology. The traditional barriers to entry for video-rental stores (heavy up-front capital investment in real estate, for example) are now obsolete, and a firm delivering video content now needs to obtain licensing deals with content providers and build a streaming website. A broad question emerges:

- What are the sources of sustainable competitive advantage (SCA) to a video service, when the traditional barriers to entry are removed?

As Hamilton Helmer posits in 7 *Powers: The Foundations of Business Strategy*,[9] competitive advantage derives from seven sources: (1) **scale economies**, meaning a reduction in unit costs of production as a firm's market share increases; (2) **network economies**, including same-side effects, in which the value of a network to a customer increases as more customers participate in it, and cross-side effects, in which the value of a network for another firm using it (like an advertiser on Google) increases as more customers participate in it; (3) **counter positioning**, or changing a business model to bring in new customers or deliver better value to existing customers; (4) **switching costs**, the difficulty for customers of changing services; (5) **branding**;

(6) **cornered resources**, or unique resources monopolized by a company; and (7) **process power**, or a unique approach to business.

This case relies on publicly available financial data for Netflix, and gives you the opportunity to draw on various learnings from this and other chapters in this book. Netflix has quickly grown to dominate the subscription-based and streaming video market. Now it has a potential competitor: Disney. Put yourself in the shoes of a Netflix marketing manager and consider your options.

- What are the keys to Netflix's success? What customer metrics are important for Netflix?
- Why is Disney launching Disney+?
- How can Netflix compete with Disney+, and what are the sources of its competitive advantage?
- What would be an appropriate measure of relative strength for a streaming service?
- How can Netflix improve its value proposition over the customer's life cycle? What are the network effects in the Netflix business model?
- Can both Netflix and Disney+ survive in the streaming industry, or is there room for only one dominant player?
- With so much content available on so many platforms, what would set apart the winners from the losers?
- Is customer discovery of new content an essential aspect of a platform's success?
- Will data and algorithms continue to offer real critical advantages, and in what way(s)?
- What would you recommend Netflix do?

CASE: NETFLIX, INC.: THE MOUSE STRIKES BACK

Mickey Mouse had plans to join the streaming game.

In 2017, the Walt Disney Company (Disney) announced it would launch a competitor to online video purveyors like Netflix in the next several years.[10]

Disney+ would be a paid subscription service offering access to all Disney and Fox Corporation content, along with new shows and movies and including 100% of the Marvel, Lucasfilm, Pixar, and *National Geographic* catalogs. Disney would also house its latest acquisitions, Hulu and ESPN Plus, on its new, web-based streaming platform.

Disney+ was slated for launch in late 2019, and consumers and investors alike were squeaking with excitement. Did Netflix, the dominant player in the streaming-video market in early 2019, have what it took to keep up with its newest competitor? And which of its existing and emerging strategic areas—its recommendation system, global expansion, original content, and so on—would be most critical in delivering value in the short and long term?

A Technological History

The Traditional Retail Rental Store

With the advent of videotape, acceptance of the VHS cassette standard, and subsequent affordability of home videocassette players in the 1980s, the movie-rental business exploded. By the 1990s, the majority of market share had consolidated to a few participants with similar business models competing on selection, price, and location. National chains, such as Blockbuster and Hollywood Video, grew by staking claims in strategically located, population-dense areas. By 1990, Blockbuster professed to have a store within a 10-minute drive of 70% of the US population.

Movie rental required customers to leave their homes with the intention of renting, then make a spontaneous decision based on what was available at the video-rental store. The cost of a video rental ranged from $3.00 per week for older movies to $6.00 per three days for new releases. Small mom-and-pop stores typically had a collection of a few hundred videos for rent; a Blockbuster store had about 2,500. Videos paid for themselves after 13 rentals, so films with mass appeal were the norm; nearly 70% of all films rented at Blockbuster were new releases. Limited selection and stock-outs were common concerns, as was the relative convenience of store hours.

Late returns were a thorny problem: a movie could not be rented to a new customer until it was back on the shelf, and a scarcity of titles might deter customers from returning. So video stores charged late fees, which monetized the delay and encouraged prompt returns. In reality, as one commentator noted, late fees called attention to customer failure, in the manner of "a disapproving librarian tallying up 35 cents in overdue fines while floating the unspoken accusation you were irresponsible on top of everything else."[11] When Blockbuster eventually dropped many forms of late fees, the move resulted in a boost to revenue of $400 million. The brick-and-mortar value proposition was eroding.

DVD by Mail

DVD mail service started to gain popularity in the early 2000s. A subscribing customer would select a movie on a website, and a DVD would arrive at their home in about one business day. The customer could keep the DVD as long as they liked, then mail it back to the provider in a prepaid envelope. By selecting multiple movies and arranging them in order of priority in an online queue, the customer could ensure prompt delivery of subsequent selections and always have something on hand to watch. Subscription tiers were based on how many movies a customer could receive simultaneously and were priced accordingly, starting at $7.99 per month for one movie at a time from Netflix.

Kiosk Rentals

Movie-rental kiosks, freestanding dispensers of DVDs, began emerging in the early 2000s. They were located in high-traffic areas such as convenience stores, grocery stores, and fast-food restaurants, and they offered extended—sometimes 24-hour—access. Redbox, the dominant player, was founded in 2003 and was originally funded by McDonald's. As of 2012, Redbox claimed to have already rented 1.5 billion movies from 30,000 kiosks nationwide and to operate a kiosk within a five-minute drive of two-thirds of the US population. Its only significant competitor at the time was a much smaller player, Blockbuster's "Blockbuster Express" kiosks. Kiosks revolutionized the rental price point (about $1.00 per night per movie) and changed consumer renting behavior by eliminating the planning ahead required by DVD-by-mail services as well as the need to go to another location as required by rental stores. Plus, 24-hour access freed customers from time constraints. Selection, however, was limited by two major shortfalls: the physical space inside the kiosk and delayed releases to kiosks by movie studios wary of cannibalizing DVD sales.

Video on Demand

The next major technological advancement was video on demand, content distribution via an internet-connected television, computer, or mobile device. The customer selected a movie from an online menu and, within seconds, the movie began streaming to their device. The customer could view the content as it was downloaded, rather than waiting for the complete file. No exchange of a data-storage medium was required, so stock-outs and late fees were avoided, and a significantly larger and more eclectic catalog could be offered.

A Dominant Player

Netflix, which began as a web-based direct mail video-rental service, joined the on-line streaming business in 2010 and soon came to sit at the top of the market. By 2016, it had captured about a third of the worldwide streaming market share, operated in more than 190 countries, and had produced more original series and films than any other media outlet.[12]

Netflix's journey to streaming dominance, however, was not without its failures. When the company announced a plan to split its on-demand video streaming and DVD mail delivery into two businesses and increase the price of its most popular service in 2012, it faced near-universal criticism. Netflix abandoned the plan within a month, having lost 800,000 subscribers and half its stock value (see **figure 10.5**).[13] Netflix faced another steep decline in the third quarter of 2018 when it reported greater losses compared to third-quarter losses in 2017. Some in the popular press speculated that the announcement in August 2017 of Disney's upcoming streaming service also contributed to the decline in Netflix's stock price.[14]

Reed Hastings had founded Netflix in 1997 in Los Gatos, California, after paying $40 in late fees to the local video store for *Apollo 13*, and later asking, "How come movie rentals don't work like a health club, where, whether you use it a lot or a little, you get the same charge?"[15] The key was to let people watch movies whenever they wanted. The Netflix DVD-by-mail model was simple, fast, and convenient: the company claimed it could ship videos to most customers in less than 24 hours. And within two years, Netflix had eliminated late fees. Customers paid a fixed monthly fee of about $16, rented as many as four movies in a single order, and kept films as long as they wanted. Longer rental periods, in fact, lowered Netflix's shipping costs. Customer retention, however, depended on more rentals per month: the more rentals per month, the more value customers placed on the service. As Hastings stated, "If [the customers] rent just two movies a month, they may decide it is not worth it."[16]

The link between number of rentals and customer retention made Netflix's movie recommendation system critical: good recommendations increased queue length, which increased retention and customer lifetime value (CLV; see also chapter 5).

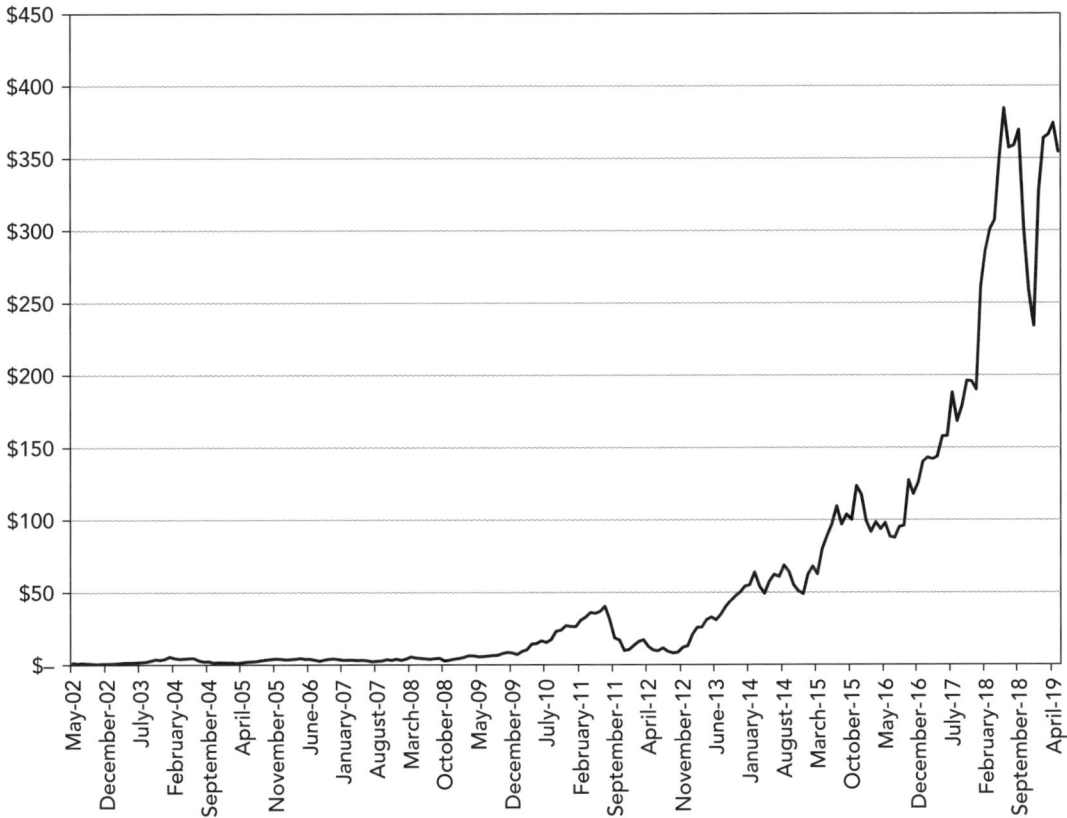

FIGURE 10.5. Netflix stock price from May 2002 to April 2019. (Data from Yahoo! Finance)

Netflix invested significantly in data-mining technology to expand its customer base and reduce reliance on popular films. The firm developed a simple but effective recommendation algorithm, which compared each user's purchases to those of customers with similar tastes, in order to suggest highly rated films and television shows that the user had not yet seen from an extensive catalog (in 2018, it included over 5,500 titles). Netflix typically picked up revenue from a broad distribution of preferences.

As the Netflix catalog grew, its recommendation system grew more robust. In January 2000, Netflix introduced Cinematch, an algorithmic recommendation system. Each customer was prompted to rate movie genres and specific movies on a scale of one to five stars. The program found other customers in the Netflix database with similar preferences and offered a predicted star value for each movie. As customers

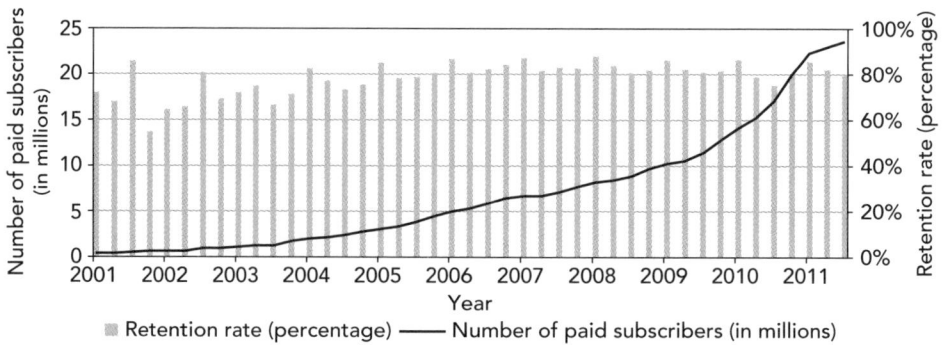

FIGURE 10.6. Paid Netflix subscribers and retention from 2001 to 2011. (Data from Netflix Q1 earnings report, 2012)

rated more films, accuracy improved substantially. "Over 50% of our traffic comes via the recommendation system," Hastings said in 2003. "It requires a lot of database work done in real-time."[17] By 2007, Netflix had close to one billion movie reviews, with customers reviewing an average of 200 movies each.

During its mail-order DVD-focused period, Netflix's CLV depended on the extent to which the firm could leverage its large catalog by encouraging customers to rent more. Its target for per-customer monthly orders was five, the Netflix corporate average. Special promotions encouraged current customers to refer the service to friends and family; efforts resulted in an upward trend in customer retention. See **figure 10.6** for a graph of retention and customer numbers, based on Netflix annual reports for each quarter; the graph ends in 2011, before Netflix began expanding globally and focusing on creating new content.

Netflix, Part II

After 2010, Netflix began to shift from being a mail-order company that also offered a streaming option to a firm focused mainly on online content delivery. By 2019, the firm would have only 2.7 million mail-order subscribers in the United States, out of a total of 58.5 million US subscribers.[18] That meant its recommendation system, original content, and international customer base had become far larger parts of its value proposition than ever before.

In 2006, Netflix offered a $1 million prize to any group developing an engine that could beat the accuracy of Cinematch, its existing algorithmic recommendation system, by 10%; for the contest, Netflix anonymized its database and made it publicly available. It took three years, but finally in 2009 a team across multiple continents came together to beat Cinematch by more than 10% and win the prize.[19] Netflix could now predict its users' preferences even more accurately, a capability worth much more to the company than $1 million.

As Netflix moved into its online streaming phase after 2010, its recommendation system continued to increase in value. Users were offered movies aligned with their preferences directly on their computer screens; all they had to do was click on a new title to continue streaming Netflix, further increasing the value of the service.

Perhaps even more importantly, the recommendation system and user preference data that it had built up became critical for Netflix's original content generation. Netflix no longer had to guess which new shows might be hits. The company could draw on the millions of reviews in its database to make informed decisions about what types of shows viewers would like, which actors they preferred, which directors to hire, and so on.[20]

In 2012, Netflix had four shows to its name. Only four years later, the company's original content had increased 3,050%. And Netflix was investing more in original content than ever before—an estimated $6.3 billion in 2017. Its next closest competitor that year was Amazon Prime, which spent $4.5 billion. Hulu, which Disney would acquire in 2019, spent $2.5 billion on original content.[21]

As it continued to invest in and focus on streaming services, Netflix's international expansion also took off. By 2014, when it was no longer tethered to physical mail, the company had surpassed 50 million global subscribers, at least 14 million of whom were located outside the United States. Netflix moved into 150 new countries in 2016.[22]

In March 2018, Netflix's stock value surpassed $300, and the firm boasted a market capitalization of $130 billion (see **figure 10.5**). Disney's market cap at the time, just months after it had announced it would roll out Disney+ in the next several years, was $155 billion.

Back to the Future: A Range of Business Models

As movie-rental content-delivery methods emerged in the late 1990s and early 2000s, the industry was in a transition time between physical and streaming content. Thus an industry participant could employ different pricing heuristics across different channels and different end-user content licenses, and could be assessed across

TABLE 10.5. Perceptual market map for the VHS and digital eras

	Revenue model		Delivery method		Content licensing	
	À la carte	Subscription	Streaming	VHS	Rent	Buy
Before 2000 (VHS)						
Blockbuster	•			•	•	
Hollywood Video	•			•	•	
Video Update	•			•	•	
Local video store	•			•	•	
After 2000 (digital)						
Amazon Prime		•	•		•	
Amazon Instant Video	•		•		•	•
Blockbuster	•	•	•	•	•	•
Cinema Now	•		•		•	•
DVD Café	•	•		•	•	•
Greencine		•		•	•	
Hulu	free	free	•		•	
Hulu Plus		•	•		•	
iTunes	•		•		•	•
Netflix		•	•	•	•	
Redbox	•			•	•	
Vudu	•		•		•	

Source: Data from company websites.

various dimensions, including revenue model, delivery method, and content licensing (**table 10.5**).

In this transitional time, there was a range of both revenue and content-delivery models. A business generated revenue either through pay-per-view fees or monthly subscriptions. The one-time fee of the pay-per-view model entitled the customer to rent one DVD by mail or online streaming access for a finite period of time. The subscription model meant subscribers had unlimited access to content, as long as they continued to subscribe. Content was either delivered by physical DVD or streamed online from the service's website to the user's computer or ancillary television device.

By 2012, the industry had, for the most part, transitioned away from physical delivery: the dominant content-delivery system was streaming and the dominant business model utilized recommendation systems. A user's right to content varied by service provider and plan but generally fell into one of three categories: rental for a finite period of time, outright purchase for unlimited personal use, or access to an entire online library from which content could be streamed.

CONCLUSION

With streaming increasingly accounting for the majority of Netflix's revenues, it remained to be seen how the company would withstand another strong market competitor like Disney+. It was possible that Disney+ would be a loss leader geared to sell customers more expensive Disney products, like the cruises. If so, Netflix's focus on only streaming content might not help it compete with Disney's diversified portfolio. Perhaps it would come down to which of the services' recommendation systems, collaborative filtering algorithms, and customer insights were superior. Or maybe they could share customer space, and each service would carve out its own niche.

As competition in the streaming industry heats up, consumer choice increases. With so much content available on so many platforms, it remains to be seen what sets the winners apart from the losers.

11

Automation of Marketing Models

At their best, the images returned for your Google query for "cuddly cats" can feel like a collection of pictures suggested by a friend who knows you well and shares your love of cats. This is an example of artificial intelligence (AI) in our daily lives, in ways that we might take for granted and that certainly don't bear much resemblance to the sentient robots we've been led to expect by Hollywood and novelists. Although it might be less flashy than we thought, AI is rapidly becoming a normal part of life, and advances in that field are accelerating.

In 2016, the ongoing tug of war between human capability and that of machines reached a critical turning point in the realm of image recognition. As recently as 2010, machine algorithms had a 30% error rate when attempting to identify images from ImageNet, a large database of over 10 million obscure images, lagging well behind the 5% human error rate. Only six years later, machines had made such strides in their image recognition capabilities that the error rate had dropped to 4% for the best systems, edging out the human eye for the first time in history.[1]

Image recognition provides just one example of how AI has progressed over the past several years and how quickly it will continue to evolve. What do these advances mean for businesses, and how will they help brands market their goods and services to new customers? This chapter surveys AI techniques and applications to marketing; mini-case studies will be included in the discussion, rather than following it. As you read this overview of AI and consider examples of its applications to marketing, try to think of other current and possible uses of AI. You might also return to earlier case studies and consider how AI might be applied to problems you've tackled using other strategies.

MARKETING AND ARTIFICIAL INTELLIGENCE

The most basic definition of marketing is a conversation between a business and its customers, both existing and potential, with the end goal of ultimately creating customer value and appropriating some of that value for the firm.[2] As you'll recall from chapter 2, one way of achieving this is through segmentation, where marketers split consumers into distinct groups and base their strategies on what would appeal to each specific group. This process enables marketers to create targeted strategies that are more effective because they are tailored to the particular needs and wants of groups of people with shared traits.

The shift of the consumer marketplace into the online world has opened up vast amounts of customer-specific information. The sheer quantity of these data theoretically allows a marketer to personalize the firm's strategy to each individual consumer,[3] leading to increased efficiency. However, this excess of available data also gives rise to new problems, in terms not only of how to decipher and sort the relevant information from the noise, but also in how to implement so many different marketing strategies at once. This is where AI comes into play.

AI has the potential to change the landscape of the marketing field. To prepare you for the marketing of the future, in this chapter we provide a basic overview of AI and its recent advancements, explore how AI is currently involved in marketing, and discuss the potential of AI-based marketing in the future.

HISTORY

The term artificial intelligence was first introduced in 1956 at an academic conference, but the idea of a machine that could "think" for itself had been around for some time. Although most people associate AI with science fiction and thus expect drastic advancements in the field, there has in fact been significant progress in what AI systems can do and in how much they are incorporated into the world around us. The three areas in which AI has progressed furthest are search algorithms, machine-learning algorithms, and integrating statistical analysis into the world at large.[4]

One of the main driving forces that shaped the field of AI and arguably kept it from remaining purely theoretical was the Turing test, created by Alan Turing, an English mathematician, in the 1950s. The object of Turing's "imitation game" was for an interrogator to distinguish which response to a single question came from a person and which came from a machine, based solely on the content of the responses, without physical clues. Although there are many problems with the Turing test, some of which were discussed by Turing himself, versions of the test continue to influence and challenge the AI field.

Because of excitement around a new field and anticipation of sentient machines, AI received large amounts of initial funding. However, with high expectations but no specific goals, financiers soon became disappointed with the lack of progress and pulled their funding. This led to what is commonly called the AI Winter of the 1970s, which finally ended when investors shifted their expectations to focus on AI's commercial potential. One of the first initiatives proving this value came in 1981, when Digital Equipment Corporation (DEC) started using RI, an expert system that helped configure orders for new computer systems. An **expert system** was a form of AI that used a knowledge base received from field experts to solve a specific problem. The system's commercial success brought funding back to the field. By 1986, RI had saved DEC an estimated $40 million annually.[5] Since then, AI research has advanced quite a bit, and it continues to evolve.

BASICS

Artificial intelligence (AI) generally refers to any situation in which machines accomplish tasks in a "smart" manner.[6] Because the term has been around for a long time and the field has expanded and differentiated, newer terms have been coined for specific applications of AI. **Machine learning (ML)** describes the process wherein machines are given data sets and asked "to learn for themselves"[7] using specifically designed algorithms in order to make predictions in the real world. ML is considered a subset of AI and has evolved with the emergence of the internet and consequent access to much larger quantities of data.[8] ML is currently the fastest-growing field of AI[9] and is thus generating significant interest from all sectors. Embedded within ML is an even more specific term: **deep learning (DL)**. Essentially, DL is the application of ML to complex problems; critically, however, it also includes a machine's ability to learn from its mistakes[10] and assess its own probability of reaching a correct result. (For a visual representation of these concepts, see **figure 11.1**.)

The story of IBM's Watson illustrates the evolution of AI. This computer was initially designed to beat humans at the game *Jeopardy!*, in the hope that it would advance technology to enable computers to find answers in unstructured data more

Artificial intelligence

Enables the computer to act in a "smart" manner, for example, by beating a human in *Jeopardy!*

AI

ML

DL

Machine learning

Equips the computer with the ability to understand question language and search for possible answers.

Deep learning

Equips the computer with a second set of algorithms that rank possible answers.

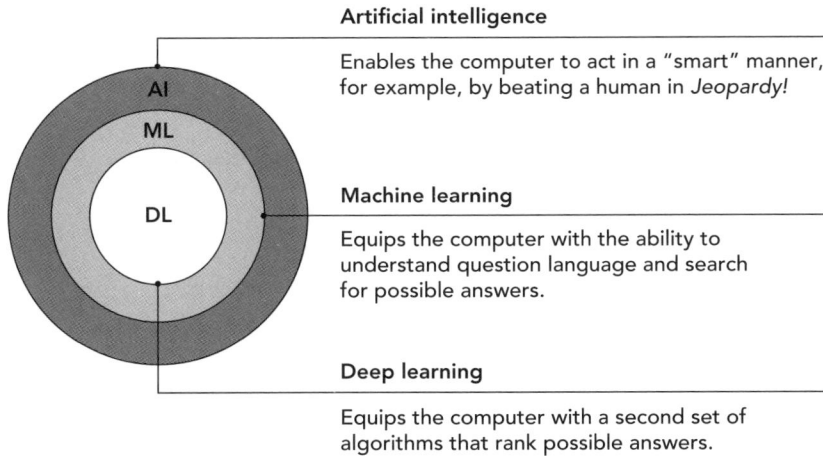

FIGURE 11.1. Categories within AI

effectively than existing search engines.[11] Developing a computer that could beat a human at a strategic game is one of the initial challenges AI sought to solve. However, *Jeopardy!* is an incredibly complex game, in that it requires the machine to understand the nuances of human language with respect to how the clues are often written. Thus the first step Watson needed to take when faced with a game clue was to analyze the language and understand the question. Watson's ability to understand what the clue was asking is an example of ML: the computer was equipped with algorithms that analyzed the various ways in which the question could be interpreted. Only once it "understood" the question did Watson search the vast amounts of data available to it for plausible answers. Considering the penalty a *Jeopardy!* player faces for an incorrect answer, Watson had to be confident in its response before buzzing in. This is where DL comes in. Watson used a second set of algorithms that found evidence to support or refute its possible answers and rank them, while also limiting its offering of an answer to the instances where it was confident in its response. As underlined by this example, the more complex the problem becomes, the more intricate the machine's programming becomes. Watson beat two human *Jeopardy!* champions in 2011 using this combination of ML and DL algorithms.[12]

Before we look at some existing applications of ML, we must understand how ML relates to predictive analytics. Technically speaking, ML is a subfield of both computer science and AI, whereas a predictive analytics statistical model is derived from pure mathematics. The CEO of Edvancer Eduventures, Aatash Shah, clarifies:

TABLE 11.1. Terminology across ML and statistics

Machine learning	Statistics
Learning	Estimation/fitting
Hypothesis testing	Confirmatory data analysis
Example/instance	Data point
Network graph	Model
Weights	Parameters
Supervised learning	Regression/classification
Unsupervised learning	Clustering
Feature	Covariate
Label	Response

Source: Data from Larry Wasserman, "Statistics Versus Machine Learning," *Normal Deviate* (blog), https://normaldeviate.wordpress.com/2012/06/12/statistics-versus-machine-learning-5-2/ (accessed Aug. 16, 2018).

Machine Learning is an algorithm that can learn from data without relying on rules-based programming,

Statistical modeling is a formalization of relationships between variables in the data in the form of mathematical equations.[13]

As statistician Larry Wasserman further explains on his blog, the same concepts are described by different terminology in the two fields. (See **table 11.1** for an illustration of statistics and ML terms.)

Both ML and predictive analytics are concerned with answering the same question: *How can we learn from data?* As we continue to advance in these different branches of predictive modeling, the lines begin to blur even more. For example, self-learning is just an advancement of humans manipulating different variables when conducting a regression analysis. Enabled by the study of data science, collaboration and overlap between these two disciplines result in better predictability and decision-making.

Initial predictions of the importance of marketing technology led to a boom in the development of marketing software based on statistical programming such as R, Python, and SQL. However, marketing software penetration across industries was minimal; in fact, by 2015, it was at less than 5%.[14] This failure to capitalize on such an opportunity may be attributed to the fact that many companies focus on increasing a task's efficiency without considering whether the task itself is an effective tool: even—or especially—in the excitement of rapidly advancing programming capabilities, marketing managers must stay grounded in delivering effective customer experiences and keep in mind the goals and priorities of their firms.

In one example of a change in programming following a change in practice, brands that initially invested in software to compose and manage regular Facebook posts[15] had to shift focus in 2014, when Facebook began curtailing posts from brands,[16] eliminating the utility of such software. Instead of optimizing online posts for consumers, advertisers began to create chatbots that interacted with Facebook's Messenger platform and took advantage of more recent advances in DL.[17] Some companies have developed their own analytic software in order to capitalize on this new technological trend in marketing. Aster, created by the company Teradata, is a kind of graphical interface with R programming in the background, which enables data scientists to take predictive models and deploy predictions on the field, without doing all the coding. For example, Aster might take predictions about customers likely to cross-buy in the next quarter and then automatically interface with the salesforce database system to provide them with call lists for the next quarter. Thus benefits of Aster include integrating big data analytics with a single interface that is user friendly and helps companies uncover insights from their data at an optimized speed.[18]

ANALYTICS TECHNIQUES AND AI

The purpose of analytics can be descriptive, predictive, or prescriptive.

Descriptive analytics refers to data explorations to summarize historical information. For example, Hilton may be interested in knowing the percentage of rooms booked in a property during the holiday season, the percentage of bookings that came through TripAdvisor, the number of Facebook posts made by customers about their stay, the value of a friend on the customers' Facebook networks, and whether the drop in bookings in a certain property in March is consistent with historical trends and with trends in other properties in that region. **Network graphs** are one interesting descriptive technique that firms are using to map customers' social relationships, identify influential folks in the network, and learn about effective ways for seeding viral marketing campaigns. Network graphs can identify influencer metrics based on social media data. These metrics then get fed into AI models for predicting customer acquisition or cross-promoting related products to existing customers, based on the preferences of their network influencers. The descriptive analytics are represented in the lower left of **figure 11.2**. Pivot tables, correlations, histograms, and

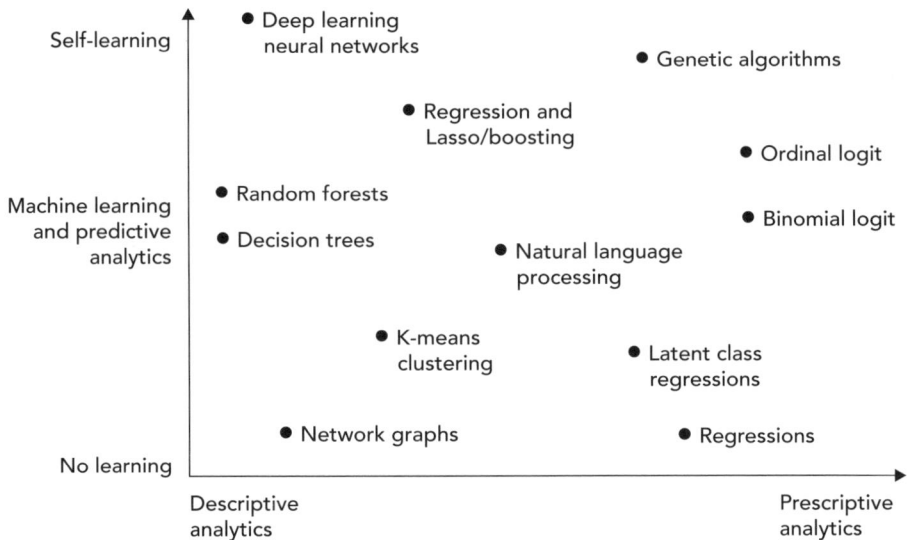

FIGURE 11.2. Organization framework for different analytics techniques

data visualizations are other good examples of descriptive analytics; these can be found in basic statistics books.

Predictive analytics refers to methods that allow managers to forecast outcomes, often as a result of different levels of inputs. Continuing the Hilton example, the hotel chain may want to predict a property's level of occupancy based on historical occupancy rates, the chain's characteristics such as star rating (five stars, four stars, and so on), TripAdvisor reviews, local events, or property features. Firms can use decision trees or an ensemble of decision trees, called random forests (see **figures 11.3** and **11.4**), for this purpose; like other descriptive statistics, these can be used for both description and prediction (even means can be used as naïve predictors). Lasso regressions allow managers to automatically select a smaller set of effective predictors from a large set of candidate variables with a specific goal of improving predictions across several possible samples of data. For example, managers at Hilton can use lasso regressions, instead of or alongside decision trees, to predict occupancy rates. As ML techniques, decision trees, random forests, and lasso regressions are sometimes considered types of AI. As is shown in **figure 11.2**, they intersect with AI and are part of that general data-driven approach.

Dependent variable: Camping

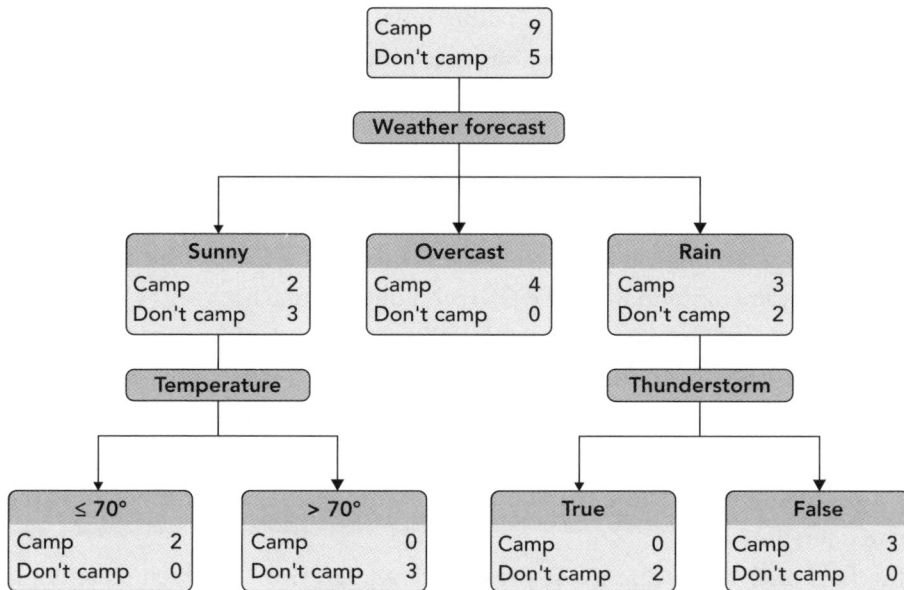

FIGURE 11.3. Decision tree

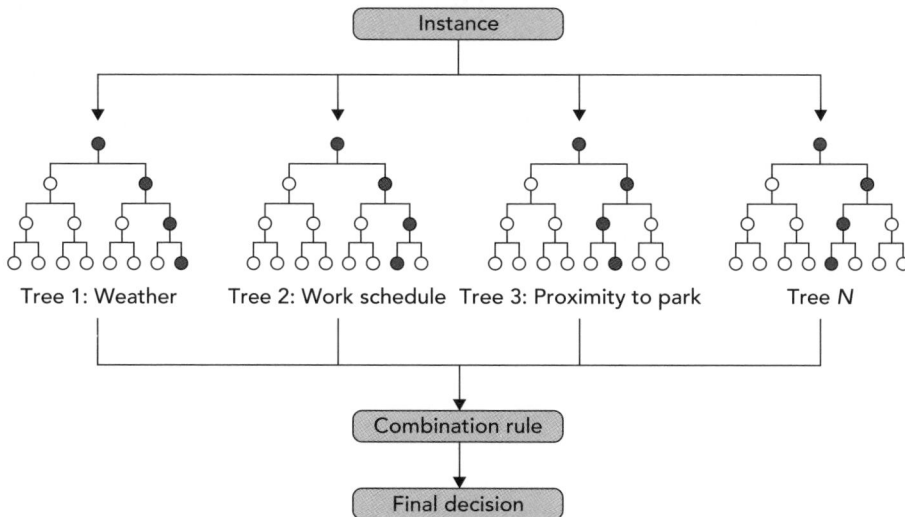

FIGURE 11.4. Random forest

Hilton would also like to know whether a customer is likely to continue booking rooms in its properties or to switch to other hotel chains or lodging options, such as Starwood or Airbnb. For these questions, it can turn to AI: **neural networks** and DL extensions of neural networks provide managers with mechanisms to incorporate all the information about the customer's interactions with the brand, including type of booking, trip type (e.g., business or leisure), day of week of the visit, customer loyalty status, trends in customer bookings, customer demographics (e.g., age or income), property manager ratings, and customer preference for the food in the hotel, in order to predict customer retention. These DL techniques, neural networks with many layers, have primarily focused on building better predictive models capable of harnessing several variables available to managers to forecast a particular event. Google's popular image classifiers (Google Images) and translation algorithms (Google Translate) also use DL algorithms. These algorithms are considered self-learning because they are capable of updating the model specification based on new data without human intervention.

The final analytics technique is **prescriptive analytics**. This technique is especially useful when managers are interested in maximizing metrics. For example, a Hilton manager interested in predicting customer churn might also want to know if certain special offers available for the company's platinum-level members, such as lounge access, are effective in building customer retention. While predictive models can predict an event, they are weak in determining whether a certain promotion is causally linked to an outcome like customer retention. A manager relying only on predictive models, then, is ill-equipped to design better offers to maximize retention. This is where prescriptive analytics, such as multiple linear regression or logistic regression (binomial, as discussed in chapter 9, or ordinal, as introduced in chapter 10), can be useful. These techniques are able to deduce the marginal effect of each individual treatment or marketing campaign on outcomes such as customer retention. The drawback of these techniques is that they are not amenable to handling a large number of independent variables, and their predictive power is typically lower than that of predictive analytics techniques.

Genetic algorithms are AI-based optimization methods that share characteristics with both prescriptive and predictive analytics. They are based on Darwinian evolution and use the concept of survival of the fittest to identify characteristics of a solution with the highest probability of survival. For example, a manager figuring out how to allocate sales calls in order to maximize profits might use a genetic algorithm to find optimal resource-allocation levels. A genetic algorithm goes through several iterations: a solution taken into the next iteration is considered to have survived, and those in the final iteration are considered optimal. This is a highly parallel search technique—meaning the algorithm evaluates multiple solutions at the same time—that can be used to search for both the best model formulation and parameters that maximize a solution. For example, genetic algorithms can be applied to design the optimal marketing resource allocation across different media channels such as television, radio, paid search, display, Facebook, print, YouTube, and mobile, and the level of discount provided for a product. For a deeper dive into genetic algorithms, we suggest Tom M. Mitchell's *Machine Learning*.[19]

One way to improve the performance of prescriptive models (and sometimes even predictive models) is to build a separate model for each customer segment. The first step in this process would be to identify customer segments. As you'll recall from chapter 2, K-means clustering can be used to identify segments in the data using customer demographics and psychographics. **Latent class models** allow managers to combine K-means segmentation and regression models into an ensemble. They involve iteratively segmenting the database, and then running separate regressions for each segment. Like decision trees, latent class models are ML techniques that are a subset of AI.

With the explosion of online business and social media, there is immense growth in customer preference data in the forms of customer reviews, blogs, and Facebook posts, among others. Managers can process this plethora of textual information and summarize these data through textual analytics (see chapter 8), or natural language processing, to get sentiment scores. These sentiment scores can then be used in predictive or prescriptive models. For example, Hilton can use textual analytics to obtain sentiment scores for each property, then use those sentiment scores to predict occupancy rates or customer retention.

EXISTING APPLICATIONS OF AI TO MARKETING

The Hilton example suggests some ways AI is currently helping businesses refine their marketing processes. From an enterprise-wide perspective, there are four main areas in which AI is being used in business today: improvement of customer service, workload automation and predictive maintenance, effective data management and analytics, and improvement in marketing and advertising.[20]

AI in Customer Service

The key advancement regarding customer service has been the chatbot, which is predicted to replace the 1-800 number in coming years.[21] Initially, chatbots operated by recognizing cue words or phrases and responding with preprogrammed responses. With the evolution of ML, they are now much more capable of evolving beyond the limitations of preprogramming and responding appropriately to user requests. Additionally, with messaging apps overtaking the use of social media, more businesses are creating chatbots. In some cases, the consumer can place an order using a chatbot within a messaging app, thus bringing the retail experience to the virtual world and increasing the convenience for the consumer.[22] For example, 1-800-Flowers launched a chatbot partnership with Facebook in 2016 that allowed buyers to purchase flowers for a friend simply by sending the name of the friend to the company's Messenger system. Facebook's Messenger platform is currently exploring partnerships with various other companies to take advantage of the many possibilities chatbots present in both customer service and e-commerce.[23]

AI in Advertising

One of Facebook's greatest assets is the vast amount of data it collects from its many users. The company has developed an AI tool called DeepText, which uses DL to figure out the meaning of words contextually from users' conversations and then directs users toward products that might interest them. This is just one way Facebook continues to use targeted advertising, in which the company uses DL to sift through the data gathered about each user to generate ads relevant to the individual's likes. Another way in which Facebook is using DL is with DeepFace, a tool that uses facial recognition to identify people in photos; this relates to marketing in terms of word-of-mouth campaigns, because it can be used to find characteristics of friends and influencers on social media. However, this tool has been controversial given the privacy concerns it raises by being able to recognize people in high-resolution crowd images.[24]

Facebook is not the only company using AI in marketing through targeted advertising and content curation. As we saw in the last chapter, Netflix uses AI to generate recommendations for users based on their viewing history. Amazon also uses AI to

Firm

Consumer A   Consumer B

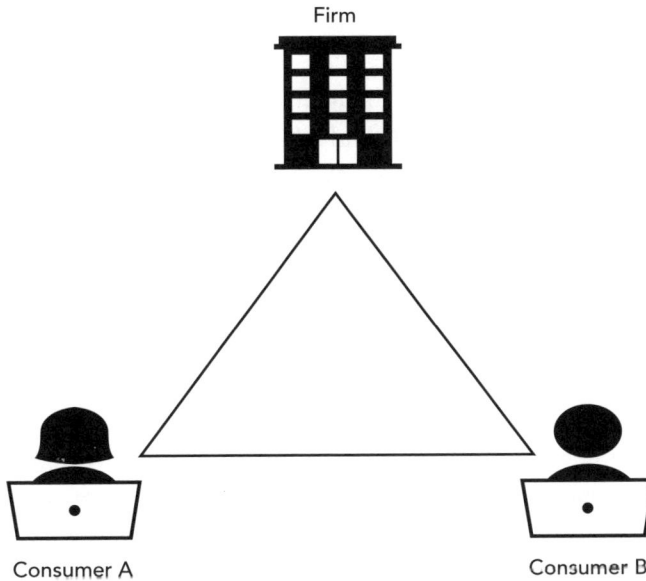

FIGURE 11.5. Model of consumer-brand conversations

suggest other products that a consumer might be interested in based on purchase and search history. Under Armour has partnered with IBM's Watson to personalize its services: the partnership combines user data from Under Armour's Record app with third-party data on fitness and nutrition to generate personalized training and nutrition regimens. This also allows the company to individualize its marketing strategy based on the user's activity.[25]

The shift of the marketplace to the internet has not only vastly increased the amount of data available to businesses; it has also led to a greater number of choices for consumers. With a seemingly endless supply of firms competing for a finite number of consumers, buyers need some way to sift through their options. One increasingly popular way is through the experiences of fellow consumers. This is where social media, and the ease it offers of communicating with other buyers, becomes very important, along with various ways to share consumer ratings.[26] Thus a triangle of conversations is created, with communication occurring not only between a business and a consumer, but among a business and multiple consumers (as shown in **figure 11.5**).

POTENTIAL APPLICATIONS

Advances in AI combined with the changing consumer landscape have already significantly altered the marketing field. And AI continues to evolve and grow, suggesting that there are more changes to come. One possible change is also to the marketing conversation: even as consumer-to-consumer interactions are increasing through social media, consumer-to-marketer conversations could be replaced by consumer-to-machine interactions. This seems like a natural progression given the growing trend of turning to Siri, Alexa, or even Google to answer any question. Since these AI forms are already answering most of our questions, it is likely that they will eventually be equipped with marketing strategies themselves to bring products forward that match specific consumer needs. In this ongoing machine-human conversation, it seems that bots will become increasingly prevalent. One advantage to bots is that they can reduce the time between a consumer's query and an answer, creating a more streamlined and efficient process.

Although this may suggest that AI will replace marketers, in reality these changes will allow the marketing teams to skip the more rote aspects of marketing and focus on the creative side. Additionally, the speed with which machines can accomplish such routine tasks will accelerate marketing and sales in general. With AI equipped to respond to changes in consumer behavior, the market will be able to adjust more rapidly, leading to adaptive pricing strategies. Furthermore, AI could customize human interaction when it comes to business-to-business (B2B) marketing by matching the most suitable salesperson to a particular client based on the data it acquires about each party.

Udacity, an online education service for professionals, offers an example that suggests that a partnership between machines and humans might be the key to effective marketing in the future. After building Udacity, the founder noticed that some chatroom salespeople were good at selling programs and some were not. The data compiled from a set of chatroom transcripts was then fed into an ML algorithm, which revealed the patterns of words and phrases that were most successful in generating sales. The company decided to build a bot that would advise its salespeople, urging them to try a certain phrase or suggest a specific course when customers asked common questions, but allowing the salespeople to rely on their own judgment for more obscure customer issues.[27]

While the possibilities of AI seem endless, there are also real concerns to be addressed alongside the field's advancement. Facebook has already faced controversy over the invasiveness of its DeepFace technology. By allowing AI access to such vast amounts of data about ourselves, are we relinquishing our privacy? Whose responsibility is it to protect the privacy of individuals, or at least to inform them of the possible repercussions of putting information on the internet where it might be accessed by a form of AI? Is there such a thing as too much access to data for AI? While questions like these reach outside the scope of this book, they are worth considering, and undoubtedly will be debated for years to come.

12

Implementing Marketing Analytics

arketing analytics powered by "big data" holds the promise to transform marketing strategy from a discipline based mostly on intuition to a fact-based decision-making process. Despite the potential of data analytics in marketing, its widespread adoption within organizations remains a challenge. Fewer than half the respondents in a survey conducted by Deloitte and Duke University reported being able to leverage marketing analytics for decisions. The trend, however, is positive: the percentage of survey respondents using marketing analytics for decisions increased from 30% in early 2013 to 42% in early 2018.[1]

Moving from traditional intuition-based marketing to data-driven, analytics-based decision-making can be a major adjustment. The roadmap for improving implementation of marketing analytics shown in **figure 12.1** is based on interactions with more than 300 executives in conferences, executive education seminars, case-study development interviews, and consulting projects; these interviews have yielded practical advice on how to successfully and profitably implement analytics in your company or business. This final chapter distills that advice to offer a survey of strategies and approaches to incorporating analytics in existing companies. Like the previous chapter, this survey does not lead to a dedicated case, but does include multiple real-life examples. As you read, consider what steps you might take to help your firm adopt marketing analytics.

The launching pad for implementation of marketing analytics is support from top management and the integration of the marketing analytics function in business processes. Firms must address issues related to organizational structures, analytics processes, and organizational change in order to foster implementation of analytics (**figure 12.1**). Within this framework, managers should ask seven key questions to start the journey toward a marketing analytics–driven culture.

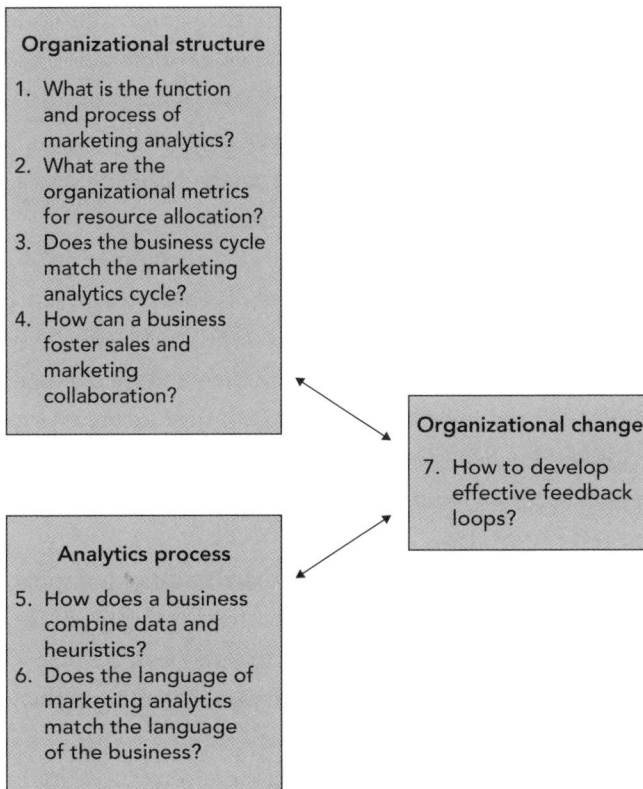

Organizational structure

1. What is the function and process of marketing analytics?
2. What are the organizational metrics for resource allocation?
3. Does the business cycle match the marketing analytics cycle?
4. How can a business foster sales and marketing collaboration?

Organizational change

7. How to develop effective feedback loops?

Analytics process

5. How does a business combine data and heuristics?
6. Does the language of marketing analytics match the language of the business?

FIGURE 12.1. Roadmap for implementing marketing analytics

The rest of this chapter explores these seven questions and offers some concrete examples to help you on your way to implementation.

ORGANIZATIONAL STRUCTURE

1. What Is the Function and Process of Marketing Analytics?

The objective of marketing analytics is to shift from intuition alone to fact-based decision-making. It is important to understand the broad range of inputs to marketing analytics. These include: attribution of sales to different marketing media; optimization of resource allocation; data related to consumer responses, which can be derived from sources including search, online chatter, store visits, and purchasing be-havior; and business outcomes, including unit sales, revenues, market share, and cus-tomer lifetime value (CLV). Other key components of marketing analytics are market conditions and competitive activities. Without such a holistic approach, organ-izations cannot see the full impact of marketing analytics, leading to a gap in its cred-ibility and reducing the likelihood of its implementation.

Once a marketing analytics team has formulated recommendations, the key first step in taking action on those recommendations is to develop field experiments. A test-and-learn environment is essential for this adoption. Practically, ongoing tests of media budgets are possible only with fluid marketing and media management. Bud-gets are often allocated (and therefore restricted) to specific media types, but a holis-tic perspective allows for flexibility across media vehicles. Conversely, marketing analytics professionals need to understand the organizational culture and capabilities of the firm's data and IT systems.

Even if an organization develops a holistic analytics function, provides fluid bud-gets to media vehicles, and embeds analytics professionals within the organization's systems and culture, management's need for control may lead the firm to reject models. A way around this is to customize models for managers and train them in how to use and interpret them.[2]

Simulation software and scenario planning is therefore crucial for implementation of analytics. Analytics professionals need to recognize the limits of the models under-lying their predictions and recommendations. Simulation software that lets managers change the business parameters or assumptions and evaluate consequences goes a long way toward developing managers' comfort with analytics.

Several firms are adopting an agile sprint–based system to allow fluid budgets; these companies cultivate a test-and-learn methodology. Online insurance-comparison business Compare.com (Compare), which you'll remember from chapter 6, credits this agile development process for its ability to use marketing analytics to optimize its purchase funnel. Every week, employees can propose tests to a senior leadership committee. If a proposed test is consistent with Compare's business objectives and has high priority, the senior leadership approves it for an agile sprint (a test run) for a period of two to four weeks. Failure of the proposed strategy at the end of the sprint is acceptable; colleagues work alongside each other without walls; and numerous storyboards, showing work in progress and goals associated with each sprint, are kept on display in the office.

Another way to develop a fact-based culture and agile methodology is to use presentations and reports to share project progress across the firm and drive alignment. One large US-based retailer has an "open house" every two weeks, where each marketing analytics team presents its objective, the metric it is trying to improve, its measurable progress over the past two weeks, its learning, its plan for the next two weeks, and how it plans to measure progress going forward. While these public accountability presentations are open to anybody in the company, representatives from the top management team always show up to provide feedback and advice, and to ensure methodological consistency. These sessions not only create a systematic and rigorous approach to managing projects, but also foster a culture centered on using data-based analytics to move projects forward.

Most broadly, to integrate a test-and-learn culture in a firm, it is important to establish a **measurement cycle**, whose five steps are: plan, execute, measure, evaluate, and learn. With this approach, a firm shifts its perspective to encourage experimentation, focus on data and data analysis, and, importantly, ground initiatives in learning from previous projects. Teams are encouraged to try out ideas, to collaborate and brainstorm, and to build on each other's work while understanding and accepting that not every idea will pan out.

2. What Are the Organizational Metrics for Resource Allocation?

Successful implementation of the budgeting process depends on focusing on better resource allocation rather than total budget optimization. Profit functions typically have a flat maximum (**figure 12.2**). In other words, it is typical to find that net profit does not increase above a certain level of marketing spending, even if unit sales continue to increase with marketing spend.

Managers are therefore better off focusing on reallocating resources across media channels for a fixed budget, rather than on optimizing the total budget.

It is important that organizations decide the metrics for evaluating the effectiveness of marketing spending up front and share those metrics widely. It is best to use a broad range of metrics to evaluate marketing investments.

Return on investment (ROI) is the most common metric in assessing the value of marketing tools because it is easiest to use in analytical marketing-mix models. **Financial ROI** is profit over investment value; because it is a yearly rate, comparable to rate of return, it is also called average ROI. To a large extent, optimization recommendations

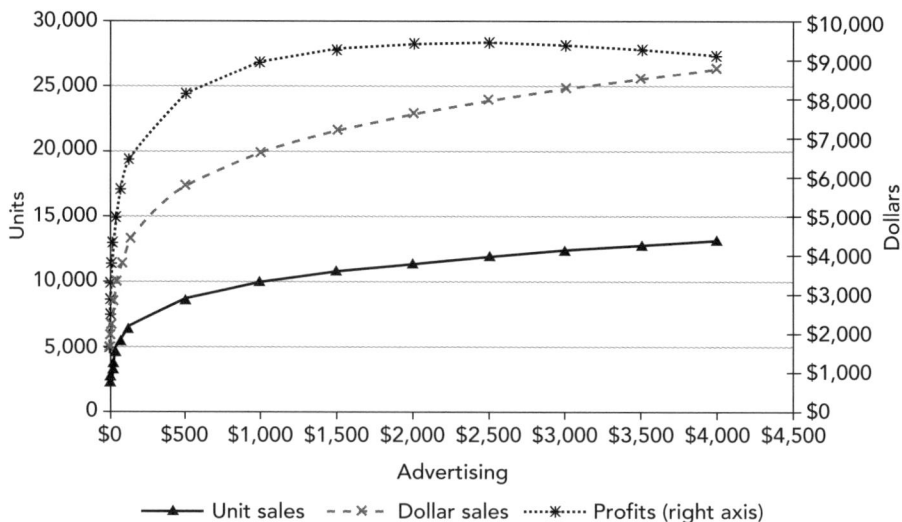

FIGURE 12.2. The flat maximum principle of profits

that use financial ROI involve reducing marketing budgets, because the returns from marketing investments are not linear as is typical in many capital projects. Furthermore, financial ROI calculations based on total returns and total marketing investments ignore the place of a brand on the market response curve.

A better metric is **return on marketing investment (ROMI)**; this is also called marketing ROI, marginal ROI, or the return on marginal investment. Market response functions typically follow an S-shaped curve (**figure 12.3**): small investments in marketing do not lead to sales response; beyond a certain threshold, incremental marketing investments start providing returns; and beyond an upper limit, additional investments do not lead to a corresponding increase in sales. Such an S-shaped function takes into account typical marketing phenomena including diminishing returns and long-term carryover.

ROMI is calculated as the "contribution attributable to marketing (net of marketing spending), divided by the marketing 'invested' or risked."[3] The challenge with ROMI is identifying sales that are attributable to marketing. Marketing analytics and smart experimental designs can be very useful in identifying the lift in sales attributable to marketing investments. As shown in **figure 12.3**, financial ROI is typically higher than ROMI. Financial ROI–based recommendations for marketing optimization would therefore normally result in a lower investment in marketing than ROMI-

Financial ROI =
Total benefits /
Total marketing
spend

ROMI is almost always
less than average.

Net economic benefit
generated by marketing

Economic benefits
of marketing efforts

Cost of marketing

Cost of marketing efforts "invested"

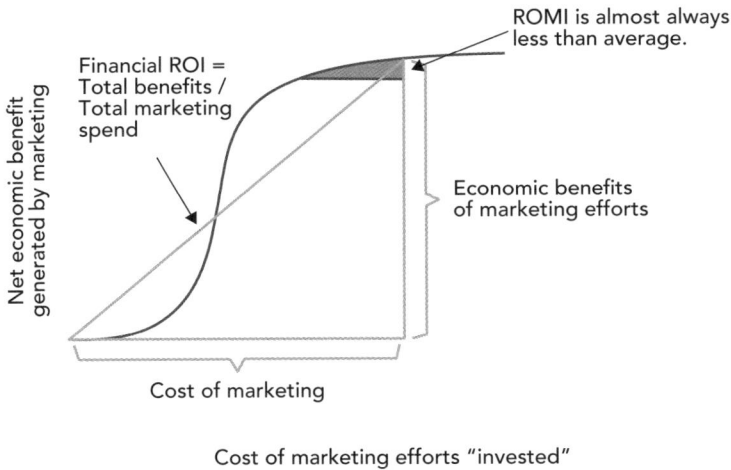

FIGURE 12.3. ROMI is not linear

based recommendations, because financial ROI attributes all of a firm's sales to marketing investments. A ROMI-based strategy is more measured and accommodates nuances in consumer response to marketing.

Even when a firm uses ROMI, the analytics function and the business teams need to be aligned on the company's strategic objectives. This is especially true during a change in business strategy. For example, consider a large media conglomerate that is developing a direct-to-consumer streaming strategy in addition to its large cable channel business. In the traditional business model, retention of a few key cable TV providers is the key business strategy. But as the company develops its new direct-to-consumer streaming strategy, it needs to include the business metrics of customer acquisition, retention, and CLV. The marketing analytics to support the business objectives need to reflect these new business metrics as well. Alignment between marketing analytics and the business teams on which metrics to use is key for successfully implementing marketing analytics in firms.

3. Does the Business Cycle Match the Marketing Analytics Cycle?

The cadence of business and analytics decisions must be synchronized. For example, purchasing television spots in advance can mean greater discounts (sometimes as high as 50%) and provide structure for media planners and the salesforce. But this

```
        Measurement

Implementation          Attribution
and budgeting           modeling

Allocation              Optimization
recommendations         modeling
```

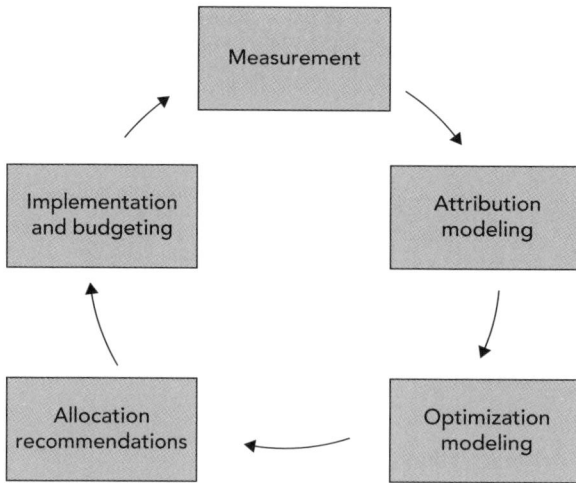

FIGURE 12.4. Synchronization of management budgeting and allocation cycles

forward-buying also establishes lock-in and comes at the expense of flexibility, which is often needed as marketing analytics teams recommend reallocations, and as the effects of those recommendations are tested. It is therefore necessary to take into account media purchase cycles and to synchronize the marketing analytics and salesforce activities with this cycle. A proposed analytics and decision cycle is provided in **figure 12.4**.

4. How Does a Business Foster Sales, Marketing Collaboration, and Technology?

Customers are increasingly conducting product research online before they engage salespeople. This is changing the nature of sales dramatically and requires salespeople to integrate data in their processes so they are better able to assist customers. Insights into customer behavior, derived from marketing analytics, can increase sales by providing qualified leads in both quality and quantity.

Organizations therefore need a unified view across all sales and marketing channels to drive predictability and improve revenue. But this is challenging because salespeople and marketers generally use different metrics. Furthermore, marketers tend to speak a language that sales teams seldom understand. It is important to communicate the value of marketing in business terms rather than marketing jargon. From the salesforce perspective, marketers who haven't walked in sales shoes lose credibility. Marketing analytics can enable alignment by creating demand, increasing collaboration, providing transparency, and mapping the marketing and sales cycle to the buyer's cycle.

In an example of successful alignment, a midsized home goods supplier enabled collaboration between marketing and salespeople through a simple experiment. A challenge for the supplier's salesforce was retention of retailers (i.e., getting retailers to reorder items) and cross-selling to retailers. The supplier had been sending emails to its retailers, and the salesforce had been calling them, but the two initiatives were completely independent: there was no coordination between the emails and the salesperson call plans. The supplier developed a simple analytical model to predict products the retailers were most likely to buy based on their email click-through and subsequent web-browsing behavior. In the experiment, the salespeople were then provided this information and asked to customize their pitch to each retailer, based on which products that retailer was predicted by marketing analytics as being likely to buy. The test was carried out with all retailers within one region. The retention and cross-buy rates of retailers in the test were much higher than in the other (control) regions. This simple experiment, which aligned marketing analytics with the salesperson call plans and used models that were consistent with the salesforce business language, led to better collaboration between marketing and sales.

ANALYTICS PROCESSES

5. How Does a Business Combine Data and Heuristics?

Marketing decisions should depend on the information gathered, but it is never possible to gather all the information. It is therefore important to blend analytics with heuristics. Integrating lessons learned over time from sources other than marketing-mix models helps create a better marketing-mix model.

Consider a situation where the goal is to use analytics across marketing elements to maximize return. The reality, though, is that according to analytics, financial ROI is higher than ROMI. This is because the sweet spot for marketing-mix models occurs when there is a high scale of execution and short time horizon of impact. Advertising does not fit this profile. While it is easier to lift sales with short-term levers like price discounts than with long-term levers like advertising, it is not the best decision to reallocate all advertising money to promotions provided to retailers. For lessons outside marketing-mix models, consider brand and advertisement awareness, correlating brand penetration with marketing activity, and understanding social media and buzz.

The biggest challenge is to incorporate heuristics into the analytics process in the long run. The solution is to learn over time. By following the measurement cycle—plan, execute, measure, evaluate, and learn—companies can apply knowledge they have learned from previous projects to compare and contrast insights into new projects.

6. Does the Language of Marketing Analytics Match the Language of the Business?

Consultants typically view messaging disconnects as the key reasons for lack of implementation of their findings. To develop a persuasive story using marketing analytics, the following three steps are key.

First, in order to tell a clear story, it is important to define and explain key resource-allocation metrics. As discussed in question 4, the more a firm's employees understand the metrics, the easier it is to explain the analytics behind developing the allocation rules. By increasing transparency and clarity, analytics teams can gain the trust of the rest of the organization and thus exert more influence on the process.

Second, analytics managers need to ensure that the model is in sync with brand strategy and other data to which executives are exposed. This will help the message of the model fit the larger story.

Finally, simple and readable models will have a much stronger impact on decision-making. Data visualization and simulation software help open the black box and enable and encourage managers to play with the marketing analytics system and thereby learn its process and benefits.

ORGANIZATIONAL CHANGE

7. How Does a Business Develop Effective Feedback Loops?

The measurement cycle of plan, execute, measure, evaluate, and learn helps companies apply lessons from previous projects to generate insights into new projects. To establish this measurement cycle effectively, a company can develop feedback loops by setting performance or ROMI thresholds, making recurring improvements, and celebrating accomplishments of both the marketing analytics and brand teams.

The key to this constant learning is to build on previous discoveries and data, and the best way to do this is to keep a library of marketing analytics models developed in the firm and a repository of insights obtained from deploying the predictive models. This enables firms not only to continuously improve upon their insights, but also to help new employees to quickly onboard into the organization. The library is most effective when the firm has consistent methods for conducting analytics and has a standardized form or canvas for recording the analytics initiative. Some of the common items to record in such a canvas include: (a) the strategic challenge addressed by analytics, (b) the options that were tested to address that strategic challenge, (c) the prior intuition or hypotheses of the organization about the relationships between marketing and business outcomes, (d) the business and financial metrics used to assess the effectiveness of the marketing analytics models, (e) the data used for marketing analytics, and (f) the analytics techniques used in the project.

To establish an effective analytics-driven learning organization, it is important to first formulate an end goal of analytics-driven organizational change. This determines the expected long-term payoff and allows management to establish key criteria for accepting initiatives proposed by analytics. Communicating the end goal and the criteria early in the journey improves the relevance of analytics activities.

Once the goal is formulated and communicated, an **organizational change journey** must be mapped to reach the end goal.

The journey begins with customer insight. Focusing only on profit will lead to low brand relevance and increased issues with customer churn and dissatisfaction. It is important to focus analytics on real data—like actual shopping behavior—rather than model sophistication. To drive customer behavior, a firm needs to understand customers' attitudes and the determinants of their attitudes. Customer transactions and profits result from a system that delivers on customer needs. Thus this first step is to understand the customer data available within an organization and to develop systems for capturing necessary data that might have been previously unavailable.

Once the company has collected these data, it can use analytics to drive customer insights. It can then test these insights, and finally combine them with management heuristics to develop customer management decisions.

The success of this process depends on managers' willingness to separate fact from fiction, to be open to changing assumptions, and to look to data to test their business and customer hypotheses. Throughout, it is key to stay focused on customer feedback as the basis for evaluating a strategy. A customer-focused incentive structure enables long-term management to focus on continuous customer feedback–based improvement.

LOOKING AHEAD

More than 40 years later, John D. C. Little's observations are still relevant today:

> People tend to reject what they do not understand. The manager carries responsibilities for outcomes. We should not be surprised if he prefers a simple analysis that he can grasp, even though it may have a qualitative structure, broad assumptions, and only a little relevant data, to a complex model whose assumptions may be partially hidden or couched in jargon and whose parameters could be the result of obscure statistical manipulation.[4]

Firms have the ability to do extensive analysis and to develop sophisticated marketing analytics tools. But there are still gaps between analytics and action, communication and buy-in, testing and learning. It is likely that firms and their analytics functions need more marketing and less science. Once organizations have learned how to measure customer value and infer insights from customer data, they must still connect these insights to the decision-makers.

By adopting an approach that is simultaneously data driven, experiment based, and customer focused, a firm can market effectively and efficiently. As you run experiments and gather data, and in the process build managerial experience and intuition, you will hone your insights and instincts, enabling you to better inform and direct these increasingly essential marketing analytics ventures.

Acknowledgments

Ẇe hope that this book takes a step toward bringing advanced analytics into the marketing process. We owe our deep thanks to many people who have made this endeavor possible.

We are indebted to the coauthors of the case studies and technical notes adapted for this book: Neil Bendle, Kelly Brandow, Kyle Brodie, Jenny Craddock, Dusan Curcic, Shea Gibbs, Noreen Nagji, Phillip Pfeifer, Daniel Shively, and Gerry Yemen. We are grateful for the opportunity to work with them and to publish, in this new format, the results of our joint work. We thank Earl Taylor and the speakers and attendants of the Marketing Science Institute Conference on Implementing Analytics for providing fodder for the chapter on implementation. Kelly Ateya, Martha Gray, Timothy Harr, Gautam Kanaparthi, Dustin Moon, Prateek Shrivastava, and Matthew Weiss provided excellent research assistance for the materials.

In particular, Shea Gibbs with Gibbscom worked tirelessly to develop several sections of the manuscript. His business knowledge and editing skills have influenced every aspect of this book.

All the source cases and notes in this book were published originally by Darden Business Publishing, http://store.darden.virginia.edu. We thank DBP not only for allowing us to use the material, but also for helping us to mold and craft these stand-alone documents into this book. We are grateful for the many contributions from the DBP team: Jennifer Hasher, Sally Hurley, Elliot Leflar, Leslie Mullin, Debbie O'Brien, Sherry Richardson, Jacqueline Smith, and Charlotte Walker. We would like to extend our deepest gratitude to our editor, Jane Haxby. Her attention to detail and the many ideas she contributed to the project greatly improved upon our original work. We also thank Julia Grammer. She not only created many of the images, but also advised on data visualization strategies; the book has immensely benefited from her creative efforts. We are also grateful to Eric Fletcher, who offered invaluable advice on legal and permissions issues.

Instrumental in making this book a reality were editors at the University of Virginia Press, including especially Eric Brandt, Anne Hegeman, and Ellen Satrom. We are delighted and honored to be the authors of the first book published under the Darden Business Publishing imprint with the University of Virginia Press.

For their helpful evaluation and critique, we thank our reviewers, J. Andrew Petersen of Pennsylvania State University, Smeal College of Business; Hai Che of University of California, Riverside, School of Business Administration; and Morris George of Baylor University, Hankamer School of Business.

We very gratefully acknowledge the many ways in which our students in marketing analytics, metrics, and pricing courses have engaged with the cases in class and thereby honed our approach and understanding of them. They are the reason we teach, and the reason we publish. The case studies have only improved with their feedback.

Of course, we take full responsibility for any errors that remain in the book.

Finally, we thank our spouses and children, who graciously tolerated the time sacrificed from home and social lives for writing this book.

Notes

INTRODUCTION

1. "Gary L. Lilien ISMS-MSI Practice Prize: 2018 Winners," INFORMS (Institute for Operations Research and the Management Sciences), https://www.informs.org/Recognizing-Excellence /Community-Prizes/Marketing-Science-Society/Gary-L.-Lilien-ISMS-MSI-Practice-Prize (accessed Nov. 18, 2019).
2. Wes Nichols, "Advertising Analytics 2.0," *Harvard Business Review*, March 2013, https://hbr .org/2013/03/advertising-analytics-20 (accessed Nov. 18, 2019).
3. Dan Kopf, "The Discovery of Statistical Regression," *Priceonomics* (blog), https://priceonomics .com/the-discovery-of-statistical-regression/ (accessed Nov. 18, 2019).
4. Thomas Davenport and Jeanne G. Harris, *Competing on Analytics: The New Science of Winning* (Boston, MA: Harvard Business School Press, 2007).
5. James Rubin, "Survey Demonstrates the Benefits of Big Data," *Forbes*, November 15, 2013, https://www.forbes.com/sites/forbesinsights/2013/11/15/survey-demonstrates-the-benefits -of-big-data/#53216b724d06 (accessed Nov. 18, 2019).
6. Louis Columbus, "53% of Companies Are Adopting Big Data Analytics," *Forbes*, December 24, 2017, https://www.forbes.com/sites/louiscolumbus/2017/12/24/53-of-companies -are-adopting-big-data-analytics/#5d0157839a19 (accessed Nov. 18, 2019).
7. Christine Moorman, "The CMO Survey Highlights and Insights Report: Feb. 2019," LinkedIn Slideshare, May 3, 2019, https://www.slideshare.net/christinemoorman/the-cmo-survey-high lights-and-insights-report-feb-2019-143475387 (accessed Nov. 18, 2019).
8. https://hbr.org/2013/03/advertising-analytics-20.

CHAPTER 1. RESOURCE ALLOCATION

1. For more details, see V. Kumar, Rajkumar Venkatesan, Tim Bohling, and Denise Beckmann, "The Power of CLV: Managing Customer Lifetime Value at IBM," *Marketing Science* 27, no. 4 (July–August 2008): 585–99.

CHAPTER 2. CLUSTER ANALYSIS

1. For more details, refer to Michel Wedel and Wagner Kamakura, *Market Segmentation: Conceptual and Methodological Foundations*, 2nd ed. (Norwell, MA: Kluwer Academic Publishers, 2000).
2. All quotations attributed to Chris DuBois and Ty Austin are from January 2014 author interviews.

CHAPTER 3. CONJOINT ANALYSIS

1. Bryan K. Orme, "Which Conjoint Method Should I Use?," Sawtooth Software Research Paper Series, 2013, https://sawtoothsoftware.com/resources/technical-papers/which-conjoint-method-should-i-use (accessed September 4, 2020).
2. Andy Giegerich, "Beleaguered Blazers Play by the Numbers," *Portland Business Journal*, October 29, 2004.
3. Todd Murphy, "Have Arena, Need People," *Portland Tribune*, August 10, 2004.
4. Pete Schulberg, "Blazers Start Losing with Viewers, Too," *Portland Tribune*, January 21, 2005.

CHAPTER 4. LINEAR REGRESSION

1. M. Berk Ataman, Harald J. Van Heerde, and Carl F. Mela, "The Long-Term Effect of Marketing Strategy on Brand Sales," *Journal of Marketing Research* 47, no. 5 (2010): 866–82.
2. *Adams Liquor Handbook 1999* (New York: Adams Business Media, 1999), 122.
3. Theresa Howard, "Absolut Puts a New Premium on Vodka," *USA Today*, March 30, 2004.
4. Beverage Information & Insights Group, Adams Business Media, https://beverage-handbook-store.myshopify.com/.
5. Noah Rothbaum, *The Business of Spirits: How Savvy Marketers, Innovative Distillers, and Entrepreneurs Changed How We Drink* (New York: Kaplan Publishing, 2007), 46.
6. *Adams Liquor Handbook 1999*, 132.
7. SVEDKA sales presentation, 2001.
8. "Best Buy," *Wine Enthusiast*, 1999.
9. "Vodka," *Drinks International*, special issue, *Millionaires 2009*, July 2009.
10. *Adams Liquor Handbook 2007* (New York: Adams Business Media, 2007).
11. Richard W. Lewis, *Absolut Book: The Absolut Vodka Advertising Story* (Boston: Journey Editions, 1996).

CHAPTER 5. CUSTOMER LIFETIME VALUE

1. Paul D. Berger, Bruce Weinberg, and Richard C. Hanna, "Customer Lifetime Value Determination and Strategic Implications for a Cruise-Ship Company," *Journal of Database Marketing & Customer Strategy Management* 11, no. 1 (2003): 49.

2. Sunil Gupta and Donald R. Lehmann, "Customers as Assets," *Journal of Interactive Marketing* 17, no. 1 (2003): 9–24.

3. See V. Kumar, Rajkumar Venkatesan, Tim Bohling, and Denise Beckmann, "The Power of CLV: Managing Customer Lifetime Value at IBM," *Marketing Science* 27, no. 4 (July–August 2008): 585–99.

4. Frederick F. Reichheld and W. Earl Sasser Jr., "Zero Defections: Quality Comes to Services," *Harvard Business Review* (September–October 1990): 105–11.

5. Reichheld and Sasser Jr.

6. Phillip E. Pfeifer and Paul W. Farris, "The Elasticity of Customer Value to Retention: The Duration of a Customer Relationship," *Journal of Interactive Marketing* 18, no. 2 (Spring 2004): 20–31.

7. Unless otherwise attributed, all quotations of company representatives are from author interviews, 2010–12.

CHAPTER 6. MARKETING EXPERIMENTS

1. Unless otherwise attributed, all quotations of company representatives are from author interviews, 2016–17.

2. Joe Mahoney, "Comparenow Trying to Change the Way Consumers Buy Auto Insurance," *Richmond Times-Dispatch*, May 12, 2014, http://www.richmond.com/article_55420f9a-d7e8-11e3-b2f8-10604b9f6eda.html (accessed Jul. 18, 2017).

3. Marketline, "Motor Insurance in the United States," March 2015, 8.

4. National Association of Insurance Commissioners data.

5. Industry Surveys, "Auto Insurance," January 2015, 65.

6. Susan Engelson, "2015 Online Auto Insurance Shopping Report," Comscore.com, November 18, 2015, https://www.comscore.com/Insights/Presentations-and-Whitepapers/2015/2015-Online-Auto-Insurance-Shopping-Report (accessed Aug. 9, 2017).

7. https://www.comscore.com/Insights/Presentations-and-Whitepapers/2015/2015-Online-Auto-Insurance-Shopping-Report.

8. "Background on: Buying Insurance: Evolving Distribution Channels," Insurance Information Institute, March 2017, http://www.iii.org/issue-update/buying-insurance-evolving-distribution-channels (accessed Jul. 18, 2017).

9. Industry Surveys, "Auto Insurance," July 2016, 40.

10. Industry Surveys, "Insurance," July 2016, 40.

11. https://www.comscore.com/Insights/Presentations-and-Whitepapers/2015/2015-Online -Auto-Insurance-Shopping-Report.
12. Visit https://www.thezebra.com/ to see its quote process.

CHAPTER 7. PAID SEARCH ADVERTISING

1. Ginny Marvin, "Report: Google Earns 78% of $36.7B US Search Ad Revenues, Soon to Be 80%," SearchEngineLand, March 14, 2017, https://searchengineland.com/google-search-ad -revenues-271188 (accessed Oct. 16, 2019).
2. "How Costs Are Calculated in AdWords," https://support.google.com/adwords/answer /1704424?hl=en (accessed Dec. 9, 2015).
3. John G. Riley and William F. Samuelson, "Optimal Auctions," *American Economic Review* 71, no. 3 (June 1981): 381–92.
4. Unless otherwise attributed, all information and quotations are from author interviews with Alicia and Chris Allen, 2015 and 2019.
5. Lizette Wilson Chapman, "Historical Emporium Is Dressed for Success in Period Styles," *Silicon Valley Business Journal*, October 17, 2010, http://www.bizjournals.com/sanjose/stories /2010/10/18/focus7.html (accessed Dec. 9, 2015).

CHAPTER 8. TEXT ANALYTICS

1. "The Real Time Statistics Project," RealTimeStatistics.org, https://realtimestatistics.org/ (accessed Oct. 16, 2019).
2. Stephanie Pappas, "How Big Is the Internet, Really?" LiveScience, March 18, 2016, https:// www.livescience.com/54094-how-big-is-the-internet.html (accessed Oct. 16, 2019).
3. Rami Nuseir, "5 Industries Taking Advantage of Text Analytics," *Lexalytics* (blog), July 3, 2014 (accessed Oct. 16, 2019).
4. To learn more about the firm and its use of sentiment analysis, visit www.sentifi.com (accessed Nov. 13, 2019).
5. Charles Dickens, *A Tale of Two Cities* (New York: Vintage Books, 1990).
6. Julia Silge and David Robinson, *Text Mining with R: A Tidy Approach* (Boston: O'Reilly Media, 2017).
7. For more detail on writing code for sentiment analysis in R, see *Text Mining with R*, https:// www.tidytextmining.com/ (accessed Nov. 13, 2019).
8. For more on AFINN, see Patrick O. Perry, "AFINN Sentiment Lexicon," http://corpustext .com/reference/sentiment_afinn.html; for Bing, see "Opinion Mining, Sentiment Analysis, and Opinion Spam Detection," https://www.cs.uic.edu/~liub/FBS/sentiment-analysis.html; and for NRC, see "NRC Word-Emotion Association Lexicon," https://saifmohammad.com /WebPages/NRC-Emotion-Lexicon.htm (all accessed Dec. 6, 2019).

9. Bing Liu, "Sentiment Analysis and Subjectivity," in *Handbook of Natural Language Processing*, 2nd ed., ed. Nitin Indurkhya and Fred J. Damerau (Boca Raton, FL: CRC Press, 2010).

10. To learn more, visit "Natural Language," AI & Machine Learning Products, Google, https://cloud.google.com/natural-language (accessed Nov. 13, 2019).

11. "Showcase Your Space," Airbnb website, https://www.airbnb.com/info/photography (accessed Mar. 24, 2015).

12. "*Pineapple*—A Magazine from Airbnb," Airbnb website, https://www.airbnb.com/pineapple (accessed Mar. 24, 2015).

13. "Airbnb Statistics," iPropertyManagement, November 2019, https://ipropertymanagement.com/airbnb-statistics (accessed Dec. 9, 2019).

14. "Study Finds That Airbnb Hosts and Guests Have Major Positive Effect on City Economies," November 9, 2012, https://www.airbnb.com/press/news/study-finds-that-airbnb-hosts-and-guests-have-major-positive-effect-on-city-economies (accessed Feb. 7, 2020).

15. "New Study: Airbnb Community Generates $61 Million in Economic Activity in Portland," Airbnb website, https://www.airbnb.com/press/news/new-study-airbnb-community-generates-61-million-in-economic-activity-in-portland (accessed Nov. 7, 2014).

16. "New Study: Airbnb Community Contributes $175 Million to Barcelona's Economy," https://www.airbnb.com/press/news/new-study-airbnb-community-contributes-175-million-to-barcelona-s-economy (accessed Nov. 7, 2014).

17. "New Study: Airbnb Community Contributes €185 Million to Parisian Economy," https://www.airbnb.com/press/news/new-study-airbnb-community-contributes-185-million-to-parisian-economy (accessed Nov. 7, 2014).

18. "New Study: Airbnb Generated $632 Million in Economic Activity in New York," https://www.airbnb.com/press/news/new-study-airbnb-generated-632-million-in-economic-activity-in-new-york (accessed Nov. 7, 2014).

19. Miguel Helft, "Growing Quietly in Airbnb's Shadow," *Fortune*, March 12, 2014, http://fortune.com/2014/03/12/growing-quietly-in-airbnbs-shadow/ (accessed Nov. 7, 2014).

20. Oded Netzer, Ronen Feldman, Jacob Goldenberg, and Moshe Fresko, "Mine Your Own Business: Market-Structure Surveillance through Text Mining," *Marketing Science* 31, no. 3 (2012): 521–43.

21. Import.io is available at https://www.import.io/ (accessed Oct. 23, 2015).

CHAPTER 9. LOGISTIC REGRESSION

1. Scott A. Neslin, Sunil Gupta, Wagner A. Kamakura, Junxiang Lu, and Charlotte H. Mason, "Defection Detection: Measuring and Understanding the Predictive Accuracy of Customer Churn Models," *Journal of Marketing Research* 43, no. 2 (2006): 204–11.

2. Kenneth Train, *Qualitative Choice Analysis: Theory, Econometrics, and an Application to Automobile Demand*, Transportation Studies Series 10 (Cambridge, MA: MIT Press, 1986).

CHAPTER 10. RECOMMENDATION SYSTEMS

1. Valen E. Johnson and James H. Albert, *Ordinal Data Modeling, Statistics for Social Science and Public Policy* (New York: Springer-Verlag, 1999).

2. "Approaching the Cold Start Problem in Recommender Systems," *InData Labs* (blog), Medium.com, September 29, 2016, https://medium.com/@InDataLabs/approaching-the-cold-start-problem-in-recommender-systems-e225e0084970 (accessed Jul. 30, 2019).

3. Joseph A. Konstan and Michael D. Ekstrand, "The Cold Start Problem," *Nearest Neighbor Collaborative Filtering* (Coursera, through the University of Minnesota), https://www.coursera.org/lecture/collaborative-filtering/the-cold-start-problem-8MtoR (accessed Jul. 30, 2019).

4. https://www.coursera.org/lecture/collaborative-filtering/the-cold-start-problem-8MtoR.

5. https://medium.com/@InDataLabs/approaching-the-cold-start-problem-in-recommender-systems-e225e0084970.

6. Kevin Liao, "Prototyping a Recommender System Step by Step Part 2: Alternating Least Square (ALS) Matrix Factorization in Collaborative Filtering," *Towards Data Science* (blog), Medium.com, https://towardsdatascience.com/prototyping-a-recommender-system-step-by-step-part-2-alternating-least-square-als-matrix-4a76c58714a1 (accessed Jul. 30, 2019).

7. Yunhong Zhou, Dennis Wilkinson, Robert Schreiber, and Rong Pan, "Large-Scale Parallel Collaborative Filtering for the Netflix Prize," in *Algorithmic Aspects in Information and Management*, ed. R. Fleischer and J. Xu, AAIM 2008, Lecture Notes in Computer Science, vol. 5,034 (Berlin, Heidelberg: Springer, 2008), https://endymecy.gitbooks.io/spark-ml-source-analysis/content/%E6%8E%A8%E8%8D%90/papers/Large-scale%20Parallel%20Collaborative%20Filtering%20the%20Netflix%20Prize.pdf (accessed Jul. 30, 2019).

8. David Carr, "Giving Viewers What They Want," *New York Times*, February 24, 2013, https://www.nytimes.com/2013/02/25/business/media/for-house-of-cards-using-big-data-to-guarantee-its-popularity.html (accessed Jul. 30, 2019).

9. Hamilton Helmer, *7 Powers: The Foundations of Business Strategy* (Los Altos, CA: Deep Strategy LLC, 2016).

10. Mike Sorrentino and Joan E. Solsman, "Disney Plus Streaming Service: Release Date, Price, Shows, and Movies to Expect," CNET, July 22, 2019, https://www.cnet.com/news/disney-plus-shows-movies-price-release-date-avengers-marvel-star-wars-black-panther-130-million/ (accessed Jul. 30, 2019).

11. Tara Lemmey, "Push the Positive for Customers," Bloomberg Business online, September 12, 2005, http://www.bloomberg.com/bw/stories/2005-09-12/push-the-positive-for-customers (accessed Jul. 21, 2015).

12. Rani Molla, "Netflix Makes Up Nearly 30 Percent of Global Streaming Video Subscriptions," Vox, April 16, 2019, https://www.vox.com/2019/4/16/18410556/netflix-30-percent-global-streaming-video-subscriptions-q1-2019 (accessed Jul. 30, 2019).

13. "Netflix, Inc.: Summary," Yahoo! Finance, https://finance.yahoo.com/quote/NFLX (accessed Jul. 30, 2019).

14. Daniel B. Kline, "Why Did Netflix, Inc. Shares Drop 19% in October?," *Motley Fool* (blog), Yahoo! Finance, November 11, 2018, https://finance.yahoo.com/news/why-did-netflix-inc -shares-004900338.html (accessed Aug. 13, 2019).

15. Chris Taylor, "The Movie Is in the Mail," *Time*, March 18, 2002, 67.

16. Alan Cohen, "Netflix: DVDs at Your Door," PC, February 19, 2003.

17. Cohen.

18. Neil Monahan and Brandon Griggs, "Why 2.7 Million Americans Still Get Netflix DVDs in the Mail," CNN, April 4, 2019, https://www.cnn.com/2019/04/04/media/netflix-dvd -subscription-mail-trnd/index.html (accessed Jul. 30, 2019).

19. "Netflix Prize: Congratulations!," Netflix, https://www.netflixprize.com/index.html (accessed Jul. 30, 2019); Preethi Dumpala, "Netflix Reveals Million-Dollar Contest Winner," *Business Insider*, September 21, 2009, https://www.businessinsider.com/netflix-reveals-million-dollar -netflix-prize-winner-announces-netflix-prize-2-2009-9 (accessed Aug. 23, 2019).

20. https://www.nytimes.com/2013/02/25/business/media/for-house-of-cards-using-big-data -to-guarantee-its-popularity.html.

21. Rani Molla, "Netflix Spends More on Content Than Anyone Else on the Internet—And Many TV Networks, Too," *Recode* (blog), VoxMedia, February 26, 2018, https://www.vox.com /2018/2/26/17053936/how-much-netflix-billion-original-content-programs-tv-movies -hulu-disney-chart (accessed Aug. 8, 2019).

22. https://www.vox.com/2019/4/16/18410556/netflix-30-percent-global-streaming-video -subscriptions-q1-2019.

CHAPTER 11. AUTOMATION OF MARKETING MODELS

1. Dave Gershgorn, "The Data that Transformed AI Research—and Possibly the World," *Quartz*, July 26, 2017, https://qz.com/1034972/the-data-that-changed-the-direction-of-ai-research -and-possibly-the-world/ (accessed Aug. 16, 2018).

2. Gil Press, "Artificial Intelligence (AI) and the Future of Marketing: 6 Observations from In-bound 2016," *Forbes*, November 21, 2016, https://www.forbes.com/sites/gilpress/2016/11 /21/artificial-intelligence-ai-and-the-future-of-marketing-6-observations-from-inbound -2016/#4deadf41441d (accessed Aug. 16, 2018).

3. Peter Isaacson, "3 Ways Artificial Intelligence Is Transforming B2B Marketing," *Martech Today*, February 21, 2017, https://martechtoday.com/3-ways-artificial-intelligence-transforming-b2b -marketing-195386 (accessed Aug. 16, 2018).

4. "The History of Artificial Intelligence," http://courses.cs.washington.edu/courses/csep590 /06au/projects/history-ai.pdf (accessed Aug. 16, 2018).

5. "AI: 15 Key Moments in the Story of Artificial Intelligence," BBC, http://www.bbc.co.uk /timelines/zq376fr#zcpkj6f (accessed Aug. 16, 2018).

6. Bernard Marr, "What Is the Difference between Artificial Intelligence and Machine Learn-ing?," *Forbes*, December 6, 2016, https://www.forbes.com/sites/bernardmarr/2016/12/06

/what-is-the-difference-between-artificial-intelligence-and-machine-learning/#54a072662742 (accessed Aug. 16, 2018).

7. https://www.forbes.com/sites/bernardmarr/2016/12/06/what-is-the-difference-between -artificial-intelligence-and-machine-learning/#54a072662742.

8. https://www.forbes.com/sites/bernardmarr/2016/12/06/what-is-the-difference-between -artificial-intelligence-and-machine-learning/#54a072662742.

9. Lee Bell, "Machine Learning Versus AI: What's the Difference?," *Wired*, December 1, 2016, http://www.wired.co.uk/article/machine-learning-ai-explained (accessed Aug. 16, 2016).

10. https://www.forbes.com/sites/bernardmarr/2016/12/06/what-is-the-difference-between -artificial-intelligence-and-machine-learning/#54a072662742.

11. "A Computer Called Watson," IBM100, http://www-03.ibm.com/ibm/history/ibm100/us/en /icons/watson/ (accessed Aug. 16, 2018).

12. Jo Best, "IBM Watson: The Inside Story of How the Jeopardy-Winning Supercomputer Was Born, and What It Wants to Do Next," TechRepublic, September 9, 2013, https://www .techrepublic.com/article/ibm-watson-the-inside-story-of-how-the-jeopardy-winning -supercomputer-was-born-and-what-it-wants-to-do-next/ (accessed Oct. 18, 2019).

13. Aatash Shah, "Machine Learning vs. Statistics," KDnuggets, November 2016, http://www .kdnuggets.com/2016/11/machine-learning-vs-statistics.html (accessed Aug. 16, 2018).

14. Bob Gilbreath, "Why AI Is the Best UI for Marketing Software," Medium.com, February 16, 2015, https://medium.com/@mktgwithmeaning/why-ai-is-the-best-ui-for-marketing-software -22ed13ea060b (accessed Aug. 16, 2018).

15. https://medium.com/@mktgwithmeaning/why-ai-is-the-best-ui-for-marketing-software -22ed13ea060b.

16. Tim Peterson, "Facebook Cuts Brands' Reach Once Again," *AdAge*, November 14, 2014, http:// adage.com/article/digital/facebook-cuts-brands-organic-reach/295881/ (accessed Aug. 16, 2018).

17. Josh Constine, "Facebook Launches Messenger Platform with Chatbots," *Tech Crunch*, April 12, 2016, https://techcrunch.com/2016/04/12/agents-on-messenger/ (accessed Aug. 16, 2018).

18. Teradata, http://www.teradata.com/products-and-services/analytics-from-aster-overview/ ?LangType=1033&LangSelect=true (accessed Aug. 16, 2018).

19. Tom M. Mitchell, *Machine Learning* (McGraw-Hill Series in Computer Science; Boston: MIT Press and McGraw-Hill, 1997).

20. Andrei Klubnikin, "Top 4 Applications of Artificial Intelligence in Business," Medium.com, November 14, 2016, https://medium.com/@andrei.klubnikin88/top-4-applications-of -artificial-intelligence-in-business-7804e3cf9bf0 (accessed Aug. 16, 2018).

21. https://techcrunch.com/2016/04/12/agents-on-messenger/.

22. Matt Schlicht, "The Complete Beginner's Guide to Chatbots," *Chatbots Magazine*, April 20, 2016, https://chatbotsmagazine.com/the-complete-beginner-s-guide-to-chatbots-8280b7b906ca (accessed Aug. 16, 2018).

23. https://techcrunch.com/2016/04/12/agents-on-messenger/.

24. Bernard Marr, "4 Mind-Blowing Ways Facebook Uses Artificial Intelligence," *Forbes*, December 29, 2016, https://www.forbes.com/sites/bernardmarr/2016/12/29/4-amazing-ways-facebook-uses-deep-learning-to-learn-everything-about-you/#3ba20eefccbf (accessed Aug. 16, 2018).

25. Ben Davis, "15 Examples of Artificial Intelligence in Marketing," *Econsultancy* (blog), April 19, 2016, https://econsultancy.com/blog/67745-15-examples-of-artificial-intelligence-in-marketing/ (accessed Aug. 16, 2018).

26. Kwon-Wai Cheung, James Kwok, Martin H. Law, and Kwok Ching Tsui, "Mining Customer Product Rating for Personalized Marketing," *Decision Support Systems* 35, no. 2 (May 2003): 231–43.

27. Erik Brynjolfsson, "How AI Is Already Changing Business," interview by Sarah Green Carmichael, *Harvard Business Review*, July 20, 2017, https://hbr.org/ideacast/2017/07/how-ai-is-already-changing-business.html (accessed Aug. 16, 2018).

CHAPTER 12. IMPLEMENTING MARKETING ANALYTICS

1. Christine Moorman, "Marketing Analytics and Marketing Technology Trends to Watch," *CMOSurvey* (blog), June 20, 2018, https://cmosurvey.org/2018/06/marketing-analytics-and-marketing-technology-trends-to-watch/ (accessed Sept. 6, 2019).

2. Gary L. Lilien, Arvind Rangaswamy, Gerrit H. Van Bruggen, and Katrin Starke, "DSS Effectiveness in Marketing Resource Allocation Decisions: Reality vs. Perception," *Information Systems Research* 15, no. 3 (September 2004): 216–35.

3. Paul W. Farris, Neil T. Bendle, Phillip E. Pfeifer, and David J. Reibstein, *Marketing Metrics: The Definitive Guide to Measuring Marketing Performance*, 2nd ed. (Upper Saddle River, NJ: Pearson Education, 2010), 351.

4. John D. C. Little, "Models and Managers: The Concept of a Decision Calculus," *Management Science* 50, no. 12 (2004 reprint; originally published 1970): 1,842.

Further Resources

CHAPTER 3. CONJOINT ANALYSIS

Green, Paul E., Abba M. Krieger, and Yoram Wind. "Thirty Years of Conjoint Analysis: Reflections and Prospects." *Interfaces* 31, no. 3 (May–June 2001): 56–73.

Lilien, Gary L., and Arvind Rangaswamy. *Marketing Engineering: Computer-Assisted Marketing Analysis and Planning.* 2nd ed. Englewood Cliffs, NJ: Prentice-Hall, 2002.

Luce, R. Duncan, and John W. Tukey. "Simultaneous Conjoint Measurement: A New Type of Fundamental Measurement." *Journal of Mathematical Psychology* 1 (February 1964): 1–27.

Orme, Bryan K. "Which Conjoint Method Should I Use?" *Sawtooth Software Technical Paper* (2013). https://sawtoothsoftware.com/resources/technical-papers/which-conjoint-method -should-i-use (accessed September 4, 2020).

A very good and surprisingly comprehensive collection of technical papers located on the site of a company that markets conjoint analysis software (http://www.sawtoothsoftware.com /techpap.shtml). These papers provide answers to many of the practical implementation questions a user may face.

CHAPTER 4. LINEAR REGRESSION

Assmus, Gert, John U. Farley, and Donald R. Lehmann. "How Advertising Affects Sales: Meta-Analysis of Econometric Results." *Journal of Marketing Research* 21, no. 1 (February 1984): 65–74.

Koyck, L. M. *Distributed Lags and Investment Analysis.* Contributions to Economic Analysis IV. Amsterdam: North-Holland Publishing Company, 1954.

Parsons, Leonard J. "A Ratchet Model of Advertising Carryover Effects." *Journal of Marketing Research* 13, no. 1 (February 1976): 76–79.

Tellis, Gerard J. "Modeling Marketing Mix." In *The Handbook of Marketing Research: Uses, Misuses, and Future Advances*, edited by Rajiv Grover and Marco Vriens, 506–22. Thousand Oaks, CA: SAGE Publications, 2006.

Tellis, Gerard J. "The Price Elasticity of Selective Demand: A Meta-Analysis of Econometric Models of Sales." *Journal of Marketing Research* 25, no. 4 (November 1988): 331–41.

CHAPTER 5. CUSTOMER LIFETIME VALUE

Berger, Paul D., Bruce Weinberg, and Richard C. Hanna. "Customer Lifetime Value Determination and Strategic Implications for a Cruise-Ship Company." *Journal of Database Marketing & Customer Strategy Management* 11, no. 1 (2003): 40–52.

Gupta, Sunil, and Donald R. Lehmann. "Customers as Assets." *Journal of Interactive Marketing* 17, no. 1 (2003): 9–24.

Peppers, Don, and Martha Rogers. *Enterprise One to One: Tools for Competing in the Interactive Age.* New York: Currency Doubleday, 1997.

Pfeifer, Phillip E., and Paul W. Farris. "The Elasticity of Customer Value to Retention: The Duration of a Customer Relationship." *Journal of Interactive Marketing* 18, no. 2 (Spring 2004): 20–31.

Reichheld, Frederick F., and W. Earl Sasser Jr. "Zero Defections: Quality Comes to Services." *Harvard Business Review* (September–October 1990): 105–11.

CHAPTER 7. PAID SEARCH ADVERTISING

Farris, Paul W., Neil T. Bendle, Phillip E. Pfeifer, and David J. Reibstein. *Marketing Metrics: The Definitive Guide to Measuring Marketing Performance.* Upper Saddle River, NJ: FT Press, 2010.

CHAPTER 8. TEXT ANALYTICS

"NRC Word-Emotion Association Lexicon." https://saifmohammad.com/WebPages/NRC-Emotion-Lexicon.htm (accessed Dec. 6, 2019).

"Opinion Mining, Sentiment Analysis, and Opinion Spam Detection." https://www.cs.uic.edu/~liub/FBS/sentiment-analysis.html (accessed Dec. 6, 2019).

Perry, Patrick O. "AFINN Sentiment Lexicon." http://corpustext.com/reference/sentiment_afinn.html (accessed Dec. 6, 2019).

Silge, Julia, and David Robinson. *Text Mining with R: A Tidy Approach.* Boston: O'Reilly Media, 2017. https://www.tidytextmining.com/ (accessed Dec. 6, 2019).

CHAPTER 9. LOGISTIC REGRESSION

Kaggle, a user-generated business analytics community: https://www.kaggle.com.

Train, Kenneth. *Qualitative Choice Analysis: Theory, Econometrics, and an Application to Automobile Demand.* Series in Transportation Studies 10. Cambridge, MA: MIT Press, 1986.

CHAPTER 10. RECOMMENDATION SYSTEMS

Helmer, Hamilton. *7 Powers: The Foundations of Business Strategy*. Los Altos, CA: Deep Strategy LLC, 2016.

CHAPTER 11. AUTOMATION OF MARKETING MODELS

Bughin, Jacques, Michael Chui, and James Manyika. "Ten IT-Enabled Business Trends for the Decade Ahead." *McKinsey Quarterly*, May 2013. http://www.mckinsey.com/industries/high-tech /our-insights/ten-it-enabled-business-trends-for-the-decade-ahead (accessed Sept. 11, 2018).

Conick, Hal. "The Past, Present and Future of AI Marketing." American Marketing Association, January 12, 2017. https://www.ama.org/publications/MarketingNews/Pages/past-present -future-ai-marketing.aspx (accessed Sept. 11, 2018).

Copeland, Michael. "What's the Difference between Artificial Intelligence, Machine Learning and Deep Learning?" *Nvidia* (blog), July 29, 2016. https://blogs.nvidia.com/blog/2016/07/29 /whats-difference-artificial-intelligence-machine-learning-deep-learning ai/ (accessed Sept. 11, 2018).

Marr, Bernard. "Fake News: How Big Data and AI Can Help." *Forbes*, March 1, 2017. https://www .forbes.com/sites/bernardmarr/2017/03/01/fake-news-how-big-data-and-ai-can-help /#73c76e70d56b (accessed Sept. 11, 2018).

Mitchell, Tom M. *Machine Learning*. McGraw-Hill Series in Computer Science. Boston: MIT Press and McGraw-Hill, 1997.

Rowe, Adam. "The 5 Biggest User Interface Trends to Look for in 2017." *Tech.Co*, December 20, 2016. http://tech.co/biggest-user-interface-trends-in-2017-2016-12 (accessed Sept. 11, 2018).

Rowe, Adam. "The Top Five Marketing Trends to Expect in 2017." *Tech.Co*, December 19, 2016. http://tech.co/top-five-marketing-trends-expect-2017-2016-12 (accessed Sept. 11, 2018).

Index

Numbers in bold refer to pages on which the term is defined.

UVA DARDEN BUSINESS PUBLISHING, an imprint of the University of Virginia Press, aims to improve the world by publishing thought-leading works in business and economics that will inspire responsible leaders. In support of this mission, UVA Darden Business Publishing recruits authors from varied backgrounds and fields to provide diverse perspectives and a wide range of ideas. DBP collaborates with authors to help them refine and effectively communicate their scholarship and expertise, then distributes their work to the widest audience possible.